D1807188

BELGIUM AND LUXEMBOURG
Practical Commercial Law

BELGIUM AND LUXEMBOURG

Practical Commercial Law

NICOLE VAN CROMBRUGGHE
Partner Lafili & Van Combrugghe, Brussels

GUY ARENDT
Partner, Bonn & Schmitt, Luxembourg

GENERAL EDITOR
ALEXIS MAITLAND HUDSON
Avocat à la cour
Solicitor

© Longman Group Ltd 1992

Published by
Longman Law, Tax and Finance
Longman Group UK Ltd
21-27 Lamb's Conduit Street
London WC1N 3NJ

Associated offices
Australia, Hong Kong, Malaysia, Singapore, USA

ISBN 085121 8962

A CIP catalogue record for this book is available from the British Library.

Typeset by York House Typographic Ltd, London

Printed in Great Britain by Loader Jackson, Arlesey.

CONTENTS

Belgium

	Page
Introduction	1
The courts	3
Lawyers	5
Approach to legal issues	6
Chapter 1: Intellectual and Industrial Property	8
1.1 Introduction	8
1.2 Patents	8
1.2.1 Definition	9
1.2.2 Procedure	9
1.2.3 Protection, exploitation and remedies	10
1.2.4 European patent	12
1.3 Trademarks	12
1.3.1 Definition	13
1.3.2 Trademark protection procedure	13
1.3.3 Protection, exploitation and remedies	14
1.3.4 International registration	14
1.4 Copyright	15
1.4.1 Definitions	15
1.4.2 Protection, exploitation and remedies	16
1.4.3 Software and semiconductors	17
1.5 Designs and models	17
1.5.1 Definition	18
1.5.2 Procedure	18
1.5.3 Protection, exploitation and remedies	18
1.6 Know-how, trade secrets and confidential information	19
1.7 Licensing	20

1.7.1 Licensing of patents   20
1.7.2 Licensing of trademarks   20
1.7.3 Licensing of copyrights   21
1.7.4 Licensing of designs and models   22
1.7.5 Licensing of know-how   22
1.8 Inventions of employees   22

Chapter 2: Competition   24
2.1 Introduction   24
2.2 Belgian competition law   24
2.2.1 Present legal situation   24
2.2.2 Law on the protection of economic competition   25
2.3 Unfair competition   28
2.3.1 Articles 1382–1384 Belgian Civil Code   28
2.3.2 Law of 14 July 1991 on trade practices and on the
information and protection of the consumer   29

Chapter 3: Business Organisations   33
3.1 Introduction   33
3.2 Legislation   33
3.3 Limited liability companies   34
3.3.1 *Société anonyme — naamloze vennootschap*   34
3.3.2 Private limited liability company   38
3.3.3 Co-operative company with limited liability   39
3.4 Partnerships   41
3.4.1 General partnership   41
3.4.2 Limited partnership   41
3.4.3 Partnership limited by shares   41
3.4.4 Co-operative company   42
3.4.5 Civil company   42
3.4.6 Temporary partnership   43
3.4.7 Partnership agreement   43
3.5 Economic interest grouping   43
3.6 Non-profit organisations   44
3.6.1 ASBL — VZW   44
3.6.2 International association   45
3.6.3 Institutions of public utility (foundations)   47
3.7 Incorporation   47

3.7.1 Incorporation of limited liability companies 47
3.7.2 Incorporation of partnerships 49
3.7.3 Incorporation of non-profit organisations 50
3.7.4 Incorporation of an EEIG and EIG 50
3.8 Shareholders' rights and liabilities 51
3.9 Directors' rights and liabilities 52
3.10 Sole trader 53
3.11 Branches 53

Chapter 4: Mergers and Acquisitions 56
4.1 The 'Community dimension' 56
4.2 Mergers 56
4.3 Share acquisitions 57
4.3.1 Privately owned stock 57
4.3.2 Shares publicly held or quoted 60
4.4 Acquisitions of goodwill 62
4.4.1 Formalities 62
4.4.2 VAT implications 65

Chapter 5: Agency 66
5.1 Background 66
5.2 Commercial agents 66
5.2.1 Absence of specific Belgian legislation 66
5.2.2 Performance of the contract 67
5.2.3 Duration and termination 67
5.2.4 Future orientation: Directive 86/653 relating
to self-employed commercial agents 69
5.3 Commission agents 70
5.4 Brokers 71
5.5 Commercial representatives ('*représentants
de commerce*' — '*handelsvertegenwoordigers*') 72

Chapter 6: Distribution 75
6.1 Introduction 75
6.2 Exclusive and quasi-exclusive distribution agreements 76
6.2.1 Scope of protection 76
6.2.2 Consequences of the termination 78
6.2.3 Enforcement of the protection 81

6.2.4 Conclusion 84
6.3 Other types of distribution agreements 85

Chapter 7: Franchising 86
7.1 Definition and characteristics 86
7.2 Franchising and competition law 87
7.3 Certificate of distribution 87

Chapter 8: Real Property and Succession 89
8.1 Introduction 89
8.2 Real property 89
8.2.1 Sale and purchase 89
8.2.2 Civil leases 92
8.2.3 Residential leases 92
8.2.4 Commercial leases 93
8.2.5 Mortgages 96
8.3 Succession 99

Chapter 9: Immigration and Employment 102
9.1 Immigration 102
9.1.1 Non-EEC nationals 102
9.1.2 EC nationals 103
9.2 Labour relations 104
9.2.1 Legislation 104
9.2.2 Employment contracts 105
9.2.3 Working regulations 108
9.2.4 Use of language 108
9.2.5 Mandatory bodies 109
9.2.6 Social security 110
9.2.7 Labour protection 110
9.2.8 Applicable law and appropriate courts in
international labour relations 110
9.2.9 Temporary secondment 111

Chapter 10: Taxation 113
10.1 Value added tax 113
10.1.1 General 113
10.1.2 The mechanism 113

10.1.3 Foreign entrepreneurs 113
10.1.4 Exemptions 114
10.1.5 Rates 114
10.2 Individual income tax 114
10.2.1. General 114
10.2.2 The mechanism 115
10.2.3 Rates 117
10.3 Corporate income tax 118
10.3.1 General 118
10.3.2 Taxable income 118
10.3.3 Tax rates 120
10.3.4 Corporations with favourable tax status 121
10.4 Tax on legal entities (non-profit organisations) 122
10.4.1 Tax on the assets 122
10.4.2 Assessment of income and tax rates 122
10.4.3 Tax in lieu of inheritance tax 122
10.5 Non-resident income tax 123
10.5.1 Non-resident individual tax 123
10.5.2 Non-resident corporate tax 124
10.5.3 Double income tax treaties 124
10.6 Transfer pricing 125

Chapter 11: Insolvency 127
11.1 Introduction 127
11.2 Tracing enterprises in difficulty 127
11.3 ('*Concordat judiciaire*' — *gerechtelijk akkoord*') composition 128
11.3.1 Conditions 128
11.3.2 Procedure 129
11.3.3 Creditors' rights 130
11.3.4 Composition by surrender of property 130
11.4 Bankruptcy 131
11.4.1 Conditions of bankruptcy 131
11.4.2 Judgment of the bankruptcy 132
11.4.3 Organisation of the bankruptcy 132
11.4.4 Consequences of the bankruptcy judgment 133
11.4.5 Termination of bankruptcy 136
11.4.6 Rehabilitation 136
11.4.7 Post-bankruptcy composition 136

11.5 Rights of creditors   137
11.6 Responsibilities and liabilities of third parties   139
11.7 International aspects   139
      11.7.1 Consequences of a Belgian bankruptcy order   139
      11.7.2 Consequences of a foreign bankruptcy decision   140

Chapter 12: Financing a Belgian Company   142
12.1 Introduction   142
12.2 Loans from a bank   142
12.3 Leasing   143
      12.3.1 Financial leasing   143
      12.3.2 Leasing of real estate   144
12.4 Factoring   145
12.5 Corporate finance   146
      12.5.1 Different methods of financing   146
      12.5.2 Capital increase   148
12.6 Banking operations   148
      12.6.1 Bank accounts   148
      12.6.2 Bank facilities   149
      12.6.3 Liability of banks and credit institutions   149
12.7 Negotiable instruments   150
      12.7.1 Bills of exchange ('*lettres de change — wisselbrieven*') 150
      12.7.2 Cheques   151
      12.7.3 Promissory notes ('*billets á ordre*' — '*order briefjes*') 153
12.8 Guarantees   154
      12.8.1 Personal and real sureties   154
      12.8.2 First demand guarantee   157

Chapter 13: Environmental planning   158
13.1 National development   158
13.2 Environmental control law   158
      13.2.1 Regionalisation and competent authorities   158
      13.2.2 Necessary permits   160
13.3 Environmental liabilities: penalties and liability   163
      13.3.1 Penalties   163
      13.3.2 Liability   164
      13.3.3 Insurance   166

Luxembourg

Chapter 14: Introduction   169
14.1 The courts   169
14.2 Intellectual property   170
  14.2.1 Trademarks   170
  14.2.2 Copyright   170

Chapter 15: Competition   172
15.1 EEC competition law   172
15.2 Luxembourg competition law   172
  15.2.1 Law of 5 July 1929 on unfair trading   172
  15.2.2 Law of 27 November 1986 listing unfair trading
    practices and penalising unfair competition 172
  15.2.3 Law of 5 June 1970 on restrictive trading practices 174
15.3 Consumer protection   174

Chapter 16: Business Organisations   177
16.1 Introduction   177
16.2 Legislation   177
16.3 Limited liability companies   178
  16.3.1 Public limited company (*société anonyme*)   178
  16.3.2 Private limited company (*société à responsabilité
    limitée* (SARL))   178
  16.3.3 Co-operative company with limited liability (*société coopérative*) 179
16.4 Partnerships
  16.4.1 General partnership (*société en nom collectif*) 179
  16.4.2 Limited partnership (*société en commandite simple* (SECS)) 180
  16.4.3 Partnership limited by shares (*société en commandite par actions*) 180
  16.4.4 Cooperative company (*société coopérative*)   180
  16.4.5 Civil company   181
16.5 Economic Interest Group (*groupement d'intérêts économiques* (GIE)) 181
  16.5.1 European Economic Interest Group (*groupement européen
    d'intérêts économiques* (GEIE))   181
16.6 Non-profit organisations   182
  16.6.1 *Associations sans but lucratif* (ASBL)   182
  16.6.2 *Etablissements d'utilité publique* (foundations) 182

16.7 Incorporation   183
  16.7.1 The main rules   183
  16.7.2 Principal costs on formation   184
16.8 Shareholders' rights   184

Chapter 17: Mergers and Acquisitions   185
17.1 Mergers and hive-offs   185
  17.1.1 Mergers   185
  17.1.2 Hive-offs   187
17.2 Share acquisitions   188
  17.2.1 General   188
  17.2.2 Transfer of shares for each company   189
17.3 Acquisition of goodwill   192

Chapter 18: Agency   194
18.1 Background   194
18.2 Commercial agents   194
  18.2.1 Absence of specific Luxembourg legislation   194
  18.2.2 Performance of the contract   195
  18.2.3 Termination of agency contracts   196
18.3 Commission agents (*commissionaires*)   196
18.4 Brokers   196
18.5 The commission agent's contract   196
18.6 Commercial representatives   197

Chapter 19: Distributorship   198
19.1 Definition   198
19.2 Legislation   198
19.3 Terms and clauses of the agreement   198
19.4 Termination   198

Chapter 20: Franchising   200
20.1 Legislation   200
20.2 Drafting of a franchise agreement   200
20.3 Characteristics   201

Chapter 21: Real property and succession   202
21.1 Real property   202

Contents   xiii

21.1.1 Sale and purchase   202
21.1.2 Business leases   204
21.2 Succession   205

Chapter 22: Immigration and Employment   207
22.1 Immigration   207
22.1.1 Non-EC nationals   207
22.1.2 EC nationals   210
22.1.3 Frontier worker's card   210
22.2 Employment   210
22.2.1 Legislation   210
22.2.2 Employment contract   211
22.2.3 Working conditions   212
22.2.4 Maternity leave   213
22.2.5 Worker representation   213
22.2.6 Social security   214

Chapter 23: Taxation   215
23.1 Introduction   215
23.2 Value added tax   216
23.3 Individual tax   216
23.4 Corporate income tax   218
23.4.1 Computation of taxable profit   218
23.4.2 Corporation with favourable tax regimes 219
23.4.3 Indirect business taxation   221
23.5 Tax on legal entities   221
23.6 Transfer pricing   222

Chapter 24: Insolvency   223
24.1 Introduction   223
24.2 Bankruptcy   223
24.2.1 Court's jurisdiction   223
24.2.2 Declaration of bankruptcy   223
24.2.3 Organisation   224
24.2.4 Consequences   224
24.2.5 Rehabilitation   225
24.2.6 Post-bankruptcy composition   225
24.3 Right of creditors   225
24.4 Responsibilities and liabilities of the management

of an insolvent business   226
24.5 International aspects   227

Chapter 25: Financing a Luxembourg company   228
25.1 Loans from a bank   228
25.2 Leasing   228
25.3 Factoring   229
25.4 Corporate finance   230
    25.4.1 Different methods of financing   230
    25.4.2 Capital increases   231
25.5 Banking operations   231
    25.5.1 Bank accounts   232
    25.5.2 Bank facilities   232
    25.5.3 Liability of banks and credit establishments   232
25.6 Negotiable instruments   232
    25.6.1 Bill of exchange   232
    25.6.2 Cheques   234
    25.6.3 Promissory notes   235
25.7 Guarantees   235
    25.7.1 Cautionnement   235
    25.7.2 Real sureties   236
    25.7.3 First demand guarantee   237

Chapter 26: Environmental Planning   238
26.1 Introduction   238
26.2 Area planning law   238
    26.2.1 Types of development plans   238
    26.2.2 Sanctions   239
26.3 Environmental law   240
26.4 Conservation law   242

Legislation Table   243

Index   249

BELGIUM

INTRODUCTION

As the host to the EC's executive body, ie the EC Commission, Belgium, and more specifically Brussels, tends traditionally to be viewed as the 'heart of Europe', and sometimes, in the minds of foreigners, its national identity tends to be restricted to, if not altogether absorbed, by the international role it has been entrusted with. Next to its role as host of the EC headquarters, however, Belgium presents specific features which should not be overlooked when doing business there.

When confronting the Belgian legal system, one must be aware that Belgium, small as it is, is far from being a monolithic country, and is far from being identical in mentality and habits to its neighbours. Too often, foreign businessmen fall into the trap of believing that they can conduct business in Belgium in the same way as they do in adjacent countries, and they discover, sometimes too late, that they have made some blatant mistakes in their assessment of the people or the legislation.

One of Belgium's most important features is probably its political structural organisation, which *de facto* reflects the divisions within its population. Belgium in effect is composed of three regions:

(1)   the Flemish Region, ie the provinces of Antwerp, Limburg, East and West Flanders, the district Halle-Vilvoorde and Leuven, headed by the Flemish Council (*Vlaamse Raad*) and the Flemish Executive (*Vlaamse Executieve*);

(2)   the Walloon Region, ie the provinces of Hainaut, Liège, Luxembourg and Namur as well as the district of Nivelles, headed by the Walloon Regional Council (Conseil Régional Wallon) and the Walloon Regional Executive (Exécutif Régional Wallon);

(3)   the Brussels Region, ie the 19 townships composing the capital of the country, headed, since 1989 by the Council of the Region of Brussels-Capital (*Conseil de la Région de Bruxelles-*

Capitale) and the Executive of the Region of Brussels-Capital (*Exécutif de la Région de Bruxelles-Capitale*).

Belgium also includes three communities: the Flemish, the Walloon and the German speaking communities. These communities have been given specific competence with regard to cultural matters, most education matters, inter-communities co-operation and international co-operation with regard to matters of their competence.

All three regions have the same fields of competence. The central State retains only residual competence over the matters which were not or are not expressly granted to the Regions or other bodies (provincial and local authorities).

One of the most important consequences of the federalisation process (started in the 1970s) is the diversity of the legislation applicable within the different regions to the various matters entrusted to the regional or community authorities, and the abundance of the legislation produced by those various bodies. Environmental issues are probably a good example of the regional complexities which the investor will sometimes have to face. Here, potentially sensitive activities spread over two regions will be subject to obtaining authorisations in both regions, according to different rules and subject to different conditions. In addition, it must be stressed that at this point in time, when a region fails to implement EC directives, the national state is powerless to sanction its failure or to take appropriate measures on its behalf. This should change in the future if the project of state reform currently discussed is implemented. In effect, in that case regions will be given direct responsibility.

Not all aspects of business life, however, are subject to the influence of Belgium's internal restructuring and linguistic variations. Belgium's legal system—which is applicable in all three regions—is still a codified system, based on the Napoleonic Code. Interpretations, however, of rules which are sometimes identical in their wording in France or The Netherlands vary from their corresponding interpretations in those countries. Even the variety of the cultures within Belgium itself can also sometimes result in differences of interpretation between northern and southern authors or jurisdictions.

A last feature which probably is common to all EC countries, is the impact on national law of the rules enacted at EC level (which sometimes are directly applicable, without any measure of implementation being required at a national level) and the pace of legislative change as a result of the implementation of provisions enacted by the EC. Here again, however, one should check the content of each national law, even on matters which were harmonised at EC level. Most of the time, EC directives grant the member states a number of options eg as to the timing of their national implementation, so that discrepancies will remain between the legislation of the member states, even as regards EC harmonised issues.

THE COURTS

In Belgium, the competence of the courts is determined on their practical field of activity (*ratione materiae*), on the one hand and on their geographical area of competence (*ratione loci*), on the other hand.

As far as the courts' practical field of activity is concerned, Belgium has three degrees of jurisdiction.

Competence to hear law suits in the first degree is granted (depending on the nature of the issue at stake and the type of measures sought) to: one of the courts of first instance (*tribunal de première instance—rechtbank van eerste aanleg*); the court of commerce (*tribunal de commerce—rechtbank van koophandel*); the labour court (*tribunal du travail—arbeidsrechtbank*); the president of one of the above mentioned courts (eg procedure in chambers, called référé—*kortgeding*); or the justice of the peace (*juge de paix—vrederechter*), who is competent to handle minor law suits.

Appeals lodged against the decisions made by courts of first degree fall to the competence of the court of appeal (*cour d'appel—hof van beroep*) or alternatively the labour court of appeal (*cour du travail—arbeidshof*), depending on the nature of the claim. (Courts of first degree are competent to hear appeals of decisions of justices of the peace.)

Pursuant to art 104 of the Constitution, Belgium has five Courts of Appeal: Brussels, which is competent for the province of Brabant; Ghent, for the two provinces of Flanders; Antwerp, for the provinces of Antwerp and Limburg; Liège, for the provinces of Liège, Namur and Luxemburg; Mons, for the prov ince of Hainaut. In cases which are reserved to the exclusive jurisdiction of the commercial court and for judgments made by the justice of the peace, the appeal court will be the court of first instance.

Decisions issued on appeal which, in the view of one of the parties, contravene the law or violate procedural requirements are referred to the Supreme Court (*Cour de Cassation—Hof van Cassatie*). Belgium has one single Supreme Court (*Cour de Cassation—Hofvan Cassatie*) which has jurisdiction, among other things, over all disputes regarding decisions made by the courts of appeal (Article 95 of the Constitution).

Administrative issues belong to the competence of the Council of State (*Conseil d'Etat—Raad van State*), which since quite recently has also provided a procedure in chambers (*référé administratif—administratief kortgeding*). The Council of State also has other areas of competence, eg to decide on the legality of laws or decrees and to determine disputes resulting from the federalisation process.

The general principles regulating any civil proceeding are as follows:

(1) Hearings and judgments are public affairs (this is generated by art 96 and 97 of the Constitution as well as by the European Convention for the Safeguard of Human Rights and Fundamental Freedoms):

(2) The parties themselves conduct the proceedings; and since a law suit is intended to obtain recognition of an individual subjective right, it is the parties who commence, pursue or abandon the proceedings as they deem appropriate. In addition, pursuant to art 1138, 2° of the Judicial Code, the judge may not make decisions on issues which have not been submitted to him:

(3) Conduct of proceedings is both written (summons, petition, submissions) and oral (hearing and pleadings); yet parties may agree between them that proceedings are to be conducted exclusively in writing (art 755 Judicial Code):

(4) The rights of the defence must be strictly complied with:

(5) Parties must adduce and prove the facts on which their action or defence is based. Also the judge may order *ex officio* measures of investigation. The judge may not, however, decide *ultra petita* (ie beyond the limits of the action or the defence):

(6) As a rule, parties should be diligent in the presentation of their action or defence. Such is not always the case, however, the courts often complain about the lack of diligence, sometimes intentional, of the parties.

LAWYERS

As a rule, only duly registered members of the bar (in French, (*avocats* and in Dutch, *advocaten*) are entitled to plead before the courts (with some exceptions, direct family members and the representative of a trade union for example, may represent a party in front of the labour court, provided a specific power of attorney has been conferred for that purpose). *Avocats* are entitled to appear before any court, with the exception of the civil chambers of the Supreme Court before which only a limited number of 16 lawyers, specifically appointed thereto, may appear.

Pursuant to art 728 of the Judicial Code, however, parties are not obliged to be represented by an *avocat*. They may appear at the hearing in person. The court may prohibit the party from presenting and defending his case, if it appears that passion or inexperience prevents him doing so properly (art 758 of the Judicial Code). In any event, it is usually inadvisable for a party to present his own case and the intervention of a lawyer on his behalf is recommended.

No distinction is made between barristers and solicitors. Traditionally, in Belgium, advice was sought from lawyers 'too late', ie when a court case was already pending or seriously threatening the parties. Belgian lawyers could therefore most usually be likened to barristers (court litigators and advocates) rather than to solicitors (clients' legal advisors). Nowadays, the situation has changed, and lawyers are consulted in their capacity both as legal advisers and as litigators. In most firms therefore, the classical Anglo-Saxon distinction has thus established itself in actual practice.

No regional qualifications are required. However, it goes without saying that it is advisable to select a lawyer who is fluent in the language in which the proceedings will be conducted.

Avocats have no monopoly on giving legal advice. Only the use of the title *avocat* is regulated by law. Legal advice therefore can be given by anyone. That has made it rather easy for foreign lawyers to be active on Belgian territory. Most foreign lawyers, of all nationalities, have established practices in Brussels, and most Belgian bars (as they are known) have proved both progressive and friendly in that respect. Lawyers are not the only players acting on the Belgian legal scene. Notaries public (*notaires—notarissen*) and bailiffs (*huissiers—gerechtsdeurwaarders*) also have an important role to play.

The Belgian notary, does not in fact fulfil the ancillary role of his English or American counterpart. The Belgian notary, who is a public officer, has exclusive competence, since the law of 16 March 1803, to approve all deeds which are to be given in authentic form. His intervention, therefore, is compulsory in several cases, such as, for instance, the incorporation of a commercial company, the sale of real estate, the creation of a mortgage, etc. Notaries are not free to render their services throughout Belgium but must exercise their functions in the specific judicial sector of their residence (*arrondissement judiciaire—gerechtelijk arrondissement*). A notary, however, can assist another notary who is active in another judicial sector. It is the latter who keeps the 'minutes' of the deed, ie the original of the executed deed.

The bailiff's role, on the other hand, is a judicial one. He is, in effect, given exclusive competence by the Judicial Code to perform all types of processes (*exploits—exploten*) in the judicial sector in which he adjudicates as per the royal decree appointing him. Bailiffs therefore will be used at several stages of the judicial procedure (eg for service of writs of summons and of court decisions, attachment orders and orders for obtaining statements of facts etc) and when other laws require their intervention (eg service of notice of transfer of claims, service of pledge agreements etc).

APPROACH TO LEGAL ISSUES

As a rule, and especially in Brussels and in the north of the country, business is conducted with very much of a 'no nonsense' approach. Belgians tend to be rather down to earth and appreciate straightforwardness in their counterparts. In court proceedings, written evidence will be of the utmost importance, since it takes precedence over all other types of evidence, but despite this, Belgians have a tendency to avoid recording everything on paper unless they particularly want to make sure of binding their co-contracting party. Especially, in the early stages of negotiations, some reluctancy to record anything in writing is to be expected. One possible explanation of this trait probably lies in Belgians' habitual flexibility. Their sense of secrecy may also be partially at stake.

But Belgians often, still consider lawyers in their traditional role, ie as that of litigating barristers, and thus tend to believe that the advent of lawyers will simply slow down the negotiation process and make it more difficult, rather than achieving the contrary. It is therefore not exceptional to see them attending negotiations on their own or together with their accountant or *reviseur d'entreprises—bedrijfsrevisor* (a sort of chartered accountant). It seems to be quite common practice, for instance, to see company *reviseurs d'entreprises* assisting the shareholders (especially in small or medium sized enterprises) in their negotiations with candidate purchasers of their shares, strange as this may seem. It is also common practice that lawyers will be acting behind the scenes, in order to give negotiations a non-aggressive but more commercial and friendly outlook.

If basic advice as to how approach Belgian operators had to be given in 'do's' and 'don'ts' form, it could be given as follows:

Do	Don't
Check the relevant legal background both before and during the course of negotiations.	Believe that Belgium is just like France or The Netherlands.
Record in writing the agreement reached.	Rely on a handshake or other verbal assurance, which are difficult to prove in possible court proceedings.
Beware of the potential variations in legal rules in the various regions and of the existing linguistic regulations.	Believe that Belgium is a monolithic country.

1
INTELLECTUAL AND
INDUSTRIAL PROPERTY

1.1 INTRODUCTION

As is the case at the level of the international conventions in this field, a distinction is made under Belgian law between intellectual and industrial property rights. This distinction is of little practical consequence. As a rule, however, the protection of intellectual property rights, as opposed to that of industrial property rights, is not subject to prior registration.

Specific legislation regarding patents, trademarks and copyrights has existed in Belgium since the end of the 19th century and, of course, has subsequently been amended several times. Designs, models and service marks were covered at a later stage. A new draft copyright law has been in preparation for a few years now. Its adoption, however, has been delayed on several occasions.

Belgium is a party to most international treaties governing intellectual and property rights. As a result of these treaties, foreign nationals of the relevant signatory states are usually granted in Belgium the same rights as Belgian nationals. In addition, provided the conditions thereto are complied with, nationals of the states who hold rights as a result of the registration of patents, trademarks, designs or models in any of the relevant signatory states, enjoy in Belgium for a certain period of time determined by law, a right of priority over subsequent applications for the same.

1.2 PATENTS

The first 'Belgian' patent law, dated 24 May 1854, was changed several times and finally replaced by the law on patents of 28 March 1984, which came into force on 1 January 1987.

Belgian law does not prejudice the application of international treaties which are enforceable in Belgium, such as the Union Convention of Paris of 20 March 1883, signed on 14 July 1967, the Treaty of Washington (Patent Co-operation Treaty) of 19 June 1970, the Convention of Munich, dated 5 October 1973, relating to European patents, or the Treaty of Luxembourg, dated 15 December 1975, relating to a European patent for the Common Market. Especially as a result of the Patent Co-operation Treaty and of the Convention of Munich which in short, provide for a single procedure pertaining to the delivery of a patent intended to be effective in all signatory states selected by the applicant, the number of national applications has decreased noticeably. According to recent studies, around 95 per cent of the foreigners who wish to obtain patent protection in Belgium in fact make use of the European procedure.

1.2.1 DEFINITION

According to Belgian law any invention can be patented provided it is new (ie not part of the current status of the technology), and can be commercially exploited. Software, presentation of data, etc, however, are expressly excluded from the scope of protection of the law of 28 March 1984. Software falls instead under the protection granted by copyright law.

1.2.2 PROCEDURE

Application for a patent must be filed by the inventor or his assignee with the Office for Industrial Property which is a section of the Ministry of Economic Affairs. The patent application must contain drawings and a description of the invention, which must be sufficient to allow the device or process to be implemented without undue experimentation by anyone ordinarily skilled in the art.

Upon request by the applicant, a search is carried out by the European Patent Office in Munich. That search, however, is not compulsory and, in any case, is essentially advisory. Even if, after completion of that search, the advice of the European Patent Office is negative, the patent will be granted. In effect, Belgian patents are granted without prior examination of the patentability of the inventions, without guarantee of their merit or of the accuracy of the description. Only the courts have a right to decide whether or not the material requirements of a patent are fulfilled. If no search is conducted, the duration of validity of the patent is reduced from 20 to six years after application is filed.

After the above-mentioned procedures have been dealt with, the patent will be granted by Ministerial Decree. Upon delivery of the patent, it is registered in the Register of Patents (*Registre des brevets d'invention—Register der Uitvindingsoctrooien*). This register is accessible to the public at the Ministry of Economic Affairs. Exclusive right to the invention is obtained from that moment on.

Application, research and delivery taxes have to be paid. From the third year on, progressive yearly taxes have to be paid in order to preserve the patent.

1.2.3 PROTECTION, EXPLOITATION AND REMEDIES

The patent gives its holder the exclusive right to exploit the patented product or process, for the life of the patent, ie as a rule, for 20 years. (In some circumstances, the duration is reduced to six years. In any case, non-payment of the annual dues will result *ex officio* in the loss of the patent).

The claims contained in the patent application establish the limits of the protection. As a rule, the holder of the patent is entitled to bar any other person from manufacturing or using the patented product or process, or from selling, using, trading or keeping in stock patented products or products which are based upon the patent. The holder of the patent may also bar third parties from indirect counterfeiting.

There are four exceptions to the exclusivity granted by a patent:

(1)   If the patent holder does not exploit his patent within the first four years after the application for the patent, or within three years after it is granted, without the justification of valid grounds, an application can be filed with the Ministry of Economic Affairs by a third party in order to obtain a forced licence:

(2)   A person who in good faith possessed or used the patented invention on the Belgian territory prior to the filing or priority date of the patent will have a personal right to continue to exploit the invention. The notion of 'possession on the Belgian territory' is broadly construed, and will cover even the situation where a foreign enterprise markets the invention in Belgium, whether directly or through a subsidiary:

(3) The inventor of a device which cannot be exploited without infringing an existing patent may seek to obtain a licence nevertheless, provided the patent he is seeking presents a noticeable technical interest:

(4) The patent protection is subject to the 'exhaustion rule'. In short, the patent holder's right to control the manufacture, marketing or application of the patented item ends (unless the product has been altered) after that product has legally been put on the market in Belgium (or elsewhere in the European Community) by the patent owner or with his express consent.

In case of patent infringement, the patent holder may apply to the court of first instance to stop the manufacture of the patented product or machine, the use or sale of patented processes, or the sale or storing of products made using the patented device or process, and claim damages. The court can provide daily penalties in cases where its order is not abided by immediately.

Confiscation of all counterfeit products and all equipment intended for their manufacture can be ordered against an intentional counterfeiter. The latter can also be sentenced to the payment of a sum equal to the price of counterfeit products already sold.

Action against a counterfeiter can be very quick and effective since the Belgian Judicial Code authorises the patent holder to apply, by *ex parte* application, for an authorisation to seize the counterfeit products as well as all documents likely to establish the infringement, in order to obtain their description by an expert. The judge ordering seizure can also prohibit the alleged counterfeiter from disposing of the counterfeit products, entrust them to a custodian and even authorise the seizure of the proceeds of their sale. In theory, the prohibition on disposing of the products can be applied, and ordered, for an indefinite duration, for example until the decision regarding the merits of the case. Bearing in mind the length of court procedures, it is, however, advisable to limit the claim in that respect to the period of time necessary for the expert to file his report. Indeed, if the judge deciding on the merits of the case rules against the plaintiff, the latter might be held liable for substantial compensation if he has frozen the activities of the defendant for a long period of time. Of course, the defendant is entitled to seek in court the release of the products seized.

A patent holder may renounce his exclusive rights by sending a written and signed declaration to the minister.

1.2.4 EUROPEAN PATENT

Pursuant to the Munich Convention of 5 October 1973, a European Patent covering the territory of any of the states which are a party to that convention, may be requested. Filing may then be made either at the European office or the local office, which will then forward the request to the European office.

Pursuant to art 64(1) of the Munich Convention, a European patent confers the same rights as those granted by a national patent, effective on the date that notice of its issue is published, and within each member state for which the patent has been issued. According to Belgian law, this protection will only be granted when the Belgian office is provided with a copy of the claims written in one of Belgium's national languages (ie French, German or Dutch).

1.3 TRADEMARKS

Trademarks are primarily regulated by the Uniform Benelux Law (hereinafter referred to as 'UBL' dated 19 March 1962, and incorporated into Belgium law by the law of 30 June 1969 which came into force on 1 January 1971). A protocol dated 10 November 1983, approved by the law dated 8 August 1986 has extended the scope of application to service marks, and came into force on 1 January 1987. Belgium is also a party to international treaties regarding trademarks, such as the Treaty of Madrid signed on 14 July 1967, concerning the international registration of trademarks, which came into force in Belgium on 12 February 1975.

EC regulations and directives must also be borne in mind in respect of trademark protection:

(1) Regulation 3842/86 of the Council of the European Communities, dated 1 December 1986, concerning the establishment of measures forbidding the free circulation of counterfeit products.

(2) Regulation 3077/87 of the Commission of the European Communities dated 14 October 1987, establishing the measures for the execution of the aforementioned Regulation 3842/86.

(3) First Directive of the Council of the European Communities, dated 21 December 1988 (89/104, Publ EEC 11 February 1989, L40/1) in order to adapt the trademark law in each of the member states.

The member states should have incorporated this directive by 28 December 1991 at the latest, but the Commission decided to give the member states an extension period until 31 December 1992.

A proposal of the Directive concerning comparative advertising and aiming to modify Directive 84/450/EEC on misleading advertising authorises the inclusion of a competitor's trademark in an advertisement, within certain limits.

1.3.1 DEFINITION

Trademark law in Belgium follows the generally accepted principles of trademark law elsewhere, ie, to avoid confusion in the market place among products or businesses. As elsewhere, any name (whether real or fanciful), design, shape, number, form of product of package or anything else which distinguishes products or services may constitute a trademark. Forms and packaging may not be registered as a mark if they are determined by the nature of the product itself, if they substantially influence the value of the product, or give an industrial advantage.

Trademarks may be individual (a name by which a company distinguishes its products and/or services from the products and/or services of other companies) or collective (a name whereby certain common qualities of products are distinguished from products of different enterprises). Bearing in mind the above, the validity of a trademark is subject to it being distinctive, not leading to confusion with existing marks actually used in connection with products or services and not offending public policy and morality. The trademark must be registered.

1.3.2 TRADEMARK PROTECTION PROCEDURE

Contrary to the practice in some jurisdictions, such as the United States for instance, trademark protection arises in Belgium only after the registration of the mark. Mere prior usage confers no right. An application for trademark registration containing the required drawing and description is filed either with the Belgian National Office or with the Benelux Trade Mark Bureau, and a search is performed against existing registered marks. If the search reveals the existence of a similar or identical trademark for the same category of products, however, the applicant may decide to maintain his application. He is liable solely for his decision.

1.3.3 PROTECTION, EXPLOITATION AND REMEDIES

Protection lasts for at least ten years from the date of the application. The design for which the trademark is being registered may not be modified either at the time of registration nor at the time of renewal. The protection can be renewed for further periods of ten years provided the formalities relating thereto have been complied with and the duties paid. An application for renewal must be made within six months prior to the expiry of the registration. The renewals will have effect as from the date of expiry.

The registration of a trademark gives priority to the holder of the registered trademark. The holder of a trademark may, based on his exclusive rights, oppose:

(1)	any use which is made of the trademark or a resembling sign for products for which the trademark has been registered or for similar products;

(2)	any other use which is made in business of the trademark or a design which resembles the design in question, without any valid reason, under conditions which may jeopardise the holder of a trademark.

Under the same conditions, the holder of a trademark may claim compensation for damage suffered as a result of such use.

The exclusive right to a trademark established in one of the national or regional languages of the Benelux, will also apply to its translation into one of the other languages. The judge will rule on the similarity resulting from translations into one or more languages which are foreign to the Benelux territory.

In case of an infringement of a trademark, the holder may seek to bar the use of the mark and claim damages. Counterfeiting or fraudulent use of a trademark, or knowingly selling or trading products with counterfeit or fraudulently used trademarks are also subject to criminal prosecution, backed by fines and imprisonment.

1.3.4 INTERNATIONAL REGISTRATION

The Treaty of Madrid of 14 July 1967, provides for the international registration of trademarks at the offices of the World Organisation of Intellectual Property ('WOIP') in Geneva. Prior to applying for an international registration, a national registration must be obtained. The application forms for the international registration will be forwarded by the competent national offices ('Ministry of Economic Affairs') to the headquarters of the WOIP.

1.4 COPYRIGHT

The Belgian law on copyrights can be found in the Copyright Law (*Auteurswet—Loi d'Auteur*) of 22 March 1886, amended by the law of 5 March 1921 (art 38) and the law of 11 March 1958 (art 21bis).

The most important international laws are:
- the Berne Convention of 9 September 1886. The rules of this convention, ratified by approximately 75 countries, may be directly invoked in Belgium when they are more advantageous for a Belgian author. This is provided by the law of 27 July, 1953.
- Universal Convention of Geneva of 6 September 1952, last revision in Paris, 1971.

1.4.1 DEFINITIONS

Under Belgian Copyright law, protection will be granted to a work if the following conditions are met:
- the 'work' is expressed in a particular *form*; and
- the work is *original*.

Copyright protects literary and artistic works, broadly defined. It protects an original expression but not the idea behind the expression. An expression is considered original if it bears the personal stamp of the author. The protection arises at the moment the expression is fixed, *without* the need of registration. The monetary value of the work, its aesthetic quality, or the purpose for which it was created are irrelevant.

Copyright protection may extend to practically any written material including: classic literary works such as plays, novels and poetry, advertising, letters and interviews, translations and adaptations, musical works whether written or not, and to architectural works, designs, photographs, paintings, clothes and jewellery. Discussion exists concerning audio-visual works, data bases and neighbour rights.

Under Belgian law, only a natural person can be an author although he may transfer certain rights to a corporation or other entity. If several people have together created a work and their contribution cannot be separated, they must act together with respect to the work. If the contributions can be separated, each may act individually with respect to his own contribution. If the work is anonymous, the editor will be considered as the author as long as the author remains unknown. If the work is posthumous, the rights belong to the owner of the work. This can be the beneficiary or another person. If several authors have worked separately, one after another, on a work, the collaboration is spread in time. The last author must have the permission of the other authors before he can make the composed work public.

1.4.2 PROTECTION, EXPLOITATION AND REMEDIES

The rules adopted in Belgium as regards the duration of the copyright protection are similar to those provided in the Berne Convention. Copyright protection lasts for 50 years following the death of the author. In the case of copyrights protecting joint works, the rights exist for 50 years after the death of the last surviving author. The protection for 'posthumous works', as for anonymous works and works created under a pseudonym, exists for 50 years after the publication, exhibition or performance of the work.

Belgian copyright law, in common with French law, distinguishes between an author's 'moral' rights, and his pecuniary (or patrimonial) rights. Moral rights are those which have to do with the author's reputation. They include the right to control whether and when a work will be made public or performed and the circumstances thereof, having his name associated with his work (right of paternity), not having the work mutilated or distorted, and the right to withdraw his work. Pecuniary rights are all other rights, including the right to profit from sale of the work.

An author may assign his pecuniary rights. In turn, it is still discussed in Belgium whether or not he is permitted to assign his moral rights in a work. If the author is an employee, the copyright in works he created generally is held to belong to the employer. The employee's moral rights, however, are retained by the employee. It is unclear under Belgian law whether, as in France, the moral rights of an author survive his death and may be exercised by his descendants in perpetuity.

1.4.3 SOFTWARE AND SEMICONDUCTORS

Until 1984 there was debate about whether software should be protected under patent or copyright law. In 1984, taking its direction from the Berne Convention, the legislature decided that copyright was the appropriate vehicle by expressly excluding software from patent protection. All aspects of software protection, including object and source codes, documentation and the like are now considered to be protected by copyright. A proposal to conform Belgian copyright law to requirements of the 1991 EC Directive on the protection of software (Lallemand proposal) is pending.

The Lallemand proposal would limit the duration of copyright protection for software to 25 years following its creation, and would give to the creator of the software the right to authorise reproduction of programs. Following the EC Directive, only the expression involved in the application programs themselves would be protected: the programming languages, interfaces, algorithms, logic or ideas underlying the programs would not be protected. Furthermore, there would be a limited right of reverse engineering where the creator of a program refused to disclose what was required to permit another to create compatible programs.

The topography of semiconductors is protected in Belgium since the law of 10 January 1990 under a legislative scheme which follows the provisions of an EC Directive. No formalities of registration are required. Protection lasts ten years from the date of first commercial exploitation, or 15 years where exploitation does not occur. Protection is conditional upon the design or topography of the semiconductor being the product of intellectual activity, and not having been previously commonly known in the industry.

1.5 DESIGNS AND MODELS

In Belgium, designs and models can be protected both by the copyright legislation and the specific rules of the Benelux Uniform Law contained in the Benelux Convention on Designs and Models dated 25 October 1966, ratified by the law of 1 December 1970 (which came into force on 1 January 1975). Protection under the Copyright Act requires the design or model to have a clear artistic character (ie to show distinctively the imprint of the artist's personality) and is limited to the artistic character of the design or model in question. Only those rules specific to the protection granted to designs and models under the Benelux Uniform Law are examined.

1.5.1 DEFINITION

Protection of a design or model requires that it gives a new appearance to a utility product (eg wrapping paper, wall paper, postcards), and is not necessary to achieve a technical effect (which would be protected by patent). A design or a model is not new if it has been previously filed, or if it was known in the Benelux countries to enterprises of the same commercial or industrial sector at any time during the previous 50 years. The design or model must actually be part of a product which has a utilitarian function and may not be strictly ornamental. Registration of a design or model may be refused on grounds of public order or morality.

1.5.2 PROCEDURE

Exclusive right to a model or design requires the previous filing, with the Benelux Office or its national representation office, of an application which should contain sufficient detail as to the characteristics of the model or design in question. In addition the application must be published (although completion of that formality may be postponed for a maximum of one year upon request of the applicant).

1.5.3 PROTECTION, EXPLOITATION AND REMEDIES

Design or model registration yields an exclusive right to exploit the design for a five-year term, subject to the exhaustion rule and the right of any third party who, in good faith, undertook on the territory of one of the Benelux countries, the manufacture of an identical or similar design or model prior to registration of the design or model in question. The registration may be renewed twice over a period of five years, by the payment of the relevant duties.

Subject to these limits, the holder of rights in the design or model may oppose the manufacture, import, sale, lease, exhibition, delivery, use, or retention of an identical or similar product for an industrial or commercial purpose and may file a suit against the counterfeiter before the court of first instance or the justice of the peace, depending on the financial importance of the case. He is also entitled to claim compensation after the application has been published or if it can be proved that the counterfeiter was aware of the existence of the design or model. Often publication of the court decision will be ordered. Reproduction for private use is not prohibited by the statute.

The holder of a drawing or a model may request the deletion of the registration at all times, or renounce the protection.

1.6 KNOW-HOW, TRADE SECRETS AND CONFIDENTIAL INFORMATION

'Know-how', trade secrets and confidential information are not the subject of comprehensive regulation in Belgium. Protection therefore must be sought under the general rules of law, including, general contract law, art 1382 of the Civil Code, the Fair Trade Practices Act, the Law on Employment Contracts and the Criminal Code.

In the absence of contractual provision, art 1382 of the Civil Code provides for the seeking of redress, provided evidence can be brought that the know-how has been unlawfully appropriated and that damage resulted therefrom for the holder of that know-how. The quantum of the damage also needs to be proved.

The Fair Trade Practices Act also offers an appropriate course of action. That Act in effect allows a seller who is the victim of unfair trade practices to apply for a court order which prevents the continuation of any such practice with immediate effect.

As far as employees are concerned, protection is granted against release of secret information under the Law on Employment Contracts which imposes on them a duty of secrecy both during the contract as well as after its termination. Infringement of that duty enables the employer to terminate the contract forthwith, without notice period or compensation, provided the conditions for immediate dismissal are fulfilled. If the employee acted fraudulently or intentionally, criminal action can also be initiated.

A third party who knowingly participated in an infringement of a contractual provision which prohibits release of confidential information, can be held liable for compensation based on the theory of third party accomplice. Often, however, the proof of the third party's knowledge will be difficult to give.

Belgian law contains no provisions specifically aimed at licences of know-how, but EC competition law and regulations address such matters in the context of licenses of other intellectual property, such as trademarks or patents.

1.7 LICENSING

1.7.1 LICENSING OF PATENTS

The holder of rights in a patent may transfer or assign them outright, or license the rights. In either case, the transaction must be recorded in a written document signed by both parties, notified to the Ministry of Economic Affairs and registered. An agreement which is not in writing will be considered void. If a licence has not been registered, the licence holder may not challenge an infringing use of the patent.

The rights of the holder of the licence to challenge an infringing use of the patent will depend on whether or not he holds an exclusive licence. Unless otherwise stipulated in the licensing agreement, an exclusive licence holder is entitled to institute court proceedings against such a use if, after due notification, the owner of the patent fails to do so. The non-exclusive holder, on the other hand, may not institute proceedings during the life of the contract. Both types of licensees are, nevertheless, entitled to take part in infringement proceedings instituted by the patent owner, in order to obtain compensation for their own damage (ie the profits the licensee could have made on the sales which he lost as a result of the infringement). Both need to prove, of course, that they hold a valid licence.

When drafting a licensing agreement, parties should bear in mind the principles of European competition law, particularly the terms of the Commission's block exemption 2349/84. This block exemption exempts certain licence agreements relating to patents on inventions from the application of art 85 para 1 of the Treaty of Rome. The block exemption regulation contains various 'white' (automatically exempted) and 'black' (non-exempted) clauses of licensing contracts.

1.7.2 LICENSING OF TRADEMARKS

The exclusive right to a trademark can be transferred or can be the subject of a licence for all or part of the products for which the trademark has been registered. In practice, the 'licence' should not be confused with other operations which do not involve any licensing. For instance the mere fact of reselling a product supplied by the trademark holder would not qualify as a licence as such. A trademark licence in fact can be defined as an agreement whereby the holder of the trademark rights authorises someone else to use the mark in connection with products which the licensee manufactured, assembled or otherwise processed.

For a licence or transfer of trademark to be valid, the following conditions must be met:

(1) The transfer *inter vivos* and the licence must be established in writing.

(2) The *transfer* must be granted for the whole territory of the Benelux countries. In the event of the *licensing* of a trademark for a limited territory, such an agreement is valid. The limitation will not, however, legally exist. This means that in the event of an infringement of this limitation, a claim based on the infringement of the trademark will not be possible. Only a claim for breach of contract will be possible.

The transfer or licence will not be opposable against third parties until after registration of the extract of the deed of transfer or licence agreement or of a declaration which the parties have signed to that effect, provided, however, that this registration is made in conformity with the formalities and against payment of duties, determined by the enforcement regulation.

The licensee has authority to claim compensation for damage suffered pursuant to unlawful use of trademark by third parties, provided, however, that he acts together with the holder of the trademark. The withdrawal of the registration of the licence can only be requested by the owner of the trademark and the licensee acting together.

In negotiating or drafting any licence of a trademark, attention must be paid to EC law as well as the Uniform Benelux Law, because of the substantial EC limitations on anti-competitive agreements or actions.

1.7.3 LICENSING OF COPYRIGHTS

Unlike the case with patents and trademarks, Belgian law does not specifically provide for licensing of copyrights, which are treated under general contract principles of the Civil Code. The exhaustion rule is applicable to copyright licences, however, so if an author has permitted the exploitation of his work in an EC member state, he will be unable to prohibit the circulation of legitimate reproductions of the work in other EC member states.

In the case of an infringement, the person holding rights in the copyright may seek an injunction to prevent further infringement, a seizure of illegally-made copies, and damages.

1.7.4 LICENSING OF DESIGNS AND MODELS

Transfers *inter vivos* must be in writing and all transfers must be operated for the whole Benelux territory. A licence can be given orally. Any limitation is null and void, with the exception of limitation in time.

A transfer or licence is not valid against third parties before registration of the extract of the deed of transfer or licence agreement or of a declaration which the parties have signed to that effect, and payment of the registration duties.

1.7.5 LICENSING OF KNOW-HOW

The know-how licensing provisions are addressed in the Commission's block exemption regulation 556/89. In order to benefit from the exemption, the know-how involved in the transaction must be secret, substantial (ie of importance for the whole or a specific part of a process, product, service or its development) and identified (ie sufficiently described or recorded).

The regulation also covers mixed agreements containing provisions relating to other intellectual property (for example, trademarks) where those provisions are ancillary, are of assistance in achieving the object of the licensed technology and contain no obligation restrictive of competition other than those also attached to the know-how and already exempted under the regulation. In particular, the regulation will also apply in the case of mixed know-how/patent licences, which are not exempt under Regulation 2349/94.

1.8 INVENTIONS OF EMPLOYEES

Belgian law does not contain specific rules regarding inventions made by employees. Inventions, processes, discoveries, creations which result from the performance of the employment contract itself are considered the property of the employer. The employee shall not have any entitlement to any other compensation than the salary he has been promised under the employment contract, unless provided otherwise by contract. On the other hand, he must supply the employer with all information which is necessary to decide on the use of the invention made. This principle is expressly reproduced by the Uniform Benelux Law on Designs and Models.

The employee's moral rights over his work are, however usually recognised. The Law on Patents, for instance, provides that, if the applicant is not the author, the latter has the right to be mentioned in the patent. The Copyright Act also allows the real author to claim authorship on the work, even after transfer, and to oppose distortions, modifications, etc.

Sometimes inventions will have a mixed status, partially a result of the performance of the contract, partially a personal invention. It will therefore often be appropriate to include in the employment contract specific provisions governing the status of inventions which could be made during the period of employment. Parties are free to insert in that respect any provision they consider appropriate. An employment contract which contains a clause according to which all inventions of the employee, even when they are made outside the office or outside working hours, belong to the employer, is valid. The validity of clauses which would enable the employer to claim the ownership of inventions totally alien to his activities or corporate object, however, is disputed.

2
COMPETITION

2.1 INTRODUCTION

This chapter deals exclusively with the rules enacted in Belgium at national level regarding competition issues. Of course, EC competition law is part and parcel of the general organised system of competition in all EC member states. Belgian courts will, therefore, refuse to grant enforcement to an agreement or provision, as the case may be, which would be void because it infringes the prohibition laid down by art 85, s 1 of the Treaty of Rome (prohibition of practices restricting competition—see introduction to chapter 6) or by art 86 (prohibition of abuse of dominant position). An infringement of EC competition rules can also trigger the application of the Fair Trade Practices Act and the cessation of the relevant practice can be claimed in court on the basis of that Act. However, since the EC competition rules are common to all member states, they shall not be examined in this chapter.

2.2 BELGIAN COMPETITION LAW

2.2.1 PRESENT LEGAL SITUATION

Belgium has, by tradition, a rather liberal approach to competition. Freedom to do business has been recognised a long time ago by a decree, called the *Décret d'Allarde* dating back to 10 November 1795, and still in force as of today. This freedom of course is not absolute and is limited by the respect of the freedom of others.

In 1960 a law regarding restraint of trade was enacted (law of 27 May 1960 regarding protection against abuse of economic power). Its purpose is to regulate practices restrictive of competition and abuses of dominant positions. That law did not prevent such agreements restrictive of competition nor did it regulate concentrations. It was limited to prohibiting restrictions of competition which conflicted with the general good. It was in effect the legis-lator's belief that agreements concluded between undertakings were concurred to safeguard the economic structure of the country against increasing competition. This law, which contains an administrative procedure and criminal sanctions, is, in practice seldom used and has for long been considered rather ineffective. The 1960 Act's days, however, are now nearly over. Indeed, on 5 August 1991 a new Act was passed on the protection of economic competition.

2.2.2 LAW ON THE PROTECTION OF ECONOMIC COMPETITION

The law of 5 August 1991 which will come into force on 1 April 1993, reproduces with some variations, for the Belgian mar-ket, the competition rules existing at EC level. In the opinion of the legislature itself, the case law established by the Court of Justice therefore should be used as a guideline for the future interpretation of the Belgian law.

Pursuant to these new provisions:

(1) Agreements, joint practices between undertakings, decisions by associations of undertakings and joint practices which aim or have as effect to restrict or distort materially the competition on the relevant Belgian market or a substantial part thereof, are prohibited and null and void. Exemptions, either indivi-dual or block exemptions, and negative clearances, as the case may be, can be applied for. The conditions to be met in order to obtain an individual exemption are identical to those provided at EC level. Implementation measures are still expected with regard to block exemptions and negative clear-ances. As at EC level, the law aims to protect workable competition, ie effective competition.

(2) Excessive exploitation of a dominant position in the relevant Belgian market or part thereof is prohibited. Negative clear-ance only can be applied for with regard to issues where a dominant position is involved.

As a rule (ie until it has been proved to the contrary), these two restrictions, however, do not apply when each party is a small and medium sized enterprise as defined by the law of 17 July 1975 relating to the bookkeeping of enterprises, ie undertakings which do not supersede more than one of the following criteria:

- Annual average of employment of 50 persons.
- Annual turnover, VAT excluded of, BF 170 million.
- Total of balance sheet of BF 85 million.

If the undertaking employs more than 100 persons on an annual basis, however, it will not qualify as a small or medium sized enterprise, irrespective its figures in respect of the other two criteria. As regards banks, credit and other financial institutions, only the number of employees and the total of the balance sheet are borne in mind.

Agreements, concerted practices or other arrangements for which individual exemption is sought, and which do not benefit from an exemption under art 85 para 3 of the Treaty of Rome, must be notified to the Competition Service (*Service de la Concurrence— Dienst voor Mededinging*). Notification is not required for agreements which are considered to contain minimal restrictions specifically listed by the new Act. Notification presents the distinct advantage that no fines can be imposed in connection with events occuring after the notification, provided they remain within the limits of the activity described in the notification. That benefit is not granted when a negative clearance is applied for. Abuses of a dominant position therefore are never exempted from fines.

The new Act also subjects operations of *concentration* carried out by one or more undertakings which together have a total turnover of more than BEF one billion and control more than 20 per cent of the market concerned, to the approval of the Competition Council. *Concentrations* that are subject to control by the Commission of the EC are not concerned with the provisions of the new Act.

The provisions of the 1991 Act, in respect of *concentrations* however, are inspired by those of the EC regulation regarding the control of large scale mergers. According to the law, a *concentration* is completed, except in some cases provided by law, when:

(1)   two or more enterprises which were previously independent, merge; or when

(2)   one or more persons already controlling at least one enterprise, or one or more enterprises acquire, directly or indirectly, the control of the whole or of parts of one or more other enterprises.

A *concentration* must be previously approved. To that end, it must be notified to the Competition Office within one week after completion of the agreement, the publication of the takeover or exchange bid or of the acquisition of a controlling interest. *Concentrations* which are the subject of an agreement must be jointly notified by the parties. Failure to notify a concentration can result in fines of BEF 20,000 to BEF one million being imposed, even if the *concentration* is found acceptable.

Pending the investigation procedure, the *concentration* operation must be suspended, and parties must refrain from taking any measure which is related to the *concentration* and which would result in being irreversible or modifying the structure of the market in a long-lasting way. After the first month of investigation, the Competition Council may decide on the acceptability of the measure contemplated. Failure to abide by that provision exposes the undertaking to fines and liability towards third parties.

The Act of 5 August 1991 creates three new bodies:

(1)   The Competition Office (*Service de la Concurrence—Dienst voor de Mededinging*) of the Ministry of Economic Affairs, which is entrusted with the investigation and statement of prohibited practices.

(2)   The Competition Council (*Conseil de la Concurrence—Raad voor de Mededinging*) created within the Ministry of Economic Affairs and operating as an administrative court.

(3)   The Competition Commission (*Commission de la Concurrence —Commissie voor de Mededinging*) created within the Central Council for the Economy (*Conseil Central de l'Economie— Centrale Raad voor het Bedrijfsleven*). The Commission has an advisory function.

Complaints, applications for negative clearance, individual exemption or approval of a concentration, etc will be investigated by the Competition Office and decided upon by the Competition Council. The investigation may not relate to events which took place more than five years previously. The Competition Office is entrusted with very broad powers of investigation (similar to those of the EC Commission) and may call upon the assistance of the President of the Competition Council if it meets with opposition from the enterprise. Failure to abide by its requests, false information, incomplete information, etc may result in fines being imposed.

The Competition Council will make a decision, based on the report drafted by the Competition Office, after having heard all parties involved. Parties will also be given access to the investigation file (confidential documents excluded). If the Competition Council decides that the practice investigated is prohibited, it may impose fines (with a maximum of 10 per cent of the turnover of the parties involved) and daily penalties (maximum BEF 250,000 per day) in cases where its decision is not immediately abided by. Decisions with regard to *concentrations* are made in two steps. First the Council conducts a preliminary investigation at the end of which either the procedure is pursued (because the acceptability of the *concentration* is seriously doubted) or is closed (because the *concentration* is outside the scope of the law or appears acceptable). That first decision must be reached no later than one month after the notification has been filed and found to be complete. Secondly, if it is decided to pursue the procedure, further investigation is carried out, after which the Council issues a decision. If no decision is issued within 75 days after the Council has decided to start the procedure. The decisions of the Competition Council and of its president may be appealed before the Court of Appeal of Brussels within 30 days of the decision being published in the Belgian Official State Journal or notified to the parties, as the case may be. The decisions of the Court of Appeal are also published in the same gazette.

When the solution of a court case depends on the lawful character of a restrictive practice governed by the law, the court can refer the question to the Court of Appeal of Brussels which in turn can request the Competition Office to investigate the situation. Interim measures may also be issued by the president of the Competition Council in order to achieve the suspension of the investigated competition restrictions, if it is urgent to avoid a situation likely to cause either a substantial, imminent and irreparable damage to the undertakings whose interests are affected by those restrictions, or if the restrictions are likely to damage the general economic interest. The decision regarding interim measures is notified to the parties concerned.

2.3 UNFAIR COMPETITION

2.3.1 ARTICLES 1382–1384 BELGIAN CIVIL CODE

The law of 14 July 1991 discussed below already gives the victim of unfair trade practices, either the seller or consumer, some remedy. That law does not, however, enable one to obtain an indemnity in respect of the damage suffered as a result of the unfair trade practice. That indemnity needs to be sought from the usual courts on the basis of articles 1382–1384 of the Belgian Civil Code, which basically provide that any damage caused to a third party must be compensated. As under French law, to be awarded an indemnity on that basis it is required to establish that.

(1) Unfair trade practices have been used.
(2) Damage has been caused.
(3) The damage results from the unfair trade practices in question.

The indemnity will as a rule be calculated bearing in mind the effect of damage suffered as a result of the unfair trade practices concerned and the loss of profit resulting from the same.

2.3.2 LAW OF 14 JULY 1991 ON TRADE PRACTICES AND ON THE INFORMATION AND PROTECTION OF THE CONSUMER

Trade practices are governed since 29 February 1992 by a new Act of 14 July 1991 concerning trade practices and the information and protection of the consumer. This Act, as was the former Act regarding Fair Trade Practices, is essentially a code of good business behaviour. However, where the former Fair Trade Practices Act chiefly aimed to regulate the relationships between competitors, the law of 14 July 1991 enlarges the scope of the former Act to the relationship among 'sellers' and includes an entire chapter on consumer protection.

Fair competition involving 'sellers'

The law of 14 July 1991 aims to regulate fair trade practices involving 'sellers', whom it basically defines as any individual or corporate body which carries out industrial, financial or economic activities and sells products or services. The law therefore does not encompass professions such as doctors or lawyers.

Information and protection of the consumer

The law of 14 July 1991 provides several measures aimed at informing and protecting the consumer, whom the law defines as any individual or corporate body which acquires or uses products or services for non-professional purposes. With respect thereto the law:

(1) Imposes on the seller the obligation to give the consumer specific information regarding prices, quantities, name, contents and labelling of products and services.
(2) Provides conditions governing the use of a label of provenance,

defined as the geographical name of a country, region or town
which is used to designate a product originating therefrom and
whose quality and characteristics exclusively or chiefly result
from the geographical environment including natural and
human factors.

(3)   Prohibits certain types of advertising. Those rules apply to any
communication which aims directly or indirectly to promote
the sale of products or services, including real estate, rights and
obligations irrespective of the place or means of communication. Pursuant thereto, advertisements which are misleading,
disparaging of another seller, the latter's goods, services or
activities, which contain deceptive comparisons or comparisons which imply without necessity the possibility of identify-
ing one or more sellers, which encourage illegal acts, etc are
prohibited.

(4)   Lays down specific rules regarding the sales of products and
goods to the consumer. Those rules basically impose a duty on
the seller to inform in his dealings with the consumer, prohibition clauses which obviously disrupt the balance between the
rights and obligations of the parties and, in some circumstances, oblige the seller to supply the consumer with a written
justification and/or an order form.

Measures other than the Fair Trade Practices Act specifically
aim to protect the consumer. Such is the case of the legislation
adopted with regard to foodstuffs or products intended to be in
contact with them. For instance, specific information must be
disclosed on the labelling of prepacked foodstuffs, or other food
products, such as diet products (for which advertising is also regulated). The contents of most foodstuffs are also regulated by law.

Credit operations concluded with consumers, defined here as
individuals whose purpose when borrowing is neither commercial
nor professional, are strictly regulated by a recent law, dated 12 June
1991, which intends to protect the consumer by imposing a strict
information duty on the lender, providing a period within which the
consumer can renounce the contract, etc.

Consumers also derive protection from the rules governing
product liability which were added to Belgian law by the law of 25
February 1991 (which implements the directive of 25 July 1985
regarding liability resulting from defective products). Basically, that
law provides that the producer (and in some cases, the supplier) is

liable for all damage caused to persons and, to some extent, to goods by products which do not offer the safety which could legitimately be expected bearing in mind all circumstances, such as the outlook of the product, its normal use, etc. The producer's liability as provided by that law may not be contractually restricted or excluded. The victim is entitled to sue the producer either on the basis of the producer's specific non-contractual liability provided by the law of 25 February 1991 or on the basis of the basic principles provided by the Belgian Civil Code regarding contractual or non-contractual liability. This means that the consumer can for instance also rely on the rule according to which professional traders (producers and sellers) are deemed to be aware of the defects (even latent defects) of the products they sell, irrespective of contractual restrictions or releases.

Regulated practices

In addition to the prohibition of some specific sales practices, the law of 14 July 1991 also provides rules regulating various sales practices, which can be grouped in the following main categories:

(1) Sales involving a reduction in price, which include straight-forward sales with a reduction in price, reduction in price through the issue of vouchers, clearance sales, liquidations and sales at a loss: all those practices are subject to compliance with strict conditions.

(2) Joint offers: there is such an offer when the acquisition of products or services by a consumer is linked to the acquisition of identical products or services. As a rule, joint offers are prohibited even when the offer is made jointly by several sellers. Certain joint offers are authorised by virtue of the law, such as the offers of products constituting a whole or products which are usually sold together as such.

(3) Sales at a distance: a sale is considered concluded at a distance when concluded outside the physical presence of both the seller and the consumer, further to an offer made through a sale system using a technique of communication at a distance. That type of sale is subject to very strict rules, aiming to make up for the fact that the consumer has no previous opportunity to see the goods before completion of the sale.

(4) Sales concluded outside the seller's premises: the provisions set out in that respect in the law aim to implement the principles

laid down by Directive 85/577 of 20 December 1985. They basically provide for the right of the consumer to renounce his acquisition, at no extra cost, providing he informs the seller thereof by registered mail within a seven working-day period starting from the day following that of the signature of the contract.

Unfair trade practices

Generally speaking, the law 14 July 1991 prohibits any unfair trade practice whereby a seller harms or could harm the professional interests of one or more sellers or consumers. Such practice includes: parasitical competition (which unduly grants someone the benefit of the efforts of a competitor); any act which creates confusion as regards the identity of the seller, its products or services; and illegal competition (ie competition made in infringement to the legal provisions of the law of 14 July 1991 or even other legal provisions).

Sanctions

In practice, one of the most important functions of the law of 14 July 1991 is to permit almost immediate relief for unfair trade practices. The Act, in effect, enables complainants to apply for injunctions ordering the immediate cessation of such practices, in accordance with procedural rules aimed at accelerating the proceedings. The injunction may also provide for daily fines imposed for failure to abide by its terms, and order the publication of its terms in newspapers or public places.

No relief can be sought through such an injunction when the practice in question consists in counterfeiting practices covered by the laws protecting patents, trademarks, designs or models.

Infringements of the law or decrees implementing it, also render the author liable to a warning issued by the Ministry of Economic Affairs to put an end to the relevant practices, and to criminal law sanctions.

3
BUSINESS ORGANISATIONS

3.1 Introduction

Before starting business operations in Belgium, the investor must choose a legal structure through which to operate. When contemplating carrying out commercial activities, basically he can decide either to open a branch or to incorporate a subsidiary under one of the corporate forms provided by Belgian company law. Or he can decide to limit his presence in Belgium to a representative office, a looser format which will be appropriate in specific circumstances only.

When other types of activities are to be conducted in Belgium, such as lobbying activities or activities ancillary to those of a group of companies, other types of set-ups, however, may be more appropriate. And sometimes, the investor might also wish to start commercial activities as a sole trader.

When making a decision concerning the appropriate business form to use, several items will be taken into consideration, including the activities to be carried out in Belgium, the different legal obligations attached to the various forms of business, the costs to be incurred, the taxation consequences, and how long the operator believes he needs a presence in Belgium.

3.2 Legislation

The main body of law regarding commercial companies is the Company Act, originally co-ordinated by royal decree of 30 November 1935 and modified on several occasions, the most recent being 8 and 20 July 1991.

Other relevant laws are:
(1) The law of 12 July 1989 containing various measures implementating Council Regulation (EC) 2137/85 of 25 July 1985

relating to the institution of a European Economic Interest Grouping.

(2) The law of 17 July 1989 on Economic Interest Groupings.

(3) The law of 25 October 1919 granting civil personality to international associations pursuing a philanthropic, religious, scientific, artistic or pedagogic purpose.

(4) The law of 27 June 1921 granting civil personality to non-profit making associations and institutions of public utility.

(5) The co-ordinated laws of July 1964 regarding the trade registry and subsequent decrees of implementation.

(6) The law of 17 July 1975 relating to the bookkeeping and annual accounts requirements for enterprises and subsequent decrees of implementation.

(7) Royal decree no 135 of 9 July 1935 on the control of banks and the rules applicable to the issue of shares and securities (modified for the last time on 4 December 1990).

3.3 LIMITED LIABILITY COMPANIES

3.3.1 JOINT STOCK COMPANY (*SOCIÉTÉ ANONYME—NAAMLOZE VENNOOTSCHAP*)

This type of company is one of the better known and more widely used forms together with the *société privée à responsabilité limitée—besloten vennootschap met beperkte aansprakelijkheid*, although there has been a recent surge of interest in the *société coopérative*.

Capital

The joint stock company must be incorporated with a minimum capital of BEF 1.25 million, fully subscribed and paid up, either privately or through public subscriptions. In addition, all shares representing cash contributions must be paid up up to 25 per cent and shares corresponding wholly or partially to contributions in kind must be fully paid up within five years of the incorporation of the company. Contributions in kind require the fulfilment of a specific procedure in order to ascertain the value of the contribution and its value for the company.

As a rule, capital increases (and capital decreases too) require a shareholders' resolution in general meeting. The articles of association, however, can provide for an established maximum authorised capital, ie within which limits the capital can be increased by a simple decision of the board of directors alone.

Shareholders

Incorporation of a *société anonyme* requires a minimum of two shareholders, corporate bodies or individuals. Shareholders' liability is, in principle, limited to their respective contribution. Founder members, in turn, will incur increased liability, for instance in the case where the company is adjudicated bankrupt within the first three years of its existence and its capital was found wholly insufficient for it to pursue its corporate activities during at least two years (see *below*). Also if all issued shares are held by in one person alone for one year or more, then the sole shareholder will be deemed liable, together with the company, for all commitments undertaken by the company while he was the only member. Until there is a second shareholder or until publication is made in the annexes to the Belgian Official State Journal that a decision has been taken to wind up the company, his liability will continue.

Duration

The company can be incorporated for either a limited or an unlimited duration.

Name

The company must be given a specific name which can refer to its corporate object. The company's name may not be that of its shareholders and must differ from that of any other company existing in Belgium. Non-compliance with these requirements authorises any interested person to request the change of the name as well as to claim damages from the court.

Shares

The capital can be comprised of registered shares or bearer shares, with or without mention of their face value. They must be registered shares until they are fully paid up. The share capital can be comprised of voting and non-voting shares. Non-voting shares may not represent more than one-third of the corporate capital and must confer specific entitlements on their holder as regards dividends, reimbursement of the capital contribution and distribution of the positive balance owing where any winding-up procedure is concluded. In addition, non-voting shares do confer voting rights in certain specific cases. Preferential shares (which do not represent a contribution to the capital fund) may be issued; the articles of association determine the rights attached thereto.

As soon as the company is incorporated and the shares have been paid up to 25 per cent of their value, both registered and bearer shares can be freely transferred (unless otherwise provided in the articles). Bearer shares are transferred by simple delivery of title. The transfer of registered shares occurs, as regards third parties, by noting the transfer in the shareholders' register. But both the articles of association and shareholders' agreements can specifically limit the transferability of shares. Such provisions must, however, comply with the rules laid down by the Company Act which basically prohibit any share transfer limitation which would result in the ownership of the shares being frozen for more than three months (increased in certain circumstances by a two-month 'remedy period').

Management

The management of the company rests with the board of directors which must consist of a minimum of three directors. They may be shareholders or non-shareholders, Belgian citizens or foreigners, individuals or corporate bodies, and they are appointed by a resolution of the shareholders in general meeting to hold office for a maximum of six years. This board of directors is empowered to delegate the daily management function to one of its members or to any other person. The directors incur liability both towards the company and third parties. Special rules are prescribed in cases where decisions must be made by the board but in which the director has a personal interest, either directly or indirectly, in a decision to be made by the board.

Although, by law, directors may resign and be dismissed without reason and at any time, actual practice can sometimes be simplistic. Company officers, and especially those entrusted with daily management duties, can be considered to be within the company's employment (even if no employment contract was specifically entered into). Such will be the case when they are subordinated to the company, ie when they perform the duties of their office under the authority of a body, another director or company officer. Although in their capacity as directors they can be dismissed at any time, as employees they may claim entitlement to a notice period or to compensation in lieu of notice under Belgian employment law. Courts sometimes require that before being recognised as employees of the company, in addition to holding office, the directors must carry out, additional technical, commercial or administrative functions. From recent case law of the Belgian Supreme Court, however, it seems that it is no longer necessary to fulfil that second condition.

Control

The control of the company's financial situation, its annual accounts and the regularity of the operations they record must, (in circumstances when the company, on a consolidated basis with companies of the same group, does not qualify as a small or medium-sized enterprise—see criteria under chapter 2) be entrusted to one or more auditors, members of the Institut des Réviseurs d'Entreprise (comparable to chartered accountants) or *commissaires-réviseurs—commissarissen-revisoren*. When one such a *commissaire-réviseur* is designated, he must be appointed for a minimum of three years. During this period, he can be dismissed for just reasons only, otherwise damages will be owed to him by the company concerned. In addition, he cannot resign during his appointed term of office unless he has serious personal reasons to support his resignation.

It should also be noted that, sometimes, the intervention of a *réviseur d'entreprises*, (whether or not the company is required by law to have its own *commissaire-réviseur*) is compulsory.

Annual meeting

The shareholders must meet at least once a year with a view to approving the annual accounts and to deciding on the discharge of responsibility of the directors and company auditor (if one exists). These shareholders' meetings must be convened in accordance with the relevant provisions of Belgian company law and of the company's own articles of association.

Publicity requirements

Publicity requirements exist and must be complied with at various stages, eg upon incorporation, after any change to the articles, upon modification of the composition of the board, and after the annual general meeting of shareholders. All documents issued by a joint stock company must contain certain specific details (eg name, VAT number, trade register number).

Winding up

The company can be wound up:

(1) Where its corporate object can no longer be achieved.

(2) By majority decision of the shareholders (in some circumstances it is mandatory for the board to propose to the share
holders that the company should be wound up.

(3) By court order: for where the company's net assets no longer
amount to BEF 1.25 million, any interested party may request
that the court pronounce that the company be wound up.

The winding up of the company invokes the appointment of a
liquidateur (*vereffenaar*), whose role is comparable to that of the
trustee of a bankrupt's estate. Compliance with the procedural rules
set out in the Company Act is necessary for such an appointment to
be validly effected.

3.3.2 PRIVATE LIMITED LIABILITY COMPANY

Most features of the private limited liability company (in
French, *société privée à responsabilité limitée*—in Dutch, *besloten
vennootschap met beperkte aansprakelijkheid*) (hereafter SPRL) are
similar or even identical to those of the *société anonyme above*. There
are some differences, however, most notably in the following
respects.

Capital

The company must be incorporated with a minimum capital of
BEF 750,000, fully subscribed and paid up up the value of to BEF
250,000. No calls may be made on the capital market for this
subscription and furthermore, every share representing a contribution in cash must be at least one-fifth paid up.

Participants

The company can have one or more participants either individuals or corporate bodies. If a corporate body is the only participant,
it will remain fully liable for all commitments undertaken by the
company until such a time as another participant is engaged. An
individual may be the sole participant but of only one SPRL. As
expected all those who participate in the incorporation of the
company are deemed founders and will therefore incur specific
liability as a result of their involvement as founders.

Name

The SPRL in addition to being able to take those names which could validly be given to an SA, can also be named after one or more of its partners.

Shares

The capital must be divided into shares of equal value (with a minimum share value of BEF 1,000. Only capital shares may be issued. The transferability of the shares is strictly governed by Belgian company law. The company's articles of association can only ever provide stricter rules (if desired), but can never relax or loosen the provisions contained in the Act.

Management

The management function can be entrusted to one or more persons, either for a limited or unlimited duration. Managers who have been appointed under the articles of association are deemed appointed for the duration of the company's existence, unless the articles of association state otherwise. They can be dismissed for serious grounds only. Rules similar to those existing with regard to the *société anonyme* are provided in cases where a manager has personal interests, either directly or indirectly in a decision to be made.

3.3.3 CO-OPERATIVE COMPANY WITH LIMITED LIABILITY

Since a law of 20 July, 1991 was passed, it has become possible to choose between two different types of co-operative company: the co-operative company with limited liability (in French, *société coopérative à responsabilité limitée*, in Dutch, *coöperative vennootschap met beperkte aansprakelijkheid*); and conversely, the co-operative company with unlimited liability (*société coopérative à responsabilité illimitée et solidaire—coöperative vennootschap met onbeperkte en hoofdelijke aanspreakelijkheid*). Where the articles of association of either of these two types of company provide that all partners will have equal voting power and that profit and loss sharing ratios between partners will be equal as regards 50 per cent of the profit made but in proportion to individual contributions as regards the other 50 per cent of the profit, then the company qualifies by law as a partnership (*coopérative de participation—coöperative vennootschap bij wijze van deelneming*).

All four types of co-operative company (noted *above*) have common features, such as:

(1) The variability of the number of their members (with a minimum of three) and of their capital value variable over and above the requisite 'fixed part' only. Admission to the company of new members is, in principle, unrestricted. However, the articles of association may exclude or limit the admission of new members within certain prescribed limits.

(2) The common prohibition on the transfer of shares to non-members, with the exception of those who are specifically nominated, or who belong to the categories defined by the articles of association.

(3) Votes in the general meeting are cast in accordance with the rule: 'one share, one vote' unless the articles of association provide otherwise.

In addition, however, the co-operative company with limited liability has specific features, for example:

(1) Its articles of incorporation and any modification thereto must be sanctioned by a notary public.

(2) The fixed part of its capital must be at least BF 750,000 (if the company is a *coopérative de participation* a figure of BF 250,000 must be subscribed and paid up) of which at least BF 250,000 must be subscribed for and fully paid up.

All shares of a co-operative company with limited liability must be paid up to 25 per cent of their value. The amount of the required fixed part of the capital must be justified in a financial plan (drafted to allow for a two year period of activities within that company) and this capital sum must then be paid into a special bank account opened in the name of the company to be incorporated:

(1) Contributions in kind are subject to a specific procedure.

(2) Some of the rules already existing for the SA are applicable to the co-operative company with limited liability; for example as regards drafting requirements and control over the accounts (such as the preparation of yearly accounts, the drafting of a management report, the distribution of profit, the role of the annual general meeting, the publication of accounts, the control over these accounts by a statutory auditor).

(3) Likewise the liability of the founders and of the managers is commensurate with the liability existing for the founders and the directors of an SA as explained earlier.

3.4 PARTNERSHIPS

3.4.1 GENERAL PARTNERSHIP

The general partnership (in French, *société en nom collectif*, in Dutch, *vennootschap onder firma*) is incorporated by means of a contract (between two or more persons) to carry out business under a corporate name. Thus it is granted a distinct legal personality. The partners are jointly and severally liable for all the debts and obligations of the partnership. This business form is very similar to that of most of the civil companies, with the exception that the general partnership may carry out commercial activities. The partners themselves are responsible for the management of this general partnership.

3.4.2 LIMITED PARTNERSHIP

The limited partnership (*société en commandite simple—gewone commanditaire vennootschap*) can be described as a general partnership to which are added one or more partners whose liability is limited to the amount of their capital contribution. There are thus two types of partner: one or more 'active' partners (*commandités—gecommanditeerden*) with unlimited liability and one or more 'sleeping' partners (*commanditaires—commanditairen*) whose liability is limited to the amount of their agreed contributions provided they refrain from taking part in the management of the partnership.

3.4.3 PARTNERSHIP LIMITED BY SHARES

The partnership limited by shares (in French, *société en commandite par actions*—in Dutch, *commanditaire vennootschap op aandelen*) consists of one or more partners (*associés—vennoten*) with unlimited liability and one or more shareholders (*actionnaires—aandeelhouders*) whose liability is limited to the capital they have agreed to contribute. This entity, which has a distinct legal personality, is, in general, governed by the rules relating to joint stock companies. Its most interesting feature is that of the role of its managers: in particular their right of veto as regards decisions concerning the modification of the articles of incorporation and acts that serve to bind the company against third parties.

Whilst the general partnership is still encountered in practice, nowadays the limited partnership and the partnership limited by shares are seldom met.

3.4.4 CO-OPERATIVE COMPANY

Specific requirements are imposed on the co-operative company with unlimited liability (in French, *société coopérative à responsabilité illimitée et solidaire*—in Dutch *coöperatieve vennootschap met onbeperkte en hoofdelijke aansprakelijkheid*), whether or not it includes the partnership element, for example:

(1) Documents operating share transfer must include the words good for an unlimited and joint commitment.
(2) The two-yearly deposit of a list of partners for the registrar of the competent court of commerce is required.

3.4.5 CIVIL COMPANY

If the activities to be performed are not commercial, parties can form a civil company (*société civile*—*burgerlijke vennootschap*). The rules applicable to the civil company are provided for in the Belgian Civil Code (art 1832–1873). Being basically an agreement between parties to carry out an activity together, it follows that no specific formalities need to be observed in the creation of the civil company. This civil company has no separate legal identity and each partner who is a party to the agreement is responsible, in proportion to the number of partners, for honouring commitments validly undertaken on behalf of the company. Parties can specifically limit or extend their exposure in that respect within the formation contract. Such restrictions on their responsibility, however, will not be enforceable against third parties unless the latter expressly accepts them.

Civil companies, however, can be created in the form of any of the commercial company types created by Belgian company law, in which case they are referred to as civil companies but with a commercial form. These companies are granted distinct legal personality and their structure and functioning are governed by the Company Act.

If commercial activities are to be carried out by the partners, the business form of the *société en nom collectif* (in Dutch *vennootschap onder firma*) is preferable, since a civil company is not authorised to carry out commercial activities. Remember Belgian law categorises certain activities as civil by their very nature such as owning land and renting out property.

This business type seems quite popular for the grouping of the practitioners of professions (such as law firms, for example). In particular, a law dated 12 July 1979 provided for the creation of a specific form of civil company, the agricultural company (*société d'agriculture—landbouwvennootschap*).

3.4.6 TEMPORARY PARTNERSHIP

The temporary partnership (in French, *association momentanée*—in Dutch, *tijdelijke vereniging*) is that one which aims to handle one or more well defined trade operations, doing so without a corporate name. All shareholders are jointly and severally liable towards co-contracting third parties. This form of partnership is often used within the framework of joint ventures relating, for instance, to public works. An example of this was the temporary partnership created for the rescue of the victims of the *Herald of Free Enterprise* a few years ago.

3.4.7 PARTNERSHIP AGREEMENT

The *association en participation—vereniging bij wijze van deelneming*, is formed by one or more persons interested in operations themselves and conducted by one or more others on their behalf. It is not granted a distinct legal personality. Terms and conditions of the partnership agreement like those of the temporary partnership are determined by the parties within the limits of the general principles of the Civil Code. As in a true partnership agreement, the partners in both cases make contributions and share in the profits and losses of the firm. The agreement, however, remains unacknowledged to third parties. For this reason such partnerships are sometimes called 'secret companies'.

As an example, partnership agreements are used by groups of banks which take investment risks. The object of the agreement could be, for example, the (common) purchase of shares.

3.5 ECONOMIC INTEREST GROUPING

On 25 July 1985, the EC Council of Ministers created the

EEIG by Regulation 2137/85. As regards the concept of this legal form, the Council was inspired by the French *groupement d'intérêt économique*. That regulation has been implemented into Belgian law by an Act dated 12 July 1989, which provides the formalities which must be complied with when registering an EEIG in Belgium.

A law dated 17 July 1989 also created a Belgian economic interest grouping, but distinct from the EEIG. The contract, functioning and winding up of the EEIG established in Belgium, are also governed by that same law (except as regards the status and legal capacity of individuals and the legal capacity of corporate bodies). The Belgian economic interest grouping is defined as having been set up by contract, for a definite or indefinite period, between two or more persons (individuals or corporate bodies) and whose purpose ranges from facilitating or promoting the economic activity of its members, to improving or increasing the results of the activity being undertaken. The activity of the grouping itself, as with that of the EEIG, must be linked with, and ancillary to, its members' activities.

With regard to tax, the EIG like the EEIG, is transparent in nature so the profits generated by their activities are taxed at the level of their members. In order to promote the establishment of EEIGs in Belgium and the creation of Belgian EIGs, the law of 17 July 1989 provides that the 0.5 per cent registration duty normally levied on contributions made to the capital of companies will not be due on contributions made to the capital of the grouping, if any; and that, in some circumstances, the retransfer of real estate from the grouping to one of its members will not be subject to the 12.5 per cent registration duty levied on the transfer of real estate in Belgium.

3.6 NON-PROFIT ORGANISATIONS

3.6.1 ASBL—VZW

The *association sans but lucratif* ('ASBL') in French or *vereniging zonder winstgevend doel* ('VZW') in Dutch, and hereafter called ASBL, is regulated by the law dated 27 June 1921, concerning non-profit making associations and institutions of public good which are granted specific legal personality.

The ASBL is not allowed to perform any commercial or industrial activities, nor to procure any material advantages for its members. Profits made by the ASBL must as a rule be used for the future realisation of its object and may in no event be distributed among the members. However, the ASBL is allowed to provide moral or material advantages (though not monetary or financial) for its members. So for example, it may provide such entertainments, as a library, facilities for scientific studies or artistic works, even sports facilities. The ASBL is also allowed to perform *occasional* and *accessory* lucrative activities provided that they are in connection with its principal object and that they stimulate or promote its realisation. (eg where the benefits of such accessory activities are utilised for the achievement of the ASBL's object). For instance, an ASBL is allowed to organise lectures, exhibitions, concerts, classes or to sell books, magazines, etc.

The ASBL is granted legal personality from the moment of publication of its articles of association and directors' identities in the Enclosures to the Belgian Official State Journal. The ASBL, however, will not be able to enforce that legal personality if it omits to fulfil the publicity requirements (imposed upon it by the law either upon incorporation or at later stages), or if three-fifths of its members are not of Belgian nationality or foreigners residing and registered in Belgium (of which either would be acceptable).

The ASBL is not entitled to own, under whatever form, any real estate, except that which is necessary for the realisation of its corporate object. Any donation made in favour of an ASBL must be authorised by Royal Decree unless it concerns transferable donations for an amount not exceeding BEF 200,000.

The law specifies only one type of member, the full member. This category consists of the founders and those admitted later as full members. They enjoy the rights specified by the articles of incorporation and take part in the annual members' meetings. The act of incorporation can, however, provide for another category of member, the affiliated member. Normally, the articles of incorporation will specify the conditions of membership. If this is not the case, the conditions will be fixed in general meeting, or by the board of directors, or even by a special body called the *comité de ballotage*. Subsequent termination of membership must be decided by a majority vote of two-thirds of members present at the general meeting. A member can also decide to terminate his own membership.

3.6.2 INTERNATIONAL ASSOCIATION

According to the law of 25 October 1919, legal personality can be granted to international associations with philanthropic, religious, scientific, artistic and educational purposes provided the conditions specified by that law are complied with.

In order to obtain this legal personality, several conditions must be fulfilled:

(1) The association must be open to Belgians and to foreigners.

(2) The association's registered office or the office for direction and administration of the company's affairs must be established in Belgium.

(3) At least one Belgian member must have a seat on the board of directors.

(4) The association may not seek any financial gain.

(5) The association must have a philanthropic, religious, scientific, artistic or educational objective.

(6) The articles of association must comply with the requirements set forth in art 2 of the Law of 25 October 1919.

(7) The articles of association, as well as the list of the identity of the directors, company by-laws and any modifications of the articles of association must be published in the Enclosures to the Belgian Official State Journal.

In practice, in order to obtain this legal personality, an application, together with the articles of association, must be sent to the Ministry of Justice. If all requisite legal requirements and conditions have been fulfilled, the articles of association will be approved by the Minister of Justice and legal personality will be granted by a Royal Decree (executed by the Minister of Justice himself). The Royal Decree, as well as the articles of association, must then be published in the Belgian Official State Journal and the association obtains legal personality status on the tenth day after publication.

The association is not allowed to own any real assets other than those directly needed for the realisation of its stated objective and the receipt of donations or legacies is only allowed if authorisation is given by Royal Decree.

International associations which have their registered office *abroad* and thus fall under a foreign body of laws are allowed (while in Belgium) to exercise the rights that their status confers them under the applicable foreign law; again provided that specific conditions are fulfilled. It is not required, however, for such international associations to have their registered office in Belgium, or to have a Belgian on the board of directors.

3.6.3 INSTITUTIONS OF PUBLIC UTILITY (FOUNDATIONS)

Foundations, such as ASBL, are governed by the law of 27 June 1921.

Anyone is entitled, on condition that a governmental authorisation is granted, to allocate all or part of his assets, by an authenticated deed or a written will, to the establishment of an institution of public utility. Sole institutions with a philanthropic, religious, scientific, artistic or educational objective, which do not seek pecuniary gain will qualify as such institutions. Obtaining legal personality requires the fulfilment of the conditions applicable in that respect and as laid down by the law of 27 June 1921 as well as the approval by the Minister of Justice of the articles of incorporation. And to render that legal personality enforceable, compliance with the publicity requirements laid down by law is also required.

Since a foundation is the expression of the final will of one person (and not of a grouping of people who actively participate in the management of an association), the law provides extensive governmental supervision and control in order to protect the realisation of the objectives for which the foundation was established. The foundation is not allowed to possess any real property assets other than those directly needed for the realisation of its declared objective.

3.7 INCORPORATION

3.7.1 INCORPORATION OF LIMITED LIABILITY COMPANIES

Incorporation requirements vary depending on the structure chosen.

Directly or by public subscription

Sociétés anonymes can be incorporated either by the shareholders making direct contributions in kind or in cash, or by public subscription. In the latter case, specific formalities must be complied with as laid down on the one hand by the Company Act and on the other hand by royal decree no 135 of 9 July 1935 with regard to the control of banks and the rules applicable to the issue of shares and titles (last modified on 4 December 1990).

Articles of incorporation

The Company Act regulates the basic contents of the articles of incorporation, which will vary depending on the type of company concerned. The articles of a *société anonyme* must contain information regarding:

(1) The form and the name of the company.
(2) The corporate purpose.
(3) The registered office.
(4) The duration of the company, unless this is unlimited.
(5) The capital.
(6) The board of directors and the controlling body.
(7) The shares.
(8) The contributions made other than in cash.
(9) The shareholders and founders and the advantages (if any) granted to the latter.
(10) The incorporation costs.
(11) The bank with which the capital sum has been deposited.

Formalities

Different formalities are prescribed by law as regards the incorporation of each type of commercial company. The incorporation of a *société anonyme* and that of a *société privée à responsabilité limitée*, however, are identical and require the following:

(1) A financial plan confirming that the capital contributed is sufficient to carry out the company's activities for the first two years, must be submitted upon incorporation to the notary public.
(2) If the capital is composed of contributions in cash, a special blocked account must be opened in the name of the company being formed and the capital sum must be paid into that account. The account may be used only after incorporation.
(3) If the capital is composed of contributions in kind, a chartered accountant must be appointed to draft a report itemising the contributions made and the methods used for their valuation. Founders must then draft a special report in which they indicate the interest for the company of the assets to be contributed and any reasons why they disagree with the chartered accountant's report (if this is the case).
(4) The articles of incorporation must be drawn up in a certified deed (ie drawn up in front of a notary public).
(5) The articles of incorporation must be published in extract form in the Enclosures of the Belgian Official State Journal.

(6) Registration must be made on the trade register and with the VAT administration.

(7) Specific authorisations may be required (eg bank, insurance, financial leasing, etc).

The articles of incorporation of a co-operative company with unlimited liability may be entered into by private deed. Those of a co-operative company with limited liability, by contrast, must be entered into by means of a certified deed. The formalities imposed in connection with the incorporation of *sociétés anonymes* regarding the bank account and financial plan must be complied with upon incorporation of a co-operative company with limited liability.

Founders

As a rule all individual persons or corporate bodies who are signatories to the incorporation deed then qualify as founders and as such incur the specific responsibilities incurred in this respect under the Company Act. However, in a *société anonyme*, the definition and thus the liability of a 'founder' can be limited in the deed of incorporation to one or more shareholders on the condition that together they represent at least one-third of the company's capital.

Pre-incorporation operations

Operations are often concluded, and commitments undertaken, on behalf of the company whilst under incorporation. Any such operation or commitment must be ratified by the company at the very latest within two months of its incorporation. On failure to make such ratification or if the company is not in fact incorporated within two years after the commitment arose, those who signed on behalf of the company under formation will be considered jointly and severally liable for the commitments undertaken on behalf of the company in formation unless provided otherwise by the contract itself.

3.7.2 INCORPORATION OF PARTNERSHIPS

Sociétés en nom collectif, sociétés en commandite simple and *sociétés coopérative à responsabilité illimitée* must be incorporated in special deeds, either certified or private, executed in as many copies as there are parties with a distinct interest. Failure to comply with that requirement results in the nullity of the incorporation deed.

However, *sociétés coopératives à responsabilité illimitée et solidaire* may be entered into by a deed executed in two copies only.

The minimum content of the articles of incorporation which must be published in the Enclosures to the Belgian Official State Journal as well as that of the articles themselves is strictly regulated by law. Failure to file for publication will result both in the unenforceability against third parties of the company's legal personality and in the company being prevented from starting court proceedings in the future.

The creation of *associations momentanées* and of *associations en participation* does not require any special documentation and can be proved by their ledgers, correspondence and even by witnesses if the court so permits.

3.7.3 INCORPORATION OF NON-PROFIT ORGANISATIONS

ASBL and international associations can be set up either by certified deed drawn up by a notary public (or any other public officer) or by a private deed. In both cases, the articles must contain the specific points provided by the Acts of 27 June 1921 or of 25 October 1919. In the event of immovable property being contributed to the ASBL, the deed must be certified.

The decision to allocate all or part of one's own assets in the creation of a corporate foundation must be entered into by a certified deed or in a will written, dated and signed by the testator (*testament olographe*). Notification must be made to the government for its approval, either immediately (if a certified deed is drafted), or after the testator has died.

In the case of a private deed, there must be as many copies as there are parties concerned and the general rules of Belgian law regulate the validity of the act.

3.7.4 INCORPORATION OF AN EEIG AND EIG

The creation of an EEIG as well as that of the EIG requires the members to conclude a written contract entered into in a certified or private deed (in the latter case the contract must be executed in as many copies as there are parties having distinct interests). Failure to comply with these requirements results in the nullity of the contract. The minimum contents of the contract are regulated by law as are the notations required to be included in the extract that must be filed for publication in the Enclosures to the Belgian Official State Journal. This must then be submitted to the registrar of the court of commerce where the grouping is established or has its registered office. The extract must be signed by a notary public, if the grouping is incorporated by certified deed, or by all members who are jointly liable or by one member specially empowered to do so if the grouping is incorporated by private deed. The extract must then be filed with the registrar of the relevant commercial court, together with a copy of the grouping's contract of incorporation ready for publication. At the same time, the grouping must apply for registration and does so at the same commercial court.

In order to obtain legal personality, the EEIG must be registered, unlike the EIG which is automatically granted legal personality upon execution of the formation contract. The enforceability of the EIG's dealings, however, is also subject to publication of the contract in the Enclosures to the Belgian Official State Journal.

3.8 SHAREHOLDERS' RIGHTS AND LIABILITIES

Shareholders' rights and liabilities differ depending on the type of company concerned and the type of shares they own. For instance, owners of bearer shares in a *société anonyme* are statutorily entitled to require the conversion of those shares into registered shares. Owners of shares without voting rights in a *société anonyme* or a *société privée à responsabilité limitée* are of course deprived of voting rights in most circumstances, but still must be granted specific entitlement regarding dividends and reimbursement of capital. The right to transfer shares in the capital of a *société de personnes à responsabilité limitée* or of a *société coopérative* is restricted by the Company Act, although the Company Act does not provide any statutory limitation to the same right in a *société anonyme*.

In a *société anonyme* or in a *société privée à responsabilité limitée*, the main rights of shareholders are as follows:
(1) Right to participate and vote at general meeting (as regards capital shares without voting rights, the right to vote is limited to specific circumstances).
(2) Right to share in the distribution of the profits (and in the net assets when the company is wound up).
(3) Right of preference to subscribe for capital increases in cash form.

(4) Right to be informed at specific moments.
(5) Right to transfer shares (as mentioned earlier that right is restricted by law as regards the transfer of shares in an SPRL, though the articles of association can facilitate the transfer in favour of specific categories of persons).
(6) Rights to challenge the directors' management of the company.
(7) Rights of control.
(8) Rights for all shareholders to be treated on an equal basis.

In those same companies, shareholders' liabilities consist mainly in:
(1) Payment of the capital.
(2) Responsibility as a founder member.
(3) Responsibility as a sole shareholder.

3.9 DIRECTORS' RIGHTS AND LIABILITIES

Again the directors' rights and liabilities vary depending on the type of company concerned. Basically either in a *société anonyme* or a *société privée à responsabilité limitée*, the main rights of directors are as follows:
(1) To manage the company.
(2) To represent the company.
(3) To increase the capital within the limits of the authorised share capital, provided that the shareholders have in fact entrusted the board with that power. This right does not exist in a *société privée à responsabilité limitée*.
(4) To limit or to set aside a share pre-emption right in the company's best interests, during a capital increase, even it is carried out within the limits of authorised capital. Here again that right does not exist in a *société privée*.
(5) To resign.
(6) To attend general meetings.

Directors have a duty to inform the shareholders at specific times prescribed by law and also must manage the company properly. They can incur liability under civil law (eg for faults of management or for infringing the articles of association or the Company Act), under criminal law, in addition to liability which may be imposed on them by specific legislative provisions.

A discharge of responsibility validly given by the shareholders having approved the annual accounts will release the directors from liabilities they can incur as a result of their management during the previous year. In some circumstances, however, the validity of the discharge given can be challenged and the directors' responsibility revived retrospectively.

3.10 SOLE TRADER

In accordance with the Code of Commerce, anyone who carries out, as his usual profession, activities which are qualified as 'commercial' by law (eg any purchase of goods with a view to reselling them, the drawing of bills of exchange, transport by air, water or land, etc) will qualify as a trader.

Special rules apply to such traders as regards the proof of commitments they have undertaken and their contract of marriage. Only 'traders' as defined *above* can be declared bankrupt. The insolvency of non-traders, quite to the contrary, is not specifically regulated. Traders, as commercial companies, must register with the Trade Register of the place where they operate and usually also with the VAT administration.

3.11 BRANCHES

A branch is a subordinate establishment set up in Belgium by a foreign company on whose account and under whose direction it operates. The branch is not a separate legal entity; it forms a single entity with its 'parent' company (possibly abroad). Two types of branches can be identified: the 'non-commercial branch', usually referred to as a 'representation office', or the commercial branch.

Representation offices

Although the most straightforward way to operate in Belgium consists either of incorporating a Belgian company or of opening an officially recognised branch, it is also possible, in some circumstances, to operate without using any of the above structures. Such will be the case when the activities of the Belgian office are limited to providing information, canvassing potential clients, etc.

This position has been confirmed indirectly by case law of the

Belgian Cour de Cassation, in a judgment dated 18 December 1941 (Pas, 1941, I, p 467) which provided that a foreign company has a centre of operations (which is governed by the same provisions as the branch) in Belgium if it regularly carries out, in Belgium, acts that fall within the framework of its commercial activities and if it is represented in Belgium by a representative who is able to bind it against third parties. Case law of the Belgian Supreme Court dating from 27 April 1896 already allowed an office (which served as an intermediary between the public and a company established abroad with regard to operations to be negotiated abroad) not to be considered as being a centre of operations (Pas, 1896, I, p 166).

The representation office is therefore not subject to the registration, publication and accounting requirements to which a commercial branch is subjected. In practice, however, it may be difficult for the office not to go beyond merely giving information to potential clients. It is thus usually rather difficult to remain merely an 'office' for any considerable period. Once the limits are exceeded, the legal status of the office becomes quite vague and the vacuum produced is then likely to cause difficulties. Furthermore, third parties can be reluctant to deal with such an office, as it has no official recognition under Belgian law. Recovery of VAT paid on purchases made in connection with the office (such as, for example, furniture, cars) also requires the fulfilment of specific formalities which are not required for branches or companies.

Commercial branch

A commercial branch is also a subordinate establishment set up in Belgium but it is one which carries out commercial activities. The Belgian branch has its own subordinate management, distinct from that of the 'parent' company which it represents and one whose behalf it is authorised to act.

Any company, which decides to open a branch in Belgium, has to publish both an extract of its most recent articles of association and of the board decision to open a branch and nominating the manager, in the Enclosures to the Belgian Official State Journal. It must also file a certified copy of the most recent articles of association and of the board decision (duly legalised either by *apostille*, if the company's country of origin has ratified the Hague Convention of 5 October 1961 on the legalisation of public acts, or by another appropriate procedure, if such is not the case). Certified translations of these, in the language of the region where the branch will be based, must also be filed. Once those formalities are fulfilled, a trade register number and a VAT number (if applicable) must be applied for. Depending on the activities the branch is to carry out, prior specific authorisation may or may not need to be obtained.

Changes to the management or address of the branch, as well as changes affecting the parent company abroad must also be filed for publication, and, as in some cases, may necessitate subsequent amendment of the branch's registration as it appears on the trade register.

As far as book-keeping is concerned, Belgian law was recently changed as a result of the implementation (by royal decree of 30 December 1991) of EC Directive 89/666 of 21 December 1989. In principle, Belgian law requires that the book-keeping of the Belgian branch or operations centre of a foreign company must comply with book-keeping requirements under Belgian law. However, this will no longer be required from branches or operations centres of foreign companies which have no income/returns from selling goods or services to third parties nor from delivering goods or rendering services to the foreign company upon which they depend, and whose running costs are borne by that foreign company. Since company law has not been simultaneously adjusted, the company's and the branch's annual accounts or the operations centre's annual accounts, however, still need to be filed in Belgium, in accordance with Belgian law, even when the branch or operations centre is normally exempt from the book-keeping requirements under that law.

4
MERGERS AND ACQUISITIONS

4.1 THE 'COMMUNITY DIMENSION'

When contemplating acquiring either shares or goodwill, or merging with another company, it will be important to examine whether or not the operation qualifies as a 'merger' and has a 'Community dimension' as defined under the EC Council regulation dated 21 December 1989. If the transaction contemplated is such a merger and has such a Community dimension, notification must be made to the EC Commission before the operation is carried out in order to obtain confirmation that the operation may be carried out, ie does not have a negative effect on the trade between the member states. Failure to notify can result in quite substantial fines being imposed on all parties concerned.

If the transaction contemplated has no Community dimension but includes provisions restrictive of competition, such as a non-competition clause, which are not to be considered ancillary to the merger, notification to the Commission can still be required on the basis of art 85 of the Treaty of Rome unless the operation is considered to fall within the scope of the *de minimis* rules provided by the Commission. In addition, when the operation has no Community dimension, notification may still have to be given to the national authorities (in accordance with the applicable national rules, see chapter 2 as far as Belgium is concerned). Failure to notify can result in parties being fined.

4.2 MERGERS

Usually a merger will be carried out either by one company absorbing another one or by one or more companies contributing their assets and liabilities to the new company which they are incorporating. In both cases, the shareholders of the company whose assets and liabilities are transferred receive shares as consideration for their contribution.

Under Belgian company law, it is still considered that a merger implies the liquidation of the company being absorbed and the contribution of its assets and liabilities to the take-over company, although that system contravenes the principles laid down by the third and the sixth EC directives. A draft bill which would adjust Belgian legislation to conform with those directives has therefore been pending for some time before the Belgian Parliament.

The new draft bill also provides simplified rules regarding the enforceability against third parties of the transfer of the assets and liabilities resulting from the merger. At present, Belgian law does not organise any system regarding the transfer of a whole estate, unless the transfer is operated as a result of the death of the owner. Some authors therefore consider that each debt and liability composing the estate must be transferred separately in compliance with the rules applicable to the transfer of each item (see 'acquisition of goodwill' below). Other authors, however, consider that a merger implies, in accordance with art 1122 of the Civil Code, the transfer of all assets and liabilities of the company merged, without any formalities being required except as regards unassignable obligations or obligations *intuitu personae* (where personal attributes are crucial).

In certain circumstances, Belgian tax law allows tax-free mergers. In addition, as in the case of the purchase of shares, notice to the employees of the companies concerned and notice to administrative authorities will sometimes be required.

4.3 SHARE ACQUISITIONS

4.3.1 PRIVATELY OWNED STOCK

As will be shown below, acquisitions of shares in privately held companies are quite straightforward transactions under Belgian law, especially when it comes to transferring bearer shares. At least two considerations, however, have prompted parties to share purchase agreements to arrive at rather lengthy documents: on the one hand, the shares and not the target are the subject matter of the sale and purchase agreement. As a result, the buyer cannot rely on the rules provided by the Civil Code to protect him against latent defects affecting the target or any of it constituent parts. Specific warranties are therefore required. On the other hand, contracts are usually shaped on Anglo-Saxon models which, as a rule, tend to be lengthier than their continental counterparts. Likewise under the

Anglo-Saxon influence, full due diligence exercises, including tax and legal audits, have become common practice.

The principles which are applicable to a share purchase agreements derive from their two basic characteristics:

(1) First, it is a *contract*. As such, when concluded under Belgian law, all usual rules of Belgian contract law apply to the share purchase agreement:

  (a) parties are free to fix the terms and conditions of the agreement as they deem appropriate, subject to the limitations laid down by public order, morality and compulsory rules (*lois impératives—dwingende wetten*);

  (b) parties reach a valid agreement by the mere exchange of their respective consents. No formalities are required. Some formalities will, however, be required when the agreement is entered into with non-traders, in order to be able to use the written agreement as the proof of the terms agreed;

  (c) the contract, when validly entered into, is fully binding on the parties and may be brought to an end only by mutual consent or in the cases provided for by law;

  (d) the agreement must be executed in good faith. (The court has jurisdiction to consider the good faith of the parties in cases of dispute.)

In addition, in order for the share purchase agreement to be valid, four basic conditions must be fulfilled:

  (e) the contract must be entered into without the parties' consent being vitiated by substantial mistake (*erreur substantielle—substantiële dwaling*), misrepresentation (*dol—bedrog*), (*lésion—benadeling*) or undue influence (*violence—geweld*);

  (f) the contract must be executed by parties legally capable of entering into a contract;

  (g) the contract must have a lawful object;

  (h) the contract must have a lawful cause. The 'cause' is generally seen as the obligation of the co-contracting party; some authors, however, define the cause as the common motivation of the parties when entering into the contract.

Failure to fulfil any of these four conditions authorises the victim to claim the rescission of the agreement and/or damages. An object infringing provisions pertaining to public policy or morality will result in the absolute nullity of the agreement (ie it must be pronounced *ex officio* by the court).

In addition, when the contract is entered into with a co-contracting party who is not a trader, some conditions of form must be complied with in order to be able to use the written contract form as a proof of the parties' rights and obligations:

(i) the contract must be executed on as many copies as there are parties having different interests;

(j) the contract must mention on how many copies it was executed;

(k) each copy must be an original and therefore must be signed by all parties.

(2) The second basic characteristic is that the share purchase agreement has a specific subject, ie shares, which implies compliance with the relevant rules of the Belgian Company Act in order to carry out a valid transfer.

These rules vary depending on the type of company and the type of shares concerned. (As regards transferability, see Chapter 3.)

In a joint stock company (*société anonyme—naamloze vennootschap*) shares can be bearer or registered shares and, as a result of a recent modification, they can carry voting rights or not. Bearer shares can be transferred simply by the transfer of the share certificates. As long as the shares are not printed (printing often proves a lengthy procedure), their transfer can be carried out by merely notifying the company. Registered shares will be transferred by entering a mention of the transfer in the shareholders' register of the company or by having a notice of the transfer served on the company by process-server. If those formalities are not complied with, the transfer will not be enforceable against the company and third parties. Transfers of shares of a joint stock company which are not paid up to the mandatory minimum (25 per cent) or which are carried out before the company's incorporation are not authorised.

In a private limited liability company, the transfer of shares needs to be entered in the shareholders' register in order to be enforceable against the company and third parties.

In addition, acquisitions of privately owned stock require notices to be given to public authorities and to the personnel of the target company in certain circumstances:

(1) Article 36 of the law of 30 December 1970, modified by the law

of 17 August 1973, concerning economic expansion, provides that the Minister of Economic Affairs, the Minister of Finance, and the Minister for Regional Economy must be informed of all transactions seeking to transfer one-third or more of the capital of any company which carries on business in Belgium, and which has at least BEF 100 million of owned assets.

(2) If the target has a works council, notice of the proposed take-over will also need to be given to that council in due course. Notice must be given before any information is released to the public about the transaction.

    This duty to inform may not, however, prevent the normal conduct of negotiations and the Works Council has no authority to oppose the deal. Failure to notify may, however, have legal consequences.

4.3.2 SHARES PUBLICLY HELD OR QUOTED

Private acquisitions

As a result of the turmoil created by Carlo De Benedetti's attempt to obtain control over Belgium's leading holding company, substantial reforms of Belgian company and financial legislation have been undertaken. As a part of this, on 2 March 1989 the Belgian Parliament adopted a law concerning the transparency of shareholdings and also the regulating of take-overs. This law has been further elaborated by the royal decree of 8 November 1989 on public take-over bids and changes in control of companies. In accordance with that decree, anyone who intends to acquire, in one or more transactions, the exclusive or joint control of a target company which calls or has called for public subscriptions, must inform the Commission for Banking and Finance (*Commission Bancaire et Financière—Commissie Bank-en Financvoorieweze n*) at least five days in advance.

    This duty to inform applies to the acquisition of a controlling participation in a quoted company and also in any company which calls or has called for public subscription for the issue of its shares or bonds, or for any other operation. In the Royal Decree of 9 January 1991 (replacing the Royal Decree dated 12 December 1969), Belgian law defines when a call on savings is deemed to have a public character. In the present case, however, the criteria laid down by that decree will only serve as guide lines to a court which would have to decide on the public character of the target. In any event, the mere fact that the target's shares are spread over a large number of holders does not necessarily imply that the Royal Decree of 8 November 1989 must be complied with.

Once informed, the Commission for Banking and Finance may either clear the operation or issue observations which can be made public if the candidate acquirer does not abide by them. In addition, the Commission is entitled, in some circumstances, to start court action before the president of the Court of Commerce or, if the situation is urgent, to order the suspension of the operation if the transaction is likely to prejudice the interests of the shareholders. Failure to inform the Commission for Banking and Finance gives rise to criminal sanctions and could even result in compensation for any damage suffered by minority shareholders as a result thereof.

The same Royal Decree also provides that if joint or exclusive control has been gained over a company which calls or has called for public subscription without a public take-over bid having taken place and if the consideration paid for the shares is higher than market value, the acquirer must give all other shareholders the opportunity to sell their shares against the same (or the highest) consideration.

Public acquisitions: public take-over bids

The Royal Decree of 8 November 1989, referred to *above*, also obliges anyone who intends to launch a public take-over bid relating to shares with voting rights or to stock entitling the holder to subscribe to or acquire voting shares, to abide by the specific procedure it provides, including notice and disclosure to the Banking Commission, publication of a take-over bid prospectus, etc and compliance with the measures of protection it provides in favour of the shareholders of the target company. In addition to the provisions laid down by the Royal Decree of 8 November 1989, those public take-over bids must still comply with the rules of Royal Decree no. 185 on the control of banks and issues of shares and stock. Public take-over bids which relate to stock other than that referred to above are subject only to Royal Decree no. 185.

It must finally be stressed that these new rules do not set aside the disclosure requirement to the works council or the information duty under the law of 30 December 1970, modified by the law of 17 August 1973, concerning economic expansion (see *above*).

Transparency of corporations

A law of 2 March 1989, complemented by the royal decree of 10 April 1989, demands, as a rule, the publicity and disclosure of all major holdings (ie 5 per cent) in companies incorporated under Belgian law and listed at the stock exchange of any EC member state. This information must be updated each time there is a new 5 per cent increase in the participation held.

4.4 ACQUISITIONS OF GOODWILL

INTRODUCTION: ACQUISITION OF SHARES OR ASSETS

The decision to acquire the shares or the assets of the target company will be influenced by several factors. Apart from purely commercial considerations on the part of both the acquirer and the vendor, the possible direct and indirect tax implications of the choice, as well as the legal considerations, will influence the parties' choice.

4.4.1 FORMALITIES

The formalities involved in the transfer of goodwill will, as a rule, be rather more cumbersome than those to be fulfilled when acquiring shares in a target company. The basic underlying reason for this is the fact that, unlike a situation where shares are taken over, the take-over of goodwill implies its transfer from one legal entity to another one. Contracts, administrative licences, claims, real estate etc will therefore need to be transferred. Under Belgian law, this means that the formalities required for the transfer of each of the items to be taken over must be fulfilled.

Transfer of claims

The transfer of a claim does not require the approval or consent of the debtor in question. According to art 1690 of the Belgian Civil Code, the transfer of a claim can, however, be enforced against third parties only on condition that notice of the transfer is served on the debtor by a process-server or that he accepts the transfer by means of a certified deed (ie a notarial act).

As long as one of these formalities has not been complied with, the debtor is entitled to consider that the transferor remains his co-contracting party and consequently he can still validly discharge his contractual obligations with the transferor.

It is recognised in practice that the procedure provided by art 1690 of the Civil Code is quite cumbersome as regards the transfer of claims within the ambit of the transfer of a branch. Therefore it is usually admitted that, even when the formalities referred to *above* are not fulfilled, the transfer of a claim will be enforceable against any third party who has recognised, even implicitly but in a definite manner, the existence of the transfer. A draft Act which modifies the system established by art 1690, is currently pending before Parliament. At present, however, enforceability against all third parties still requires compliance with its provisions.

Belgian law also contains several exceptional rules which aim to facilitate the transfer of specific claims, such as, for example, the transfer of invoices in the favour of banks or other recognised credit institutions, of bills of exchange, etc.

Transfer of claims guaranteed by a mortgage

Article 1692 of the Civil Code provides that the transfer of a claim includes all the accessories of the claim such as personal guarantees, priorities and mortgages.

The transfer of a claim guaranteed by a lien or a mortgage which is registered at the Mortgage Bureau is only enforceable against third parties if there is mention of the identity of the transferee and the date and nature of the transfer act in the margin of the register (art 5 of the Mortgage Act).

Transfer of debts

There are no particular formalities required for the transfer of debts. The original debtor (the transferor), however, remains liable for the debt unless the creditor agrees that the original debtor can be discharged. In other words, if the creditor does not give his agreement to the substitution of one debtor for another, the original debtor remains liable for the debt. Likewise, the transfer of sureties given as a guarantee of the debt requires the agreement of the person who granted them.

Transfer of contracts

Yet again, there are no general rules under Belgian law which relate to the transfer of contractual obligations. As a rule, the transfer of a bilateral contract can be carried out by the transferor and the transferee without the agreement of the co-contracting party being required. However, if his consent is not secured, transferor and transferee remain responsible jointly and severally as regards performance of the contract transferred. As regards third parties, the enforceability of the transfer in principle requires compliance with the formalities provided by art 1690 of the Civil Code.

The transfer of a contract concluded *intuitu personae* (that is to say, concluded because of a person's specific qualifications or characteristics) or of a contract whose provisions expressly disallow its transfer, requires the agreement of the co-contracting party. In addition, the enforceability of the transfer of guarantees provided by a third party as a security for the performance of the obligations of the transferor's co-contracting party, requires compliance with art 1690 of the Civil Code.

The law organises the transfer of contracts in some cases, such as, for example, the transfer of credit contracts (1), employment contracts (2) and commercial leases (3).

(1) In accordance with art 26 of the Consumer Credit Act of 9 July 1991, the transfer of a credit contract is only enforceable against the consumer after the latter has been notified of the transfer by *registered mail*, except if the immediate transfer is expressly provided in the credit contract and the identity of the transferee is mentioned in the credit offer.

The consumer may still use against the transferee all means of defence (including the possibility of off setting the debt) that he could have used against the transferor.

(2) When a branch of activity is transferred, the employment contracts concluded with the staff employed within that branch are transferred to the transferee without the latter's agreement being necessary. If an employment contract is terminated because the transfer results in the terms and conditions of the employment contract being substantially changed, termination is deemed to occur at the initiative of the employer. Both transferor and transferee are liable towards the transferred staff as regards past debts.

(3) Regardless of any contractual provision to the contrary, the transfer of a commercial lease is always allowed if it takes place in connection within the transfer of the whole business.

Article 11 of the Commercial Lease Act establishes that in case of transfer of the lessee's rights, the transferee becomes the direct lessee of the lessor. However, the original lessee remains jointly and severally liable for all obligations resulting from the original lease unless the lessor expressly discharges him.

If the lease agreement contains a clause which prohibits its transfer, the draft transfer act must be served on the lessor by bailiff or notified to him by registered mail. The lessor may oppose the transfer for 'fair reasons' (such as the fact that the lessee has carried out commercial activities on the premises for less than two years), to be evaluated by the judge, by informing the lessee of these reasons by bailiff or by registered mail within 30 days of receiving notification. The lessee then has 15 days to take the matter to court.

If the lease does not contain a clause stating that it may not be transferred, there are no formalities to be complied with regarding the lessor (in application of Cass, 19 March 1971, Pas, I, p 674). Obviously, for all sorts of practical reasons, the lessor must nevertheless be informed of the transfer.

4.4.2 VAT IMPLICATIONS

Unless the whole of the estate of the target company or of one of its divisions is taken over, the transfer of assets will be subject to VAT. Such is, of course, not the case where shares are transferred, when even no stamp duties are due.

5
AGENCY

5.1 BACKGROUND

The legal treatment of commercial intermediaries is one of the major characteristics of the Belgian legal system. Indeed, in Belgium as opposed to the situation in other European countries other than the UK and Ireland, no specific protection has been granted by law to commercial agents. As long as the EC directive is not implemented in the Belgian legal system, it will therefore be important for agents to obtain a written agreement making up for that loophole. On the contrary, the distributor, who in most countries is not the beneficiary of any specific protection, is in most circumstances able to claim the benefit of the entitlement which has been provided by the law of 27 July 1961 (as modified in 1971).

5.2 COMMERCIAL AGENTS

5.2.1 ABSENCE OF SPECIFIC BELGIAN LEGISLATION

Belgian law does not as yet contain specific rules regarding commercial agency agreements or their termination. The rules applicable to these relations are, therefore, to be found in the general law of contract, case law and in legal doctrine.

On an international level, the Benelux countries entered, on 26 November 1973, into a convention regulating the status of the commercial agent. This, however, has never been, and will never be, ratified by Belgium since a directive was issued at EC level on 18 December 1986. At this point in time, Belgium has not yet implemented that directive into Belgian law although this should be done by 1 January 1990. The directive will however have direct effect. A draft bill has been prepared but its further study has been postponed as a result of the last Belgian Government's collapse at the end of 1991 and it is unclear when the bill will be passed.

5.2.2 PERFORMANCE OF THE CONTRACT

As a result of the absence of specific statutory provisions regulating the status of the agent, the rights and obligations of the agent and of the principal are governed by the agreement concluded by the parties within the limits imposed by public policy and general principles of law. If there is no written agreement, the rights and obligations of the parties will be determined by trade practices, general principles of law and case law.

Generally speaking, it is accepted that:

- the agent must carry out his duties with diligence, in close co-operation with the principal and in good faith; and that
- the principal must facilitate the activities of the agent and pay his remuneration.

Authors disagree as to the exact legal definition of the agency contract under Belgian law, especially where the agent is entrusted with a power of attorney which entitles him to bind the principal. Most authors, however, agree that the agency agreement has an *intuitu personae* character (ie that the identity of the co-contracting party is of utmost importance). This has major consequences as far as the termination of the contract is concerned.

5.2.3 DURATION AND TERMINATION

Duration

An agency agreement may be concluded for a fixed or indefinite duration. A verbal agreement may be agreed for an indefinite duration. An agreement for a fixed period but tacitly extended after its expiry, in circumstances showing the will of the parties to continue the agency, will usually be considered as continued for an indefinite period.

Termination

General rules. As mentioned *above*, the agency agreement is held to be concluded by the parties because of their mutual identity. As a result thereof, either party's death, bankruptcy or incapacity will result in the dissolution of the agreement. In addition, as any other agreement, the agency agreement will come to an end whenever its subject matter disappears, ie in cases where the products are no longer manufactured or where the principal loses the right to distribute the products. In such cases, the principal will, however, as a rule, remain liable for damages as soon as his own decision making power is involved in the disappearance of the contract's subject matter, eg when he decides to discontinue the production of the products.

Determinate duration. An agency agreement for determinate duration ends upon expiry of its term. Unilateral termination of the agreement by the principal before expiry of its term entitles the agent to compensation in respect of any profits he would have obtained from the performance of the agreement for its full term (*lucrum cessans*), as well as any losses resulting from such early termination (*damnum emergens*). Likewise, the agent, who terminates the agreement before expiry of the term, is liable to compensate any damage the principal might suffer as a result thereof.

Bearing in mind the *intuitu personae* character of the agent/principal relationship, it is sometimes considered that both parties are entitled to terminate the agreement with immediate effect when the co-contracting party commits a serious fault (*faute grave—zware fout*), whether a breach of contract or not (eg criminal indictment of the agent).

Indefinite duration. As with any other agreement concluded for an indefinite duration, an agency agreement for indefinite duration can be terminated unilaterally by either party, provided notice is granted sufficiently in advance. If no such notice is given and the termination occurs abruptly, the agent or the principal, as the case may be, is entitled to compensation. The amount of compensation will often be determined *ex aequo et bono* taking into consideration, among other things, the duration of the agreement, the turnover achieved by the agent, the period of time the agent needs in order to adapt to the new situation. In principle, however, the judge must attempt to determine the amount of the compensation to be awarded on the basis of positive data.

Notice periods usually vary between three and six months but have even reached 12 months and more but such only in exceptional circumstances (Antwerp, 4.2.1980, BRH 1980, I, 456; Commercial Court Brussels, 21.1.1981, BRH 1981, I, 493).

There are conflicting court decisions on whether or not the agent is entitled to compensation for loss of goodwill (*contra:*

Commercial Court Brussels, 21.1.1981, BRH 1981, 493; the indemnity for loss of goodwill claimed by the plaintiff is not justified since in the agency agreement the goodwill is owned by the principal and not by the agent' (free translation) in Commercial Court Brussels, 3.9.1981, BRH, 1982, 631; *pro*: Antwerp 4.2.1980, BRH, I, 456). It is usually considered, however, that the agent is not entitled to any compensation on that basis. One of the reasons alleged to support that position is that the goodwill is bound to the enterprise of the principal and not to the agent.

It is also argued that the agent, whose contract is terminated by the principal, could require in court that the agreement be further carried out during the notice period which should have been granted, subject to the penalty of a fine (*astreinte—dwangsom*). Again, it is sometimes considered that if the termination is justified by a serious fault or even by a legitimate interest (such as a justified reorganisation of the principal's distribution network), no notice period or compensation would be due. Utmost care should be exercised when terminating an agency contract on that basis, however, since the judge retains full power to determine whether the decision made was adequate and to grant compensation if he deems it appropriate.

5.2.4 FUTURE ORIENTATION: DIRECTIVE 86/653 RELATING TO SELF-EMPLOYED COMMERCIAL AGENTS

Directive 86/653 co-ordinates national laws only with respect to the main points of the status of commercial agents. It provides protection for the agent mainly in the area of remuneration (one-third of the provisions of the directive) and termination of contract (more than one-third of the directive's provisions).

The rights and obligations of the parties during the contract (except as far as remuneration is concerned) are only summarily sketched: the directive only provides that the principal and the agent must act dutifully and in good faith. The regulation does not contain either any provisions with regard to the termination of the contract without notice, the bankruptcy of either the principal or the agent, or the attachment of the agent's remuneration.

It is to be noted that although this directive aims to bring the legislations of the EC member states on self-employed commercial agents into conformity, its enforcement by the various states will most probably result in quite a number of discrepancies remaining:

(1)   First of all several aspects of the relationship agent/principal
      are not ruled by the directive, as above mentioned.
(2)   The directive contains several fields where the member states
      are entitled to make their own rules, eg level of remuneration,
      existence of commission on transactions in the case either of
      exclusivity or when a specific mandate has been granted to the
      agent with regard to a specific area or group of customers, right
      to inspect the principal's books, requirement of a written
      contract, etc.

As a result, when drafting an agency agreement which will
have effect in EC territory, account should be taken of the fact that
even where member states have implemented the directive, the
legislations of the various EC member states will still show discrepancies. Given that operators may have the impression that the law
in the whole of the EC is now the same, these discrepancies are
probably more dangerous because they are less expected and less
obvious.

5.3   COMMISSION AGENTS

The commission agent (in French, *commissionnaire*—in
Dutch, *commissionaris*) undertakes to carry out, in consideration for
remuneration, one or several commercial operations in his own
name but for the account of a principal whose name is not to be
disclosed by the commission agent.

Under Belgian law, the commission agency is governed by art
12–17 of the law of 5 May 1872 (Book I, Title VII of the Commercial Code) and the current commercial customs and practices
resulting from it. The provisions of the law of 5 May 1872, however,
only define the commission agency and provide for a legal priority
interest in favour of the commission agent (and his financial backer,
if any) on the goods he is entrusted with as a guarantee of all claims
he (or his backer) may have against the principal when the contract
is performed.

The existence of a commission agency contract implies the
fulfilment of three conditions: first, the commission agent must deal
with third parties in his own name, second, his task must involve the
completion of one or more legal transactions regarding the move-
ment of goods, and, third, he must be paid for his services. (As a

general rule, the principal must also reimburse all costs and expenses incurred by the commission agent and losses suffered by the latter, unless they result from his own fault. In turn, no commission is due if the transaction is not concluded).

The commission agent incurs several obligations towards the principal, such as compliance with the instructions he has been given, to inform and report to the principal and to refrain from carrying out, with himself as a co-contracting party, the operation he is entrusted to execute, with a third party. If several commission agents are entrusted with one and the same operation they incur joint liability towards the principal.

As a rule, the commission agent is not responsible for the non-performance by the third party of the contract he concludes with him on behalf of the principal, unless that third party was known to be insolvent at the time the operation is carried out. The commission agency agreement can of course enlarge that responsibility by including a clause whereby the commission agent guarantees the solvency of the third party (*clause de ducroire—delcrederebeding*). The bankruptcy of the commission agent does not leave the principal defenceless since, as a rule, he will be able to claim either those goods which the commission agent held on his behalf and whose nature has not been altered, or their sale price if still owed by the purchaser.

As an agency agreement, a commission agency agreement is concluded *intuitu personae* and therefore, in principle, comes to an end as a result of either party's death, legal incapacity or bankruptcy. It is also terminated in the cases provided by the Civil Code for all contracts, ie expiry of the term, breach of contract (as a rule, this requires the prior authorisation of the court), etc. It is accepted that the principal is entitled to terminate the contract forthwith, irrespective of the fact that the commission agent is not liable for any fault, provided he compensates him. That same right is not granted to the commission agent.

5.4 BROKERS

The broker (*courtier—makelaar*), is an independent commercial intermediary who undertakes to put two or more parties in contact with the prospect of their concluding a commercial deal to which the broker himself is not a party. Brokerage activities within such sectors as the stock exchange, commodities, insurance etc, are covered by specific laws. As with commission agents, the broker is entitled to remuneration for his services, unless the operation is not carried out. In that case, however, courts sometimes grant the agent remuneration for services already performed. As a rule, the commission is due to the broker upon execution of the deal. Sometimes local practices make payment of the commission subject to the payment of the price by the third party. Generally speaking, in order to avoid subsequent disputes, it is advisable for the broker to determine in advance, by written contract, the conditions, time of payment and amount of commission he will be due, as well as the other terms and conditions of his task.

As a rule, either party may terminate the brokerage agreement at any time without any notice period or compensation.

5.5 COMMERCIAL REPRESENTATIVES (*REPRÉSENTANTS DE COMMERCE—HANDELSVERTEGENWOORDIGERS*)

The commercial representative (*représentant de commerce— handelsvertegenwoordiger*) acts in the same way as the agent. However, he is employed contractually by the principal. A commercial representative is, in fact, subordinated to the principal who is his employer.

Commercial representation is governed by the law of 3 July 1978 on employment contracts. It is important to note that under that law, anyone who is appointed to canvass customers with a view to negotiating or concluding commercial transactions (except for insurance contracts) and who is remunerated therefor is deemed bound to the principal by a contract of employment. The principal who wishes to challenge that legal definition will have to prove that he does not exercise employer's authority over the 'agent'.

Generally speaking, the commercial representative is subject to the same rules as any other employee (as opposed to manual workers, see chapter 9). The commercial representative, however, is granted specific protection in several respects. First, several provisions of the law are devoted to protecting his right to commission (if any, since the contract can also provide for a fixed salary, without entitlement to commission). For instance, commission is due on any order accepted by the employer even if the transaction is subsequently not concluded (unless that is a consequence of a fault of the representative). In some circumstances, commission can also be due on all orders accepted during a period of three months after termination of the employment contract.

Upon termination of his contract, the representative, who brought clients to his employer and has been in the latter's employment for at least one year, is also entitled, in addition to the usual notice period (or compensation in lieu) to an indemnity for goodwill (*indemnité d'éviction—uitwinningsvergoeding*). The representative forfeits that right if he terminates his contract in the absence of a serious fault of the employer, if he is dismissed because of a serious fault or if the employer can prove that the termination does not prejudice the commercial representative in any way. If compensation for goodwill is due, it is equal to three months' remuneration, for the first five years of employment, and is increased by one month's remuneration for every new five-year period of employment with the same employer. If the commercial representative terminates the contract because of a serious fault by his employer, he may, in addition, claim damages if compensation for goodwill does not compensate his loss in full.

Non-competition clauses are invalid if the representative earns less than BF 796,000 (index-linked) gross per year, as are non-competition clauses which are not recorded in writing. When the remuneration is in excess of that amount, the non-competition clause is valid provided it relates to similar activities, is not in excess of 12 months and is limited to the territory where the representative operates.

Both non-competition clauses included in employment contracts of employee or manual workers and non-competition clauses contained in employment contracts with sales representatives, have no effect when the contract terminates during a probation period, and thereafter, at the employer's initiative without the representative being liable for any serious fault, or at the initiative of the representative as a result of a serious fault committed by the employer (as regards employees, a derogating system is possible in specific circumstances). The compensation provided by contract for breach of the non-competition clause may not be greater than three months' remuneration. The employer, however, may claim additional damages in court if he can prove that the damage exceeds such

amount. Finally, as with commission agents, the commercial representative is not liable for the insolvency of the clients he refers to his
employer. Any clause whereby he guarantees the solvency of those
clients must be recorded in writing. His exposure under that clause
may not, under any circumstances, be higher than the amount of the
commission pertaining to the sum unrecovered.

6
DISTRIBUTION

6.1 INTRODUCTION

Belgian law contains no statute regarding distribution contracts *except* with regard to their termination, which is the subject of a very well known Act dated 27 July 1961 (modified on 13 April 1971) concerning the unilateral termination of exclusive distribution agreements. Parties to such an agreement are therefore entitled to agree any terms and conditions within the usual limits with the exception of those which are regulated by the above-mentioned Act.

Attention also needs to be paid, when entering into a distribution agreement, to the competition rules provided for by the Treaty of Rome, and especially its article 85 which basically holds as automatically void all agreements, joint practices, etc which may affect trade between member states and which have as their goal or effect the prevention, restriction or distortion of competition within the Common Market. An exemption can, of course, be obtained, either on an individual basis (this course requires notification of the agreement to the Commission) or as a result of block exemptions (no notification required). As a rule, distribution agreements can be caught by art 85, unless they comply with the provisions contained in the block exemption regulations provided by the EC Council (Regulation 1983/83 on Categories of Exclusive Distribution Agreements; Regulation 1984/83 on Exclusive Purchasing Agreements) or unless the size of the enterprises concerned entitles them to benefit from the *de minimis* rule provided by the Commission (Commission communication dated 3 September 1986).

If careful examination of the contract and of the parties' respective importance does not give certainty as to the non-applicability of art 85 of the Treaty of Rome to the distribution agreement, it is advisable for parties to consider applying for an individual exemption and to notify their contract to the Commission. Absence of notification can result in very heavy fines being imposed on the contract partners if the agreement is considered to infringe art 85.

6.2 EXCLUSIVE AND QUASI-EXCLUSIVE DISTRIBUTION AGREEMENTS

6.2.1 SCOPE OF PROTECTION

Only those distribution agreements which are within the definition of the law of 27 July 1961 and fall within one of the categories it specifies, will entitle the distributor (or the principal) to claim its protection. In addition the entitlement provided in favour of the distributor (and of the principal) means that the contract lasts for an indefinite period.

Categories of distribution agreements covered

The law defines distribution agreements as agreements whereby a supplier grants to one or more distributors the right to sell in their own name and on their own account, the products which he manufactures or distributes.

There are three types of such distribution agreements entitling the distributor to claim protection under this law:

(1) Wholly exclusive distributorships, ie distributorships under which no other distributor is appointed within the contractual territory.

(2) Quasi-exclusive distributorships, ie distributorships under which the distributor sells more or less all of the contractual products which are sold within the contractual territory.

(3) Distributorships imposing such substantial obligations on the distributor that the latter would suffer considerable hardship in the event of termination of the distribution. The following obligations have been considered 'substantial':

- Obligation to make investments, eg with respect to the storage of products.
- Obligation to promote the trademark of the manufacturer.
- Obligation to have a stock of products, etc.

The agreement does not need to be entered into in writing. In that case, the distributor will, of course, need to prove that he holds distribution rights and that his verbal distribution agreement falls within one of the categories defined *above*. Such will result from the actual circumstances, eg the continuous and organised character of the relations existing between the parties is usually considered a proof of the existence of distribution rights; the fact that commissions are paid to the distributor on sales made directly by the manufacturer (and without any intervention by the distributor) in the territory has been deemed a proof of the exclusive or quasi-exclusive character of the parties' relationship.

Sometimes the distributor will act at the same time as agent of the same manufacturer. The question therefore arises as to whether or not he will be entitled to the protection of the 1961 Act. Courts usually consider in this respect that that protection will benefit the distributor provided his activities as agent are ancillary to those as distributor.

Fixed or indefinite duration

The law grants the distributor (and to a lesser extent the principal) a specific protection upon termination of a distribution contract concluded for an indefinite duration. It is generally accepted that a distribution agreement is agreed to be for an indefinite duration when this is provided by the contract itself or when it is not possible to determine from the language of the agreement on what date the contract comes to an end. These, however, are not the only cases when a distribution agreement subject to the 1961 Act will be of indefinite duration. The law in fact also determines cases where a contract initially agreed to be for a fixed period will convert automatically into a contract for an indefinite length of time.

A distribution agreement for a fixed period which is subject to the 1961 Act, does not automatically come to an end upon the expiry of the agreed term. If either party wants the agreement to come to an end upon the agreed term, such a party will need to serve notice of termination on his co-contracting party be registered letter at least three months and at the most six months before the end of the term. Failure to send such a letter results in the agreement being deemed to have been renewed either for an indefinite period or for the period stipulated in the renewal clause. In addition, a distribution agreement entered into for a fixed duration is by law considered converted into an agreement for indefinite period upon the third renewal, even when modifications have been made to the agreement.

The distribution contract will therefore be of an indefinite duration when:

(1) It is verbal.
(2) It is concluded without specific indication of duration.
(3) It provides for a fixed duration and contains a tacit renewal clause, but is renewed for a third time; the agreement will be considered to be agreed for an indefinite duration from the third renewal onwards.
(4) It is of a fixed duration, does not contain any clause of tacit renewal for a specific period and is not terminated in accordance with the rules provided by the 1961 Act.

6.2.2 CONSEQUENCES OF THE TERMINATION

If an exclusive distribution agreement for an indefinite period is terminated by either party, a reasonable notice period must be given. If no such notice period is given, an adequate compensation must be paid in lieu. If however, termination is for serious breach of contract, notice may be immediate and without compensation. The 'serious breach of contract' is that which results in the further continuation of the parties' contractual relations being impossible. Courts have considered as a 'serious breach of contract', the sale of competing products, non-performance of quotas, failure to pay invoices, etc.

In addition to his right to a notice period or compensation in lieu, the distributor, as opposed to the supplier, is entitled to claim free compensation if:

(1) He terminates the contract on the grounds of the supplier's serious breach of contract; or
(2) the supplier terminates the contract for reasons other than for serious breach of contract.

Reasonable notice period

The length of the notice period can only be determined upon agreement by the parties *as from the moment when notice of termination is served*. If the parties fail to reach an agreement, the matter will be referred to the court which will make a decision *en équité* (on equitable principles) and, if appropriate, bearing in mind usual practices. Courts have provided several criteria to be borne in mind when assessing the length of the 'reasonable notice period'. As a general rule, it is considered that the notice period must be such as to enable the distributor to find a new product for distribution, similar to that which has been terminated.

In assessing the length of the notice period to be given, the following items are taken into consideration by case law:

(1) The overall effect of the termination on the distributor's activities: the larger the amount the distribution accounts for in the whole of the distributor's activities, the longer the notice period will be.

(2) The extent and sophistication of the distributor's set-up and the obligations he has assumed in order to perform the contract.

(3) The length of the period during which the exclusive distribution has been in existence.

(4) Compensation for promotional efforts and expenses, eg canvassing and promotion costs, expenses for renting, costs of material, storage of goods, etc, the possibility of further use of materials after the termination of the contract.

(5) The reputation of the products of the supplier and the possibility of selling similar products.

(6) The extent of the territory for which the exclusive distribution was granted.

(7) The obligations and duties relating to the distribution and the burden assumed by each party.

(8) The importance of the supplier's trademark.

During the notice period, each party must comply with his contractual obligations. Failure to do so might authorise the co-contracting party to terminate the agreement forthwith for serious breach of contract.

Compensation in lieu of notice period

If no notice period is granted or when the notice period granted appears to be insufficient, the distributor (or the supplier as the case may be) is entitled to compensation for the damage suffered as a result of the insufficient notice period. Again the law does not indicate how this compensation is to be computed. It is, however, generally accepted that the amount of compensation should be calculated in such a way as to compensate for the profit which would have been earned during the notice period, which should have been received.

When assessing the amount of the compensation to be paid the courts use different parameters: average gross profit achieved by the distributor, gross profit or net profit. Most court decisions use the average net profit realised over the two or three years preceding the termination, increased by the fixed overheads relating to the distribution. Often the court will also refer the determination of the amount of compensation to an expert.

In the absence of contractual rules relating to the condition of the stock upon termination of the agreement, most courts order the supplier to repurchase the stock still in the possession of the distributor at the time of termination. Again expert valuation will very often be used.

Complementary indemnity

In cases where the supplier terminates the distribution other than for serious breach or where the distributor terminates the agreement for serious breach of contract by the supplier, the distributor, can, in addition to the reasonable notice period or the compensation on termination, claim a complementary indemnity according to the particular circumstances of the case.

For the calculation of the complementary indemnity, one should take into consideration the following factors:

(1) Significant additional clientele brought in by the distributor, which remains with the supplier after the termination of the contract. Evidence thereof must be brought by the distributor. The court will often refer the valuation of the compensation due in respect thereof to expert appraisal. Sometimes, however, the court will make an assessment *ex aequo and bono*, in which event the clientele indemnity will usually be considered as equal to once or twice the net average profit of the two or three years preceding the termination.

(2) Expenses incurred by the distributor as a result of the distribution and which benefit the supplier after the termination of the contract, eg advertising and promotion costs when required by the supplier. Usually the main problem will consist in proving whether there will be any benefit after termination;

(3) Costs incurred by the distributor in connection with redundancies as a result of the termination of the contract. As a general

principle of law, in this case the distributor needs to seek to limit the exposure of the supplier as much as possible. He must therefore take care to lay off his personnel in such a way that their notice period ends as close as possible to the end of his own notice period under the distribution agreement.

6.2.3 ENFORCEMENT OF THE PROTECTION

Rules provided by the 1961 Act

In order to ensure that distributors really benefit from this protection even on the international level, rules have been clearly incorporated into the law:

(1)   A distributor who has been prejudiced by the termination of his distribution agreement relating to part or the whole of Belgium may always refer the dispute to the courts of his domicile or of the manufacturer's domicile. The purpose of this provision is to give the distributor the right to refer the dispute regarding the termination of his contract to his own, ie Belgian, courts (art 4, para 1).

(2)   The Belgian court hearing the matter must compulsorily apply Belgian law (art 4, para 2).

(3)   The provisions of the law are applicable to all agreements notwithstanding any agreements to the contrary that are concluded before the end of the distribution agreement (art 6).

As a result of the above, upon termination of his contract, a distributor whose agreement is within the scope of the law of 27 July 1961 is entitled as a rule to refer a related dispute to the Belgian courts which will decide according to the rules of Belgian law. Any waiver of this right is invalid if made before the distribution is terminated, but may be relied upon if made afterwards.

Special cases

Jurisdiction clause as per the Brussels Convention. A clause, however, whereby parties to a distribution agreement, one of whom at least is domiciled in an EC member state, grants jurisdiction to the courts of an EC member state in accordance with art 17 of the Brussels Convention of 27 September 1968 on Judicial Competence and Enforcement of Civil and Commercial Court Decisions, must be recognised as valid by Belgian courts.

Pursuant to art 17, such an agreement attributing jurisdiction must be made either in writing, or verbally with written confirmation, or be made in the course of international trade in a form customarily accepted in the trade and of which the parties are aware or should have been aware. As a result, when the parties have validly inserted such a jurisdiction clause, a Belgian court to which any application has been made on the basis of art 4, para 1 of the 1961 law, will have to decline jurisdiction in favour of the court provided by that jurisdiction clause, community law taking precedence over national law. In this way parties can set aside the exclusive jurisdiction of Belgian courts.

Applicable law. If, in accordance with a jurisdiction clause, foreign courts are given jurisdiction, the question arises as to whether or not they will apply the rules contained in the 1961 Belgian Act on the termination of the distribution agreement. In other words, will the foreign court grant the distributor, whose contract is terminated, the benefit of the protection provided under the 1961 Act? In theory, the answer to that question will differ depending on whether or not the Rome Convention of 19 June 1980 on the Law Applicable to Contractual Obligations was in force at the time when the distribution agreement was concluded. In effect, the Rome Convention provides for specific rules to apply when determining the law applicable to a contract.

In Belgium, the general rules applicable to the determination of the law applicable to a contract are as follows:

(1) Contracts concluded before 1 January 1988 are governed by the rules of the autonomy of will as they existed before that date.

(2) Contracts concluded between 1 January 1988 and 30 March 1991 are governed by the law of 14 July 1987 which incorporates most provisions of the Rome Convention.

(3) Contracts executed after 1 April 1991 are governed by the Rome Convention as approved by the UK.

In practice, there are two possibilities:

• Parties have not made a clear choice of the law applicable to their contractual relations.

• Parties have made such an explicit choice.

If parties have not made a clear choice of law, the law applicable to the contract and its termination will be determined in accordance with the rules of conflict of law applicable in the country where the court proceedings are pending. Usually this will have as a consequence the application of the law of the country of the distributor. If the distributor was active on the Belgian territory, the Belgian Act of 1961 should therefore be applied.

If parties have granted jurisdiction to foreign courts and simultaneously provided for the application of a foreign body of law, the question arises as to whether the foreign court will have to apply the Belgian 1961 Act. For instance, if a distribution agreement between an Italian manufacturer and a Belgian distributor provides for the jurisdiction of the courts of Milan and the application of Italian law, will the Milan courts agree to apply Belgian law to the termination of the distribution agreement, or will they apply Italian law? For agreements concluded before the entry into force of the Rome Convention of 19 June 1980, this question will very probably be answered negatively by most foreign courts.

As far as agreements concluded after the Convention of Rome came into force are concerned, the answer is less certain. In effect, art 7 of the Rome Convention provides that courts can apply compulsory provisions (*dispositions impératives—dwingende bepalingen*) of another country which is closely related to the situation, provided those compulsory provisions would apply irrespective of any contractual provision to the contrary. As a result, in our example, the Milan courts, which would have to decide on a dispute regarding the termination of the distribution agreement concluded after the Rome Convention entered into force in that country, are authorised to pay attention to the Belgian 1961 Act and give it effect. However, the Milan courts have no obligation to do so and the Convention does not provide any criterion of assessment.

Arbitration. Since the terms of the law of 27 July 1961 are mandatory no arbitration clause may be inserted in a distribution agreement for all or part of the Belgian territory and where both parties have Belgian nationality. After termination of the agreement, however, parties may validly agree to refer their dispute to arbitration. The question has arisen as to whether an arbitration clause, agreed in a distribution concluded with a foreign supplier, is enforceable. The question has long been a controversial one and still is to a certain extent. It once appeared to have been settled by the *Cour de Cassation* (ie the Belgian Supreme Court) in a case concerning the termination by the manufacturer of a distribution agreement for Belgium, governed by the law of 27 July 1961. The court held that the termination could not be referred to arbitration under a clause agreed before the end of the contract, and which purported to apply a foreign law (28 June 1979, Pas, 1979, I, 1260). This case, however, concerned the recognition of an arbitration award already issued.

In a later case the Court of Appeal of Brussels was required to decide whether a Belgian court is competent to hear a dispute relating to the termination of a distribution agreement, despite the existence of an arbitration clause. It held that the legality of arbitration clauses must be determined in accordance with the law which governs the contract, ie as agreed by the parties. In other words, pursuant to that decision, a Belgian court could decide that it is not competent to hear a dispute arising out of the termination of a distribution agreement, if that agreement contains an arbitration clause which is perfectly valid in the eyes of the law which the parties have agreed should apply to it. An award, however, made by the appointed arbitration tribunal, could not be enforced in Belgium for the reasons stated *above*.

Authors consider that this last solution is in conformity with the provisions of the New York Convention of 10 June 1958 on the Recognition and Enforcement of Foreign arbitration awards but would not be obligatory in disputes where the European Convention on the International Commercial Arbitration of Geneva (as approved by Belgian law of 19 July 1975) applies.

The present state of the law therefore offers no guarantees as to the treatment by Belgian courts of an arbitration clause contained in an 'international' distribution agreement. The latest status of case law should therefore be ascertained prior to including an arbitration clause in a distribution agreement executed in respect of all or part of the Belgian territory.

6.2.4 CONCLUSION

If a manufacturer or an exporter wishes to terminate a distribution of indefinite duration granted for the whole or part of Belgium without the distributor having committed a serious breach of contract, such a manufacturer or exporter should:

(1) Not terminate the agreement without giving a reasonable notice period (or equivalent compensation) and not forget that the distributor is entitled to compensation for goodwill, costs and redundancy payments.

(2) Make sure that the distributor's acceptance of the notice period and the compensation scheme are obtained in writing.

(3) After notification of the termination, have the distributor sign a document renouncing any further claims, specifically under Belgian law, regarding the exclusive distribution agreement.

When entering into a distribution agreement of fixed duration, manufacturers and exporters should:

(1) Make a note in their diaries regarding the termination date, and confirm termination by the agreed term three to six months before the stated term lapses.

(2) Be aware that to renew the agreement for a third time will result in the agreement being deemed as lasting for an indefinite period and that all the rules on protection of this type of distribution arrangement will then become applicable.

6.3 OTHER TYPES OF DISTRIBUTION AGREEMENTS

Types of distribution agreements other than those described *above*, are governed by the general principles of law, and thus the parties are entitled to regulate the terms and conditions of their relationship as they deem appropriate within the general boundaries of Belgian public policy, morality and other general principles of law. Considering the very wide characteristics of the definitions contained in the 1961 Act, very few distribution agreements will be outside its scope. It should be carefully checked with local legal advisers as to whether or not the contract qualifies as a distribution contract under the 1961 Act, and which attitude should be adopted either upon the execution or termination of a distribution contract relating to all or part of the Belgian territory.

7
FRANCHISING

7.1 DEFINITION AND CHARACTERISTICS

Under Belgian law, there are no specific rules governing franchising, although a draft bill on franchise agreements has been pending before the Belgian Parliament since 1980. It is unlikely, however, that the draft will ever be passed.

It is sometimes argued that the national Code of Ethics drafted by the Belgian Franchising Association supplemented by the European Code of Ethics is sufficient to deal with the situation. The European Code has been submitted to the European Commission, which considers that it does not contain any clause which would conflict with arts 85 or 86 of the Treaty of Rome.

Franchising agreements are generally defined as an agreement concluded between independent parties, in which one (the franchisor) grants to another (the franchisee) for a consideration, the use of his know how, trademark and/or brand name and any other symbols, developed by the franchisor, which have been tested and found to work. Additionally, support and regular services may be provided for. As a result of such an agreement, the franchisee becomes part of a co-ordinated system. Franchising agreements can either relate to the distribution of products or services or to the manufacturing of products.

It is important to stress that under Belgian law, a franchising agreement, as an agency agreement, is considered concluded *intuitu personae*. As a result, the rights and obligations deriving from the agreement cannot be transferred without the other party's consent. Likewise, if the contract is entered into with an individual, the latter's death implies the termination of the contract.

The view has been expressed by some authors that the law of 27 July 1961, as modified by the law of 13 April 1971 on the termination of distributorship agreements, would apply also to franchise agreements which are exclusive or quasi-exclusive distributorships of goods. In that case, franchisees involved in the distribution of goods would therefore be able to claim the benefits linked to the protection granted by this law (see chapter 6). To date however, there is no case law to support this theory.

7.2 FRANCHISING AND COMPETITION LAW

Franchising agreements can be affected by EC competition law and, from 1 April 1993, by the new Belgian competition provisions.

EC law considers as null and void, as has been explained earlier, all agreements, concerted practices, etc which may affect trade between member states and which aim or have as effect to restrict or materially distort the competition respectively within the Common Market. As from 1 April 1993, similar rules will be applicable in Belgium (see chapter 2). Although in the famous *Pronuptia* decision (161/84 ECJ), it has been admitted by the European Court of Justice that franchising agreements do not as such affect competition, their validity under art 85 of the Treaty of Rome will depend on the contractual provisions they contain and on the economic context.

In case of doubt, parties to a franchising agreement can seek the benefit of an individual exemption. however, franchising agreements which comply with the provisions of regulation 4987/83 dated 20 November 1988, will benefit from the block-exemption provided by that regulation.

Franchising agreements which do not affect trade between member states and which cannot benefit from the *de minimis* rule provided by the Belgian law, could theoretically fall under the prohibition provided by the Belgian law on the protection of economic competition. It will therefore be prudent when concluding a franchising agreement as from 1 April 1993, to ascertain also whether or not the agreement in question should be notified with the relevant Belgian authorities.

7.3 CERTIFICATE OF DISTRIBUTION

If the franchising agreement implies the performance of retail trade activities of products such as foodstuffs, tobacco, shoes, clothes, luxury products, cars, etc and provided the franchisee employs less than 50 persons, he will need to obtain a certificate of distribution which proves that he has a minimum management knowledge. This certificate will be required at the time the franchisee registers at the trade register.

Foreigners who want to set up such a retail trade in Belgium, will also need to give evidence of their management knowledge, either at the time they apply for a professional card if they are not citizens of EC member states or, as required from Belgian citizens, at the time they apply for an entry in the trade register, if they are citizens of EC member states.

8
REAL PROPERTY AND SUCCESSION

8.1 INTRODUCTION

Investing abroad can sometimes result in the investor or members of his staff being moved to the foreign country in which the investment is being made. At that time, questions will necessarily arise regarding the purchasing or leasing of adequate business and housing premises. Some of those questions will now be addressed. In this chapter, attention will also briefly be paid to Belgian laws on succession.

8.2 REAL PROPERTY

8.2.1 SALE AND PURCHASE

Notary public

As a rule, under Belgian law, the conclusion of a sale is not subject to the completion of any specific formalities; in accordance with the Civil Code, once parties agree on the item to be sold and on the sale price (and, as a result of case law, on all other essential provisions of their agreement), the sale is considered completed.

The sale of real estate, however, requires the additional intervention of a notary public. Although this requirement will not affect the validity of the agreement between the parties, it will affect the enforceability of the agreement against third parties. In other words, the agreement is enforceable against third parties only on condition that the agreement is made with the intervention of a notary public. The notary public will check whether or not the real estate to be sold is subject to an existing mortgage and he will notify the tax administration with a view to ascertaining the existence of any tax debts of the seller to any of the departments of that administration. If there is any such mortgage or tax debt, the notary public must deduct the amount of the existing debt from the amount of the purchase price on sale, and transfer the relevant sum respectively to the creditor or to the department of the tax administration concerned.

Registration duties

The sale of real estate will entail the consequent payment of a hefty registration duty at the rate of 12.5 per cent of the sale price of property in question (or on its real value, in the event where the tax administration considers that this is higher than the sale price as agreed between the parties). Payment must take place within four months from the completion of the sale. (If a *compromis de vente—verkoopscompromis*, has been signed, payment must take place within four months of the signature of that document.)

If real estate acquired with the additional payment of the 12.5 per cent registration duty is sold by the original purchaser within three months of completion of his own purchase deed, four-fifths of the registration duties originally paid by him can be refunded. If the resale takes place within five years of completion of the original purchase deed, then three-fifths of those duties will be refunded.

Authorised real estate dealers (*marchands de bien*) benefit from specific rules which enable them to pay a reduced registration duty of only five per cent. Obtaining the status of a real estate trader requires a written and dated undertaking to be engaged in the real estate trade to be filed with the relevant registration office, and the deposit of a guarantee of at least BEF 200,000. That guarantee is intended to cover the reimbursement of the registration duties which would again become due if the real estate on which a reduced tax rate was paid is not resold within a period of ten years after the initial purchase deed. If the applicant is not domiciled in Belgium, he will also need to appoint a representative to be jointly and severally liable with the real estate trader for the payment of the latter's tax liabilities. If the authorised real estate trader is not able to prove, within five years from the undertaking mentioned above, that he regularly trades in real estate, then the full amount of the unpaid registration duties will become due, increased by a fine equal to the same amount again.

Considering the high level of the registration duties, parties are sometimes seen to structure the operation as a sale of the shares of the company to which the real estate was previously deliberately transferred. Since, as a rule, no taxes are due on the capital gains made on the sale of shares by private individuals, the benefit of such an operation for both the seller and the purchaser are immediately obvious. One should however be wary of such a structure, since tax authorities are entitled to challenge the reality of this share operation on the grounds of false pretences (ie the tax authorities might allege that the sale structure chosen is a mere sham used to evade the payment of taxes). This will be the case especially where the real estate in question is the sole asset of the company whose shares are being sold and where that company is not engaged in any other activities.

VAT

Sales are subject to VAT instead of registration duties when the object concerned is a new building or a building still to be erected, and when the seller meets specific requirements (either he is involved in the building sector or fulfils specific administrative conditions).

Practical procedure

In practice, in Belgium, the acquisition of real estate usually involves two stages:

(1) The signature of a *compromis de vente—verkoopcompromis*, which records the main terms and conditions of the sale. From the time of signature of that document onwards, the sale is complete as between the parties, and signature of the *compromis* also constitutes the starting point of the four month period within which registration duties must be paid.

(2) The signature of the sale agreement in certified form.

The reason for those two steps lies basically in the need for the notary public to have a period of time in which to prepare the documentation, to check whether or not any mortgage burdens the real estate and to discover whether or not the seller has outstanding tax debts.

Costs of sale

In addition to the registration duties to be paid, transfer of real estate also entails the payment of the notary's fees and costs. This will bring the total additional costs of the transaction (registration duties included) to approximately 15 per cent to 17 per cent of the purchase price. In accordance with the Civil Code, all those costs are borne by the purchaser. If the purchaser, however, fails to pay the registration duties (for instance because the purchaser changes his mind after signature of the *compromis* but before execution of the certified deed), the seller will be held liable to pay them.

8.2.2 CIVIL LEASES

Pure civil leases, ie leases which are neither residential leases, commercial leases nor farming leases, are subject to the general rules enacted by the Civil Code and by the terms and conditions agreed upon by the parties. They can be entered into either in writing or verbally, and for a fixed or indefinite period. If the lease is entered into by a written agreement, it must be registered in order to be enforceable against third parties, for example the purchaser of the premises.

As a rule, an inventory of fixtures and fittings (*état des lieux—plaatsbeschrijving*) should be made either before or immediately after the lessee has entered the premises. This, however, is not compulsory and if no such statement has been made, the lessee shall be deemed to have received the premises in the same state in which he returns them to the lessor at the end of the lease. By law, the lessor is bound to make all necessary repairs, with the exception of those which result from the very occupation of the premises by the tenant and day-to-day maintenance (repairs resulting from normal wear and tear, however, are to be borne by the lessor).

An annual adjustment of the rent in line with the retail prices index (*indice des prix à la consommation—consumptieprijsindex*) is authorised by law.

The lessor is by law granted a lien over the furniture that the lessee keeps in the premises, and the lessee is bound by law to furnish the premises in such a way that that lien is effective. Usually, however, the lessor will in addition require the lessee to set up a guarantee (either in cash, shares or by bank guarantee) which is usually intended to cover the damage which might be caused to the premises by the lessee while in occupation.

Leases agreed for an indefinite period may be terminated at any time by giving one month's notice. Leases for a fixed term automatically come to an end upon expiry of the agreed term.

8.2.3 RESIDENTIAL LEASES

The law of 20 February 1991 (amended by the law of 1 March 1991) created a specific type of civil lease: the residential lease, ie the lease which relates to the main residence of the lessee. Increased protection is granted to the beneficiary of the residential lease as regards:

(1) Duration of the lease: residential leases are by law deemed to be for a duration of nine years and are automatically renewed for successive periods of three years unless notice of termination is served by either party at least six months before expiry of the current term. Shorter or longer terms (shorter terms may not be agreed for a total period in excess of three years) may be agreed by the parties.

(2) Early termination: the lessee is entitled to terminate the lease agreement at any time, by giving three months' notice. If termination takes place at the initiative of the lessee during the first three years, the lessee is liable to pay compensation equal to one, two, or three months' rent, depending on whether the lease is terminated during the third, second or first year of its existence. Early termination by the lessor requires a six month notice period to be given and is authorised in specific circumstances only. In some cases, the lessee will be entitled to compensation for early termination.

(3) Rent adjustment: adjustment of the rent according to the retail prices index and revision of the rent are subject to rules similar to those provided for commercial leases. Adjustment in line with the retail prices index, however, is no longer automatic.

(4) Transfer of the property: if the lessee has been living in the premises for more than six months, the acquirer will be entitled to terminate the lease agreement, upon acquisition; but only in those circumstances where the original lessee was entitled to do so. The same rule applies if the lease had not acquired a fixed date before the transfer of the property (eg as a result of the registration of the agreement). However, in that case the acquirer is entitled to terminate the lease agreement by giving the lessee three months' notice to the lessee no later than three months after the transfer of property is completed and by failure to do so, he will forfeit that right to terminate.

8.2.4 COMMERCIAL LEASES

Commercial leases are the subject of specific rules laid down by the law of 30 April 1951 which was intended to protect traders against real estate owners. Commercial leases are also required (as does any other lease agreement), to be registered with the Registration Administration in order to be enforceable against third parties (such as, for instance, against a new owner of the premises). Duties must be paid upon registration, which are calculated according to the amount of the rent over the duration of the term of the lease as increased by ancillary costs. Failure to register the agreement within four months of its completion will expose the lessee, in addition, to payment of fines equal to the amount of the registration duties themselves.

The provisions of the law of 30 April 1951 law are mandatory, unless it is clearly specified to be otherwise. Parties to a commercial lease agreement therefore cannot contract outside the provisions of the law. But on the other hand, the parties may agree, that although the conditions required for the law to be applicable are not fulfilled, the law will nevertheless still be applicable to their contractual relationship.

In order for the law to apply, a total of five conditions must all be fulfilled:

(1)   There must be a lease.
(2)   The lease must relate to real estate.
(3)   The premises must primarily be intended for retail or manual work, eg such as a hotel, a cinema, diamond cutting, plumbing, or a garage.
(4)   The public must have access to the premises.
(5)   The commercial purpose of the premises must be agreed on execution of the agreement (explicitly or implicitly) or during the period of the lease (in that case explicitly).

The law itself, however, sums up a limited number of situations in which (although all five conditions are fulfilled) the law itself is still not applicable. This is usually the case, for instance, with lease agreements which are habitually granted for periods of less than one year.

Commercial leases are compulsorily agreed for a minimum duration of nine years. Longer periods are of course permitted. A commercial lease agreement whose duration is in excess of nine years, must be registered with the Mortgages Registrar, as with any other type of lease contract in the same circumstances, and therefore must be recorded in a certified deed.

The tenant is always allowed to terminate the lease agreement upon expiry of every third year of the term, on condition that he gives notice of his decision to terminate at least six months before the end of every third year, by means of registered post or by a bailiff. The lessor can be granted the same right by the contract. However, the lessor is entitled to use that right only in circumstances where he or members of his direct family plan to start a commercial activity in the leased premises. The parties, of course, can at any time decide to terminate the lease agreement by mutual consent, provided that that consent is recorded in a certified deed or in a declaration made before the court.

The law expressly recognises the right of the lessee to apply for the renewal of his lease, with a maximum of three renewals being available. Renewals, as a rule, have a duration of nine years. Parties, can, however, by mutual consent, agree upon longer or shorter periods, provided again that their consent is recorded in a certified deed or in a declaration made before the court. If the tenant wants to make use of this right to renewal, he must apply for it between the 18th and 15th month preceeding the expiry of the current lease period. The lessor will be authorised to refuse the renewal only in quite specific circumstances.

The lessee will be entitled to compensation upon refusal of renewal or upon any early termination of the lease agreement. The lessee's entitlement is regulated by law, and no arrangement to the contrary may be agreed upon before the lessee's entitlement has effectively arisen. And, in all cases, the lessee's claim must be lodged not later than one year after his entitlement becomes exercisable.

Parties are free to fix the rent as they deem appropriate at the beginning of the lease agreement. Most commercial lease agreements will contain a clause organising automatic annual increases of the rent on the basis of the retail prices index. In addition, upon the expiry of each three year period, each of the parties is entitled to claim a revision of the rent, provided the conditions prescribed by law to attain that end are fulfilled. If the parties cannot agree, they may refer their claim to the judge who will make a decision based on equitable principles. A price revision can also be requested at the time the contract is renewed. Again, intervention of the court can be sought if no agreement can be struck by the contracting parties.

If the lessor transfers the property containing the leased premises, the rights of the lessee will vary depending on the following considerations:

(1)   For how long has he occupied the premises at the time of the transfer?

(2)   Does the lease agreement expressly make provision for obtaining possession from expelling the lessee in the case where the premises are to be sold?

(3)   Has the lease agreement acquired a fixed term before the transfer of the property? In other words has the lease agreement been registered, have its main provisions been laid down in a judgment or another certified deed, or are any of the parties now deceased?

As a rule, the lessee is entitled to transfer the lease agreement or to sublet the premises, unless he is prevented therefrom by the terms and conditions of the lease agreement. As a rule, such a contractual ban, does not, however, prevent the lessee from transferring the lease agreement or from sub-letting, if this occurs together with the transfer of the lessee's goodwill and relates to all of the lessee's rights. In some circumstances, the lessor, who must be notified of the lessee's intentions, is entitled to oppose such transfer or subletting proposed by his lessee.

8.2.5 MORTGAGES

Mortgage loans

Mortgage loans or credit openings have long been and for a short time will remain, the subject of legislation dating back to 7 January 1936. As a result, among other things, of the re-regulation taking place in the credit sector of EC level, new legislation regarding mortgage lending has recently been passed (4 August 1992) coming into force on 1 January 1993. This new law will basically apply to loans for non-professional purposes, secured directly or indirectly by a mortgage or other right imposed on real estate, with a view to financing the purchase or preservation of intangible fixed assets, which are granted to individuals usually residing in Belgium. Credit granted by lenders established abroad who have not advertised in Belgium in any way and who do not conclude their loan agreements in Belgium, will not, as a rule, be concerned with these new provisions. Pursuant to the law of 4 August 1992, companies which grant mortgage loans are not entitled to operate nor to pursue their operations without being first registered with the Insurance Control Office (*Office de Contrôle des Assurances—Controledienst voor de Verzekeringen*).

Operations of mortgage companies are and will be subject to several obligations aiming at enabling the relevant Belgian authorities to control these lending activities and thus to protect the consumer. Loan agreements, for instance, must include specific provisions in order to grant the borrower full information as to the terms and conditions of the operation.

Mortgages

The creation of a conventional mortgage as such requires the intervention of the notary public and the registration of the mortgage with the Mortgage Registrar (*Conservateur des Hypothèques—Hypotheekbewaarder*).

Power of attorney to mortgage

Sometimes, lenders will accept that the loan be secured by a simple and irrevocable power of attorney, enabling the lender to secure a mortgage over a specific piece of property (*mandat hypothécaire—hypothecair mandaat*). If the borrower fails to comply with his commitments under the loan agreement, such a power of attorney grants its beneficiary, usually the lender, the right to vest a mortgage in his own favour over the real estate concerned. This formula is sometimes used in order to avoid the costs and registration of a mortgage. Unlike the mortgage promise, the above mortgage proxy is valid only if embodied in certified deed. This proxy, however, does not grant full security to the creditor:

(1) If the debtor grants a mortgage to a third party before the power of attorney has been implemented, the beneficiary of the power can seek relief only by claiming damages in court, unless specific conditions are fulfilled (eg when proof can be given that the third party, the beneficiary of the mortgage, acted fraudulently).

(2) In situations where other creditors of the debtor can claim entitlement to the same real estate (*concours—samenloop*) prior to the mortgage having been registered, the mortgage cannot be enforced against them. Likewise in the case of the bankruptcy of the borrower, the mortgage can be nullified where it was entered into in the period immediately before the debtor is declared bankrupt (*période suspecte—verdachte periode*). (The exact duration of this period is fixed by the court when declaring the bankruptcy.) Non-enforceability can also arise when more than 15 days elapses between the date of the

mortgage deed and the date of the registration of the mortgage with the Mortgage Registrar.

If the borrower who granted such a power of attorney dies, the Supreme Court considers that the mortgage must be constituted and registered within three months after the death.

Mortgage promise

The mortgage promise (*promesse d'hypothèque—hypotheekbelofte*) gives the lender even less security. Such a mortgage promise is an agreement whereby a debtor undertakes to his creditor, to mortgage a specific piece of real estate as security for the payment of a specific amount at a later stage, and in the creditor's favour. This agreement is lawful. It is a simple contract which is not subject to the rules for the grant of an actual mortgage, but it is subject only to the general conditions of validity governing any commercial promise. Therefore:

(1) A mortgage promise may be given in the form of a private deed (as opposed to the certified deed which must be signed before a notary public).

(2) The rules relating to the identification of the property and of the claim as provided by the law on mortgages need not be complied with; but both the real estate which is to be mortgaged according to the earlier promise, and the claim to be secured, must however be valid, determined or at least determinable.

Although the informal character of this mortgage promise might seem attractive, this formula does not really offer the creditor the security he desires, in the event that the debtor does not carry out his commitments. This is because:

(1) Since the creation of the mortgage requires certified deed, the promisee will be unable to require that the court's judgment should amount to an actual enforceable mortgage. (Such a solution is generally possible as regards promises of contract.)

(2) The creditor is entitled only to damages and, according to authors and case law, to the reimbursement of his debt.

Undertakings not to alienate or mortgage

Sometimes undertakings not to alienate or mortgage a specific piece of real estate are requested by the lender. Such an undertaking is valid, since the inalienability comes to an end when the debtor has reimbursed all sums due to the beneficiary of the undertaking. But breach of that undertaking could result in the immediate obligation to repay the loan in accordance with art 1188 of the Belgian Civil Code. It cannot, however, be enforced against third parties, unless it can be proved that they were aware or should have been aware of the existence of that preventative undertaking.

8.3 SUCCESSION

Freedom to dispose of one's assets is strictly limited by the Belgian Civil Code. Rules vary depending on whether or not a will has been made.

In the absence of any such will, the law determines who is an heir and what each will inherit. If the deceased did not leave any heir, his or her estate will be inherited by the state. Where the deceased died intestate, the surviving spouse's entitlement differs depending on whether he or she must share the deceased's assets with existing children or with other surviving relatives. If there are children, the surviving spouse will be entitled to a life-interest (*usufruit—vruchtgebruik*) in the whole of the deceased's own estate. If there are no children and the assets are to be shared with relatives, the surviving spouse can claim entitlement to the assets of the joint estate and a life interest on the personal assets of the deceased. The importance of the 'joint estate' and of the assets of each spouse will vary depending on the marriage contract agreed by the spouses. (Under Belgian law, if the spouses do not enter into any marriage contract, assets acquired after the marriage with incomes resulting from the spouses' professional activities will by law constitute the joint estate.)

It is possible to depart from the rules provided by the Civil Code by drafting a will. A will, however, can in no event deprive the deceased's children (or their descendants), the deceased's ascendants or the surviving spouse from the entitlement they are provided by law. As a result, children are always entitled to half, two-thirds or three-quarters of the deceased's estate depending on whether the deceased leaves one, two, or three or more children. Likewise, the surviving spouse may always claim a life interest in half the estate (therein included at least a life interest in the family residence).

Only in specific circumstances will it be possible to deprive the surviving spouse of that entitlement.

No one is obliged to accept an estate which can also be refused altogether, or accepted or refused later on the basis that further information is required as to its composition (*acceptation sous bénéfice d'inventaire—aanvaarding onder voorbehoud van boedelbeschrijving*).

Death duties are payable, the rates of which will vary depending on the closeness of blood relationship between the beneficiaries of the deceased and on the value of the estate received. The same duties, as a rule, are levied on gifts whose validity, in addition, requires that they be made by a certified deed with the exception of manual, indirect or disguised gifts. Non-registered gifts, made less than three years before the donor's death, are also included in the value of the estate for calculation of death duties purposes.

Belgian law does not acknowledge trusts. Systems however have been devised with a view to avoiding inheritance duties. General partnerships, for instance, are often considered an adequate vehicle to that end. General partnerships in effect grant the company's manager a veto right on all operations binding the company towards third parties or attempting to modify the articles of incorporation. A testator can therefore incorporate such a general partnership and thereafter donate all the shares of the partnership but one, (since the manager must be a share holder and thus own one share at least) to his heirs-to-be through a manual gift. If the parent survives his gift for at least three years, no succession duties will be levied against the beneficiary of the gift. (Manual gifts need not be entered into by a certified deed and therefore can be left unregistered.)

If the spouses opt for estate settlement as provided for by the Civil Code, each of them will have full power to manage the joint estate (it being understood that certain operations will require both spouses' consent). When considering executing a transaction with a person who is married, it can therefore be important to ascertain the type of marriage contract he or she has entered into. Information in this respect is available from the trade register as far as traders and persons entrusted with the daily management of commercial companies are concerned.

As a rule, each spouse will be able to carry out professional activities. Within that framework, each of them may manage his or her professional belongings and perform all acts of management which are necessary (as opposed to simply desirable) to his or her profession. The other spouse may however require the court to prohibit the performance of any act of management which would harm him (or her) or the family's interests as a whole.

9

IMMIGRATION AND EMPLOYMENT

9.1 IMMIGRATION

Access to the labour market in Belgium is regulated mainly by a system controlling entry and residence on the one hand, and employment on the other hand.

9.1.1 NON-EC NATIONALS

Work permit—professional card

Non-EC nationals who intend to work in Belgium will need to obtain a work permit, if they are to be employed either as manual or intellectual workers; or a professional card, if they are to become self-employed.

Belgian law provides three different types of work permit:

(1) work permit A: for an indefinite duration and for all types of salaried profession;

(2) work permit B: for a limited duration and restricted either to one employer, or to one branch of activity; and

(3) work permit C: for a limited duration and for professions in which workers are not usually employed by only one employer.

The delivery of permits B and C is subject, in addition to compliance with several other conditions, to the employer obtaining an authorisation for employment. Both the work permit and the authorisation for employment must be obtained from the Ministry of Employment and Labour. In practice, they are granted by the regional authorities governing Brussels, Wallonia or Flanders, depending on the place where the employer has his registered office. An employer who fails to comply with the legal requirements relating to the authorisation to employ, can be sentenced to pay all the expenses that the employee (and his family) may incur by returning to their original country of residence, in addition to a penalty.

Work permits B and C are granted for a period of twelve months but can be renewed upon request by the employer. An employee, who can show that he has been employed in Belgium under a B permit for an uninterrupted period of at least five years prior to making the request, will be entitled to apply for work permit A. Five years uninterrupted residence in Belgium will also entitle the foreign national to apply for work permit A. That period is reduced by one year if the foreign national is accompanied by his family.

It is currently becoming increasingly difficult to obtain work permits or professional cards. Subject to strict instructions given to the administrative authorities in charge, work permits or professional cards are granted only to highly specialised workers or important investors. In practice an applicant employee can be considered 'highly specialised' if his gross monthly salary exceeds BEF 90,000, and he has specific qualifications.

Once the authorisation to employ has been obtained, the work permit will follow. Work permits are obtained for a period of 12 months but can be renewed. Professional cards, by contrast, are valid for a maximum of five years and these too are renewable.

Residence permit

Non-EC nationals must file an application for a residence permit at the Belgian consulate of their country of origin once they have received a work permit or a professional card (in practice, this can sometimes be done by mail, depending on the consulate). If the application is accepted, the Minister of Justice issues the applicant with a visa which allows him to enter Belgium. Then, within eight days of having entered the country, the foreign national must still request registration from the Town Administration under which he is newly domiciled.

The residence permit will remain valid for the duration of the work permit; thus for a maximum of one year but like the work permit, it too can be renewed. Then, having resided in Belgium for five years, the worker may file an application for establishment by which he can obtain a five year residence permit.

9.1.2 EC NATIONALS

The Treaty of Rome provides both the right for nationals of its member states to stay in any other member state in order to work there and also the abolition of any discrimination on the basis of nationality between workers of the member states as far as employment, remuneration and other conditions of work are concerned.

Work permit—professional card

As a rule, EC nationals are no longer required to apply either
for a work permit or for a professional card in order to have access to
the Belgian labour market, pursuant to the Treaty of Rome and
Directive 1612/68.

Residence permit

EC nationals, who enter Belgium to perform either a salaried or
a non-salaried function, are entitled to stay in Belgium. They must
provide proof of their employment by showing a declaration from
their employer. This very declaration will allow EC nationals to
receive a residence permit.

9.2 LABOUR RELATIONS

9.2.1 LEGISLATION

The obligations of parties involved in labour relations in
Belgium are governed by:

(1) The law itself; eg the law on employment contracts, laws
     regulating the duration of the work (which basically prohibit
     work on Sundays and on public holidays, regulate night work
     and limit daily and weekly working allowances), law governing
     annual holiday entitlement, etc.

(2) Joint bargaining agreements, ie agreements concluded at the
     level of each sector of activity or of an enterprise, between
     employers (at either individual or collective level) on the one
     hand; and one or more workers' organisations, on the other
     hand. Such joint bargaining agreements can be concluded at
     the level of the undertaking, or of a specific sector of activity,
     or at national level (within the national labour council). Joint
     bargaining agreements concluded under the auspices of a joint
     bargaining body (regrouping employers' and workers' bodies in
     a same sector of activity) may be the subject of a Royal decree.
     In that event they will acquire binding force as regards all
     employers, employees or workers operating in that specific field
     of activity, regardless of whether they were directly represented
     during the antecedent negotiations.

(3) Individual labour contracts whether written or not.
(4) Working regulations.
(5) Custom and practice.

9.2.2 EMPLOYMENT CONTRACTS

Labour agreements are governed by the law of 3 July 1978. A contract of employment (or labour contract) is a contract by which a party is hired to work, under the *authority direction*, and *control* of an employer, in consideration for payment. If there is no authority or no payment, then there is no contract of employment.

Very broadly speaking, Belgian law may be said to differentiate between two types of staff: either 'workers' or 'employees', and in addition there may be those who are employed for a limited period or those hired for an indefinite period. The word 'workers' generally speaking refers to manual workers, while the term 'employees' covers intellectually skilled workers. The law distinguishes also other categories, such as sales representatives, ie employees who work most of the time outside of the company visiting clients and negotiating contracts with these clients, students and some other categories of staff, who are subject to specific rules. Significant consequences flow from these classifications. For example, the definition of the employment relationship existing will affect instances such as probationary periods, paid vacations, paid leaves in case of work-related accidents or illness, contract termination, non-competition and arbitration clauses, notice periods and compensation in cases of dismissal.

Generally speaking, unless express written agreement is made in advance of the commencement of work, one is presumed to have been hired for an unlimited period. Likewise the act of renewing a contract, though initially concluded for a limited period of time, will result in the contract being considered to have acquired the character of a contract for an indefinite period. Terms and conditions of employment must strictly comply with the applicable legal provisions. Probationary periods of employment, for instance, are permissible but are limited in time according to the nature of the position held and the level of pay. Non-competition clauses are also permitted, but only for relatively well-paid staff. Such clauses can have a maximum duration of 12 months and their validity is subject to the fulfilment of strict conditions, one of which is the necessity for a written document recording such terms. Unless the employer waives the benefit of the non-competition clause within 15 days of termination of the contract, he will be required to pay a one-off lump sum to the 'retiring' party in compensation. Any non-competition clause which does not follow such strictly prescribed legal conditions would be null and void. Arbitration clauses may only be included in contracts of employment concluded with top-level employees.

Workers and employees are strictly protected against dismissal by their employer and unilateral modification by the employer of any significant terms of their employment. Their rights, however, will vary depending on their level of qualification and on whether they have been engaged under a fixed term or non-time limited contract.

Assuming that an employee (an intellectually skilled worker) who has been hired for an indefinite duration of employment has not given his employer substantial cause that would make the continuation of the employment relationship impossible, the employee is entitled to reasonable written notice of his dismissal. Notice must be given by registered letter or served by a process server and indicate the starting point and the duration of the notice period. Reasonable notice is a period sufficient to find similar employment, taking into account the length of the employee's service and the inevitable difficulties of finding an equivalent position, including age of the individual, his function and compensation. The absence or insufficiency of the notice period will entitle the employee to compensation in lieu. An intellectually skilled employee must by law receive a minimum of three months' notice for each five year period of continuous employment. The notice to be given on termination may only be agreed upon once the termination itself has taken place. Any agreement fixing the notice period to be given fixed in advance of actual termination is null and void. In case of disagreement about what constitutes reasonable notice, the matter can be put before a special labour court where the emphasis to be attached to each element of the contract may be argued. Employers may release the employee from his duties during the notice period with immediate effect, in which case they will immediately have to pay him compensation in lieu of notice.

A employee hired for a fixed term and laid off before the expiry of the agreed term will receive a compensatory payment equal to the value of the unexpired period of his contract of employment, with a ceiling of twice what he would have received had he been hired for an unlimited period of time. The law applies in reverse where an employee resigns without proper notice or just cause, thus requiring the employee to pay compensation to the employer.

By contrast, a manual worker is entitled by law to a minimum of 28 days' notice, and after 20 years' service, to 56 days notice. In circumstances where his dismissal can be considered unfair, the manual worker employed for an indefinite duration is entitled by law to additional compensation equal to six months' salary. The law does not provide the concept of 'unfair dismissal' compensation as far as employees are concerned. Courts, however, might grant a specific compensation to an aggrieved employee where his dismissal is considered unfair. Furthermore, despite the apparent discrepancy in the degree of protection afforded as between 'workers' and 'employee's, as a practical matter, collective bargaining agreements won by trade unions generally provide additional protection to the manual worker.

If the staff member commits a repudiatory breach (*faute grave— zware tekortkoming*) which results in the furtherance of the employment relationship becoming immediately and definitively impossible, his employer is entitled to terminate the contract forthwith without notice period or compensation. Notice of the serious reasons relied on and of immediate dismissal must then be served on the worker or employee within a very short period of time after the employer has gained knowledge of the facts to be alleged against the worker or employee. Failure to comply with these deadlines will result in the employer being prevented from availing himself of the right of summary dismissal. It must be stressed that courts are usually very cautious when assessing the grounds alleged by the employer upon which he relied without having to give notice or pay compensation. If the justification relied on by the employer is not found to constitute a repudiatory breach of contract by the worker or employee, the employer may then be ordered to provide additional compensation to the staff member whose rights have been adjudged to be unfairly prejudiced, in addition to the payment of the usual compensation in lieu of notice. This is because the circumstances of the dismissal were found to have been prejudicial to the employee or worker in question.

In the case of pregnancy, special rights are provided in favour of a woman concerned once the pregnancy is known to her employer, including a prohibition on terminating her contract of employment except for serious grounds or for reasons which are distinct and separate from her mere physical state. If those reasons cannot be proved and if therefore the dismissal is founded on her pregnancy alone, the female employee or worker will be entitled to compensation equal to three months' gross salary.

Specific protection has also been provided in favour of staff whose contracts are terminated as a result of a collective dismissal, or of the closure of their employer's business. Likewise, specific measures have been enacted in order to protect such members of the staff when all or part of their original employer's business or branch of activity is transferred to a third party. In that case, the staff and their contracts of employment will be automatically transferred to the purchaser and will continue to enjoy all the rights and benefits they were able to enjoy with their original employer, including the fact that their length of service acquired with the transferor prior to the transfer will remain unaffected, uncurtailed and operative as against the transferee.

9.2.3 WORKING REGULATIONS

All employers employing staff in Belgium must establish internal working regulations, in accordance with the relevant provisions of the law of 8 April 1965. Those regulations must be approved by the staff and made available for inspection on the working premises.

9.2.4 USE OF LANGUAGE

Strict attention must be paid to the language used in the contract of employment as well as in any other document addressed to or intended for the staff. Failure to comply with the legal rules applicable to this issue can result in the nullity of the document. As a rule, the language should be Dutch if the company's operational headquarters are located in Flanders. If the seat of activities is located in the Walloon region, the language to be used within the framework of labour relations should be French. However, in this last case the relevant decree adds that this is without prejudice to the complementary use of another language, thus this is generally taken to mean that some other language may be used.

In bilingual Brussels, French or Dutch may be used, depending on the mother tongue of the worker. In the German speaking part of Belgium, German alone must be used. But in that region as in the Brussels region, failure to comply with this language direction is not penalised by nullity of the contract and the contract can at any time be replaced by a version in the correct language, according to the terms of the relevant law.

9.2.5 MANDATORY BODIES

In the interests of industrial harmony, Belgian law, like that of France, requires employers to deal directly with the members of their staff at management level regarding certain aspects of the business. All undertakings with a total of more than 100 employees have a *conseil d'entreprise—Ondernemingsraad* or works council. Representatives are appointed to the council by the management, and are elected by the employees. The works council meets at least once a month to consult and advise, primarily with respect to economic matters such as working conditions, hiring and firing decisions, social legislation and collective bargaining agreements. It also receives reports from the management and communicates these to the employees. It must be consulted in the event of management entertaining notions of closure or mass redundancies.

In addition, every employer, who employs 50 or more employees is required to implement a body for safety, hygiene and conditions of work in his premises (*Comité de Sécurité et d'Hygiene— Comité vodr Veiligheid en Hygiene*). This committee, which basically has an advisory function, has a structure similar to the works council, but concerns itself primarily with hygiene, health and safety matters. Usually, when the undertaking has less than 50 employees, the functions of the committee on safety and hygiene will be performed by the trade union representatives.

Trade union delegations, however, must be created only by those undertakings which are members of the employers' organisations which have signed the Joint Bargaining Agreement no 5 dated 24 May 1971. Members of the works council, of the committee for safety and hygiene or of the trade union delegation enjoy special protection against dismissal where they are, or have been members of those bodies, and where they are or have been candidates in the elections for the same.

9.2.6 SOCIAL SECURITY

Pursuant to the law of 27 June 1969 revising the Decree Law of 28 December 1948 concerning social security, all members of the staff employed in Belgium or attached to a centre of activities established in Belgium are subject to social security rules, unless the contrary is provided by international conventions or regulations concerning social security. Several treaties have been signed by Belgium, at EC level and otherwise, excluding at least temporarily the application of Belgian social security law relating to seconded visiting employees (ie employees who have been sent over to Belgium for a limited period of time).

Social security contributions will be required to be paid both by the employer and by the seconded member of personnel, at rates which differ depending on whether the worker is a manual one or an intellectually skilled employee. Likewise entitlements will differ depending on the category to which the member of staff belongs.

9.2.7 LABOUR PROTECTION

Several provisions of Belgian labour law aim at creating acceptable working conditions. To this end, rules have been enacted with a view to restricting the duration of working hours, imposing rest periods, ensuring staff safety and health, preventing unjustified discrimination and limiting, as much as possible, heavy and unhealthy work.

9.2.8 APPLICABLE LAW AND APPROPRIATE COURTS IN INTERNATIONAL LABOUR RELATIONS

Competent courts

As a rule, the Belgian labour courts have jurisdiction to deal with disputes arising from an employment relationship in Belgium. However, in accordance with the Brussels Convention of 1968 on Jurisdiction and Recognition of Judgments, parties may agree on the competence of foreign courts to preside over possible disputes.

Applicable law

In principle, the Belgian legal system applies to anyone who is employed in Belgium. Nevertheless, Belgian law does not prevent parties from electing that their relationship be governed by foreign laws. Indeed, the EC Convention on the Law Applicable to Contractual Obligations, which came into force on 1 April 1991, stipulates that the wishes of the parties shall be recognised unless otherwise prohibited by Belgian mandatory and public policy laws. (At present in Belgium, most of the provisions of that EC Convention have already come into force on 1 January 1988 by means of a law of 14 July 1987.)

If, for example, an employee has been temporarily assigned to a Belgian-based company by his own foreign company, without him being effectively integrated into the staff of the Belgian company and if he receives instructions directly from the foreign company, the foreign legal system could be considered as the proper law to regulate his contract. The instances of this possibly valid choice of foreign law are, however, limited by Belgian coercive rules (*lois de police et de sûreté—wetten van politie en veiligheid*), which apply to foreigners working in Belgium (for example, social security laws, the language decrees, etc).

9.2.9 TEMPORARY SECONDMENT

The temporary secondment by an employer of a member of his staff to work with another employer is strictly regulated by law. As a rule, it is prohibited. Contracts of temporary secondment therefore are null and void and the second employer is considered legally bound to the worker or employee by a separate contract of employment as of the first day of service. The original and the temporary employer are jointly liable for the payment of the salary, social security contributions, etc due to the seconded member of staff.

In exceptional circumstances, however, temporary secondments to the service of another employer will be authorised, provided the prior approval of the relevant government department is obtained. That requirement is replaced by a simple duty to report in advance whether the member of staff is exceptionally and temporarily seconded within the framework of a co-operation between businesses which belong to the same economic and financial organisation or where he has been seconded in order to carry out specialised tasks which require particular professional qualifications. In any event, a written contract must be concluded between the original employer, the seconded member of staff and the temporary employer. Again both the original and the temporary employer are jointly liable for the payment of all sums due to the member so seconded.

Any infringement of the provisions of the above result in hefty criminal fines.

10
TAXATION

10.1 VALUE ADDED TAX

10.1.1 GENERAL

Value added tax, VAT (*taxe sur la valeur ajoutée—belasting over de toegevoegde waarde*), is charged on: the delivery of goods and the performance of services in Belgium by tax payers within the framework of business activities, and on the importation of goods, except those retained in bonded warehouses.

Delivery means sales, leasing, exchange, and sometimes contributions in kind to a company, while tax payer means anyone, whether an individual, company or legal entity without legal personality, regularly carrying out taxable transactions.

Although a person who regularly carries out taxable transactions becomes automatically subject to VAT, registration must still be applied for.

10.1.2 THE MECHANISM

VAT is levied on each transaction and is collected by the government through the seller who adds VAT onto the sales price or onto the price of the service rendered. The purchaser, however, does not suffer any real burden of VAT since he receives a credit or a refund from the government for the VAT he paid to the seller. VAT may therefore not be considered as part of the cost price but is only a burden for the ultimate consumer.

10.1.3 FOREIGN ENTREPRENEURS

Credit is available to taxpayers regardless of whether they are Belgian residents or not. In order to be eligible for credit, non-residents must either have a permanent establishment or appoint a responsible person resident in Belgium.

If the taxpayer has a permanent establishment in Belgium, he must apply for a VAT registration number and file VAT returns quarterly or monthly if the annual turnover exceeds BF 20 million.

If the non-resident has no permanent establishment or has not appointed any responsible person resident in Belgium, he will be authorised, under certain circumstances, to request a refund of the VAT he has paid.

If a foreign entity conducts an activity in Belgium which is subject to VAT, the credit will only be allowed for the pro rata portion of the VAT previously paid on goods and services which are used in both taxable and/or tax-exempted transactions with credit for previously paid VAT, or on the exempt transactions without credit for previously paid VAT.

10.1.4 EXEMPTIONS

There are two types of exemptions:

(1) The true exemption which does not allow for credit for previously paid VAT (exemptions of that type have been provided for activities such as the supply of immovable property (except on new buildings); the leasing and renting of immovable property, the transfer of an entire business, services rendered by lawyers, etc).

(2) The exemption with credit for previously paid VAT. Such is the case as far as export activities are concerned, deliveries to bonded warehouses, the sale of newspapers and magazines, etc.

10.1.5 RATES

As per 1 April 1992 the standard VAT rate is 19.5 per cent under which applies to all services and goods which do not benefit from a reduced rate. Reduced rates are provided as follows: 0 per cent for newspapers and magazines, 1 per cent on monetary gold, 6 per cent on products such as meat, fish, milk and milk products, etc and 12 per cent on tobacco, margarines, etc.

10.2 INDIVIDUAL INCOME TAX

10.2.1 GENERAL

Individual income tax is levied on the worldwide income earned, and on some capital gains realised, by residents, as defined in art 3 of the Income Tax Code (ITC),

(a) any individual who has his residence or the centre of his economic interests in Belgium; and

(b) Belgian diplomatic and consular agents who are accredited abroad.

Non-residents are liable for income tax on their Belgian source income only, after deduction of related expenses.

Tax treaties, based on the OECD model, have been concluded between Belgium and most industrialised countries in order to avoid one and the same invoice being subject to taxes several times over. Those treaties must be checked in order to ascertain whether or not Belgium is entitled to levy income tax (see also 10.6. below).

10.2.2 THE MECHANISM

The taxable basis on which taxes are levied comprises four types of income:

- Incomes produced by real estate.
- Business income.
- Movable income (from investments).
- Miscellaneous income.

From these incomes, deductions are allowed.

Immovable income

Immovable income includes only those incomes arising out of the real estate held, in Belgium or abroad, by an individual for private purposes. Revenues produced by real estate held for business purposes, will be treated as business income.

Business income

Business income includes:

- Trading income.
- Employment income.
- Professional income.
- Professional income from a profession which is no longer exercised.
- Pension income.

Trading income includes income from a commercial, industrial or agricultural enterprise and is taxed on an accrual basis.

Employment income includes salaries and remuneration to company directors.

Professional income is the income earned by an individual

from his profession which is not a trading activity nor an employment income and is taxed on a cash basis. Professional income from a profession which is no longer exercised is taxed on an accrual basis and is taxed at a separate rate.

Pension income is taxable and will be added to gross income and be subject to the progressive tax rates if paid in the form of an annuity. If paid in one lump sum payment, it may be transformed into a deemed annuity which must be added to the income.

If the payment takes place at normal pension age, it may be taxed at a separate rate of 16.5 per cent.

Movable income (from investments)

As a rule, movable income is subject to a withholding tax if paid in Belgium. This tax is final for dividends, royalties and foreign interest. The rate applicable varies depending on the type of movable income in question:

(1) Interest on bonds, debentures, deposits or other loans are, as a rule, subject to a 10 per cent withholding tax. An additional tax of 25 per cent may be levied on Belgian source interest exceeding BF 523,000, unless the individual undertakes to reinvest all amounts received. Generally this withholding tax is final, unless the individual's total tax rate is lower than 10 per cent, in which case the individual may elect to submit this income to be taxed at the progressive income tax rate. He may then ask for a possible refund of the withholding tax paid.

(2) Dividends and any distributions by a foreign or Belgian company are subject to a 25 per cent withholding tax unless the tax payer elects to include this income in his tax return, in which case, the progressive income tax rates will then apply. The reimbursement of paid capital and income resulting from liquidation of companies is, however, tax exempt. There are also some temporary exemptions.

(3) Royalties which do not derive from the exercise of professional activities are taxable at the progressive income global tax rate as movable income from investment.

Miscellaneous income

Miscellaneous income includes:

(1) Profits resulting from activities outside any professional, trading, employment relation or other business activity and which

cannot be considered the result of a transaction in the daily course of management of a private property.
(2)   Alimony.
(3)   Income from subletting immovable property not in the scope of a professional activity.
(4)   Capital gains realised on the sale of unbuilt land within a period of eight years after its acquisition.
(5)   Capital gains on substantial shareholdings in a Belgian company if sold to a foreign company.

The tax rates applicable to miscellaneous income vary depending on the type of income concerned. However, most of these items are taxable separately at a flat rate of 16.5 per cent if the progressive income tax rate is higher.

Deductions from total income

Some expenses may be deducted from total income, unless they have already been deducted from one of the above-mentioned separate categories:
(1)   Certain mortgage interest.
(2)   Donations to social, cultural, scientific and foreign aid organisations listed in the ITC, up to 10 per cent of total income or BF 10 million, with a minimum of BF 1,000.
(3)   80 per cent of payments to close relatives who are not part of the immediate family unit (*gezin*) and 80 per cent of alimony payments to a separated or divorced spouse.
(4)   Payments up to BF 21,000 per taxpayer under a tax favoured pension saving fund.
(5)   The purchase price of shares acquired by the employees in the company in which they are employed.
(6)   80 per cent of the daily expenses incurred in minding children under the age of three with a maximum of BF 345 a day.

10.2.3 RATES

The individual's tax rates vary from 25–55 per cent increased by municipal taxes of around 7 per cent on the rate.

taxable income (BF)	rate
up to 245,000	25 %
245,000–325,000	30 %
325,000–464,000	40 %

464,000–1,067,000	45 %
1,067,000–1,600,000	50 %
1,600,000–2,347,000	52.5 %
over 2,347,000	55 %

There are Personal Allowances of BF 176,000 for a single person and of BF 139,000 per person for a couple.

10.3 CORPORATE INCOME TAX

10.3.1 GENERAL

According to art 94 of the Belgian Income Tax Code, all companies, associations, establishments, which are corporate bodies and which have their registered office, their most important establishment or their seat of actual management in Belgium, and which carry on a business or perform activities of a profit making character, are subject to corporate income tax.

10.3.2 TAXABLE INCOME

In Belgium the taxable income of a company is determined in six steps. The amount reached after completion of the six steps constitutes the taxable income which will be subject to Belgian corporate income tax. Items, however, that are taxed separately must be taken out of the company's income.

First step

In the first step the taxable income is assessed by calculating:
- Reserved profit (retained earnings).
- Non-deductible expenses, (income taxes).
- Dividends (income from invested capital).

Certain items which are included in this income must be deducted, including:

(1) Tax-free reserves
   (a) for risks and charges which became certain during that year
   (b) for probable losses, only on commercial receivables and within certain limits.
(2) Exempted capital gains (see 3.1.2).
(3) Premiums and subsidies received from the State.

Second step

The profits are subdivided as a function of their origin:

(1) Profits of Belgian origin, ie incomes earned or redeemed in Belgium and which are normally taxed at the full rate.

(2) Profits taxable at a reduced rate, ie incomes earned and taxed abroad, for which corporate tax is reduced to one quarter.

(3) Profits exempted as a result of treaty provisions, ie incomes earned abroad and exempted from taxes by virtue of a double tax treaty.

Third step

Deductions may be operated, such as:

(1) Deduction of profits exempted due to treaty provisions.
This has as a result the elimination of the profits which are exempted further to a double income tax treaty.

(2) Deduction of exempted gifts, within certain limits.

(3) Deduction of BF 100,000 for any additional staff member assigned for scientific research.

These deductions are operated in total from the balance of the profits and up to that balance. If part of the profits come from countries with which Belgium did not conclude a double income tax treaty, the deductions are first made from the Belgian profits.

Fourth step

The fourth operation aims to avoid the taxation of:

• Incomes resulting from holdings in Belgian or foreign companies which, as a rule, are already taxed at the level of the paying entity.

• Dividend payments after liquidation.

This deduction, a ratio of 95 per cent, is granted on condition that:

(1) The participation is held fully beneficially or for life.

(2) The dividends are paid by a company subject to a corporate taxation similar to the Belgian system.

(3) The company is the final beneficiary of that income.

(4) Payment of these dividends does not induce a capital loss of the participations to which the payment relate.

The deduction of those incomes is operated by preference from the Belgian profits, when the incomes are of Belgian origin and from the profits arising from countries with which Belgium has no double corporate tax treaties, when the income arises from those countries.

Fifth step

Tax losses which were incurred during previous fiscal years and which were not previously deducted or covered previously by profits exempted as a result of treaties are deducted from the balance of the taxable profits. As from income year 1990 tax losses may be deducted without any time limit.

Specific rules apply to companies which made a tax-free take-over of a business or a tax-free merger. The origin of the losses is also important since losses are deducted by preference from profits of the same origin.

Sixth step

In the last step, companies may operate an additional investment deduction which corresponds to a percentage of the depreciable amount of the purchase price or of the cost price of some specific investments made during the fiscal year. The investment deduction rate is fixed each year at the inflation rate of the previous year plus 1, with a minimum of 4 per cent and a maximum of 11 per cent (the rate for 1991 is 4 per cent).

10.3.3 TAX RATES

Resident companies are in the income year 1991 subject to a corporate income tax rate of 39 per cent.

taxable income (BF)	rate
up to 1,000,000	28%
1,000,001–3,600,000	36%
3,660,001–13,000,000	41%
above 13,000,000	39%

In the following cases, however, the lower tax rates are not applicable, irrespective of the amount of the taxable income:
(1) When at least half of the shares of the company are held by another company.
(2) When the distributed profits are higher than 13% of the fully paid up capital.
(3) When the company is a 'financial company', ie a company which has holdings worth more than 50 per cent of:

(a) either the paid up capital (updated if the company was incorporated before 1950); or

(b) the paid-up capital increased by the reserves which have been taxed and the capital gains which have been booked.

In order to determine whether the 50 per cent threshold is exceeded, active and permanent holdings which represent at least 75 per cent or more of the issuing company's capital are not taken into consideration.

10.3.4 CORPORATIONS WITH FAVOURABLE TAX STATUS

Several tax incentives are available for Belgian as well as for foreign companies. The most important incentives under Belgian law are:

- Accelerated depreciation.
- Investment deduction.
- Allowances for specified investments.
- Regional investments.
- Incentives applicable to small and medium sized enterprises.
- Innovation companies.
- Job creating incentives.

No additional incentives are granted to foreign joint venture partners. However, the following specific tax incentives are available for multinationals that wish to set up a company (or a branch) in Belgium:

(1) The coordination centre: the advantages granted in that respect are available only to corporations which belong to large international groups and which carry out specific activities for the sole benefit of the companies of the group

(2) The distribution centre: again the advantages provided in that respect are available only to companies which are part of a large international group. Also the activities which the co-ordination centre may carry out are limited to specific activities. Generally speaking, this system is considered to be of rather limited interest;

(3) Foreign Sales Corporations: Belgium is one of the countries which meet the requirements of the US foreign sales corporations tax treatment.

10.4 TAX ON LEGAL ENTITIES (NON-PROFIT ORGANISATIONS)

Non-profit organisations in Belgium are subject to two different taxes:
- a tax on the assets, ie a tax in lieu of inheritance tax;
- a legal entity tax, ie a tax on income.

10.4.1 TAX ON THE ASSETS

All assets of non-profit organisations, with the exception of some assets, are subject to this tax as from 1 January after their incorporation.

10.4.2 ASSESSMENT OF INCOME AND TAX RATES

The taxable income of a non-profit organisation can be split up into the following categories:
(1) Immovable income.
(2) Movable income (stock, bonds, securities, etc): movable income is taxed under the form of a withholding tax of 25 per cent on dividends and 10 per cent on bonds and securities.
(3) Business income. As a rule, non-profit organisations are not authorised to conduct business activities. Exceptional business activities or operations which are not making use of industrial or commercial methods, however, are authorised. As long as those rules are complied with, incomes deriving from those activities are not taxable.
(4) Miscellaneous income: capital gains on undeveloped land situated in Belgium and sold within a 3- or 8-year period after the acquisition are taxed at a rate of respectively 33 and 16.5 per cent. Capital gains, realised on the sale of a substantial shareholding (exceeding 25 per cent of the share capital) to a foreign company are taxable a rate of 16.5 per cent.

10.4.3 TAX IN LIEU OF INHERITANCE TAX

Pursuant to art 148 of the Income Tax Code, non-profit organisations are liable for an annual tax in lieu of inheritance tax at a rate of 0.17 per cent on the assets owned by the organisation in Belgium.

This tax is not due if the assets do not exceed BF 1,000,000.

10.5 NON-RESIDENT INCOME TAX

10.5.1 NON-RESIDENT INDIVIDUAL TAX

Business income

Trading and professional incomes are taxed in Belgium if earned through a permanent establishment. The definition of permanent establishment conforms to the OECD model definition, with some small exceptions. For example, a building site or a construction project which lasts more than 30 consecutive days is a permanent establishment in Belgium. In contrast, double taxation treaties as a rule provide that a duration of six months or longer is required.

Other Belgium-source income such as the following will also be taxable in the absence of a permanent establishment:

(1)   income from real estate.
(2)   income of artists and athletes.
(3)   professional income earned in Belgium.
(4)   income from a profession carried out in Belgium.

Employment income

This income will be taxed if paid by a resident, the Belgian government or a branch of a non-resident in Belgium. Employment income paid by a foreign employer is taxable in Belgium if the employee is present in Belgium for more than 183 days in the taxable year.

Movable income

Movable income paid to a non-resident is taxable and is collected through a final withholding tax.

Immovable income

Incomes generated by rented immovable property are generally taxed in the same way as for residents. Tax on non-rented property is payable through withholdings.

Capital gains

Capital gains on assets used for business purposes are taxable as business income. Gains made from assets, which are not investment nor professional income, may be taxed as miscellaneous income by way of withholding (33 per cent).

Gains made in normal transactions in the daily course of management of private property are tax free in Belgium.

10.5.2 NON-RESIDENT CORPORATE TAX

A foreign company is only liable for income tax in Belgium if it is doing business in Belgium through a permanent establishment.

The following are regarded as permanent establishments whether they have a representative who is authorised to conclude transactions or not:

(1) the seat of actual management;
(2) branch offices;
(3) factories;
(4) workshops;
(5) agencies;
(6) warehouses;
(7) offices;
(8) laboratories;
(9) all establishments of a productive nature, etc.

The branch is, in principle, taxed on the same basis as a Belgian company.

The normal income tax rate of the branch is 43 per cent but, where there is a double tax treaty, it is normally reduced to 39 per cent. The tax rate is only reduced to 42.05 per cent in the case of the double tax treaties with the Netherlands, France and Luxembourg.

10.5.3 DOUBLE INCOME TAX TREATIES

Treaties mainly follow the OECD model draft treaty and have been concluded with:

Australia	France
Austria	Germany
Brazil	Greece
Canada	Hungary
China	India
Czechoslovakia	Indonesia
Denmark	Ireland
Finland	Israel

Italy	Portugal
Ivory Coast	Romania
Japan	Singapore
Luxembourg	South Korea
Malaysia	Spain
Malta	Sri Lanka
Morocco	Sweden
Netherlands	Switzerland
New Zealand	Thailand
Norway	Tunisia
Pakistan	(USSR)
Philippines	United Kingdom
	Yugoslavia

Belgium has entered into negotiations for the conclusion of double taxation treaties with Algeria, Cyprus, Kenya, Kuwait, Mexico, Niger and Vietnam.

In order to avoid double taxation, Belgian tax treaties contain the provision that, where the treaty assigns certain income to taxation in the other contracting state, such income will be exempt from tax in Belgium.

10.6 TRANSFER PRICING

The arm's length principle in Belgian tax law is inserted in three articles, arts 24, 46 and 250 CIR.

The most important is Article 24, which states that when a Belgian company has, directly or indirectly, any links of interdependence with a foreign enterprise, any abnormal or gratuitous advantage which, because of this relationship, it grants to the latter or to any person or enterprise sharing common interest with it shall be added to its own profits.

The preceding paragraph also applies to any abnormal or gratuitous advantages granted to a person who, or an enterprise which, pursuant to its domestic legislation, is governed by a tax regime considerably more favourable than that which governs the Belgian enterprise.

Article 46 states that certain expenses (interest on loans,

royalties, etc) paid to a holding company or a foreign company in a country considered as a tax haven will only be deductible as costs if the taxpayer demonstrates that the transaction corresponds to normal and regular operations and does not exceed normal limits.

Article 250 states that the sale, assignment or contribution to the capital of a holding company resident in a country which has a favourable tax regime will not be deductible for tax purposes unless the taxpayer demonstrates that the transaction is in response to legitimate financial or economic needs or that he has received a real countervalue producing income that is subject to Belgian taxes. The key problem is to ascertain what is understood by abnormal or gratuitous advantage.

With respect to art 24, it must be noted that case law considers that abnormal or gratuitous advantage has been granted if a transfer of taxable income has taken place. No proof of intended fraud or an intention to reduce tax need be given by the authorities in order to ascertain that such advantage was granted.

11
INSOLVENCY

11.1 INTRODUCTION

Whether operating at home or in a foreign country, and even when concluding contracts with other commercial operators, the possible financial difficulties of one's business venture or with one's contract partner are usually considered merely hypothetical if not altogether disregarded. Often too little attention is paid to the consequences those difficulties might have. This chapter is intended briefly to highlight the particularities of the Belgian insolvency system.

11.2 TRACING ENTERPRISES IN DIFFICULTY

The early detection of a business in difficulty allows it to continue its activities, with or without subsequent in-depth reorganisation. This detection may occur at different levels. Creditors (such as banks or the tax and social security administrations), and often the organisation itself may be in a position to determine whether or not its business is floundering.

In addition, the initiative of the Court of Commerce of Brussels has produced a 'detection device'. It operates as a service for commercial investigation within the Court of Commerce. Originally the service was implemented with a view to detecting imminent bankruptcies at an early enough stage to prevent the creditors' rights from being further prejudiced. The structure of this service has now been altered so that it can also give advice and make recommendations to businesses in need in order to assist them in their efforts to avoid possible insolvency.

In practice, the commercial investigations service will invite companies it considers to be in financial trouble to appear before it and to provide an explanation as to their financial situation and the remedial measures they envisage. The invitation to appear is usually the consequence of, for example, a substantial large number of judgments (especially default judgments) issued against the business, any late filing of annual accounts, a decrease in the net assets to below half the level of the share capital etc. Then, unless this service is satisfied with the explanations supplied to it by the business concerned, it will fix a further hearing date in order to monitor the situation.

11.3 COMPOSITION ('CONCORDAT JUDICIAIRE'— 'GERECHTELIJK AKKOORD')

The Belgium Bankruptcy Act does not contain a provision for the economic restructuring of the organisation. It merely aims to guarantee the realisation of the business's assets at the best possible price, and then to secure the equitable distribution of the proceeds among the creditors.

Pre-bankruptcy restructuring is to some extent possible. This will be by means of an arrangement made between the indebted enterprise and his creditors, known as the *concordat judiciaire— gerechtelijk akkoord*, similar to the 'voluntary arrangement' existing in the UK. The *concordat* (voluntary petition for restructuring) can be defined as an agreement between an unfortunate but *bona fide* debtor and his creditors, which requires the approval of the court and which is subject to the court's control. Agreeing such a *concordat* is the only method whereby a debtor, who cannot pay his debts and who thus cannot obtain credit, may avoid bankruptcy. In practice, though, this route will be successfully followed in a very limited number of cases.

11.3.1 CONDITIONS

Only a trader (including commercial companies) may file an application for a *concordat judiciaire*, on condition that:

- he is virtually bankrupt, ie has stopped paying his creditors and is unable to obtain further credit;
- he has been unfortunate and has acted *bona fide* (ie in good faith); and
- his proposals have been accepted by his creditors and by the court.

11.3.2 PROCEDURE

Obtaining the *concordat* requires first the filing of an application with the commercial court of the applicant's domicile or registered office, together with:

(1) A summary of the facts on which the application is based.

(2) An estimated itemised statement of the applicant's assets, defining any part of the assets which are subject to a mortgage, or a privilege or which are secured, and further noting the extent of debts and liabilities incurred.

(3) A list of all creditors, noting their domicile and the amount of their claims.

(4) The applicant's reimbursement proposals (*propositions concordataires—concordataire voorstellen*).

Once the application has been filed, it is for the court to decide whether it has jurisdiction, how far the application conforms with the legal requirements imposed, and if necessary to decide whether the applicant may apply for a *concordat*. The justice's decision must be taken not later than eight days from the filing of the application.

If the application is declared admissible, the court will decide (on the basis of a report by *juge-commissaire—rechter commissaris*) whether or not the applicant's situation permits the granting of a *concordat*. This second decision must be made within 14 days of the first judgment which allowed the admission of the petition. If the application passes that second test, the court, among other matters, will invite the creditors to meet, so that they may vote on the proposals put forward by the debtor.

The arrangement will be accepted if the majority of the creditors (whole claims represent at least two-thirds of the whole amount owed by the debtor) approve the proposals made by the applicant party. However, debts towards creditors who have not participated in the vote or who have not voted validly; are not included in the calculation of the required majority. Creditors with a lien or a privilege who cast a vote will lose the benefit of their lien or privilege. In practice, therefore, they will not participate in the procedure.

Once the creditors have approved the proposals made by the applicant, the court will confirm the composition arrangement by issuing a judgment. To that effect, the decision is then published, in extract form, in various newspapers.

11.3.3 CREDITORS' RIGHTS

Once the composition is confirmed by court decision, it is binding on all creditors with regard to all claims existing prior to the court's approval. The creditors, therefore, are no longer in a position to enforce their claims individually. This principle, however, will not apply with regard to:

- Taxes and public charges.
- Amounts guaranteed by privileges, mortgages or pledges.
- Amounts due as alimony.

Consequently, neither co-debtors nor sureties will be released from their commitments to the main debtor's creditors once the arrangement has been implemented.

The debtor, in turn, can no longer transfer, mortgage or undertake commitments in any way without the authorisation of the *juge-délégué* (the member of court appointed to control the composition's procedure). He will recover full active capacity, only after the judgment confirming the *concordat* is given. Strictly speak ing, the authorisation of the *juge-délégué* is no longer absolutely required; however, the *juge-délégué* must still be able to ensure compliance with the approved composition conditions.

Furthermore if the applicant's situation improves, he will then have to pay all his creditors in full, notwithstanding the terms of the prior arrangement.

11.3.4 COMPOSITION BY SURRENDER OF PROPERTY

The composition effected by surrender of property is a special type of composition arrangement whereby the debtor proposes to surrender all his property to his creditors in satisfaction of their claims against him. In that case, the judgment confirming the composition's validity will need to appoint one or more liquidators and entrust them with the sale of the debtor's assets held under the control of the *juge-délégué*. Once the liquidation procedure has been concluded, a creditors' meeting will be convened by the *juge-délégué* in order for them, officially, to terminate the composition arrangement.

In practice, this type of composition is usually considered the most efficient, since it can even be enforced against preferential creditors; for example, against employees social security, VAT and tax administration bodies. It does, however, require a rather lengthy procedure involving several court hearings. Likewise, the application for composition by surrender of assets also often gives rise to the need for experts' reports.

11.4 BANKRUPTCY

This matter is governed by the law of 18 April 1851 which covers bankruptcy, criminal bankruptcies and suspension of payments. The law now forms art 437 onwards of the Commercial Code.

11.4.1 CONDITIONS OF BANKRUPTCY

Unlike in other systems, bankruptcy, under Belgian law, is not a question of insolvency, but rather a question of illiquidity. Thus bankruptcy can be said to result when payments have ceased and when credit can no longer be obtained. Liquid cash flow is thus impossible to maintain.

It must be stressed that, under Belgian law, it is only traders that will be concerned by the Bankruptcy Act, ie the Act will affect only:

(1) Individuals carrying out functions, which qualify in law as commercial activities, which make up their profession in either a main or an ancillary form.

(2) Commercial companies, as opposed to non profit-making companies which have civil activities as their corporate aim despite the fact that they are incorporated under one of the forms provided by the Company Act.

Yet, even where the above conditions are satisfied there will normally be no reason to declare a trader bankrupt as long as he maintains the confidence of his bankers and creditors (Brussels, 15 December 1981, JT, 1983, 175). The credit which allows continued payments may, however, not be artificial nor be illicitly obtained. Thus where this is the case, the court will normally make a bankruptcy order (Comm Namur, 25 February 1982, Rev Rég Dr, 1982, 243).

The cash flow crisis must be permanent in order for the courts to establish the insolvency of the debtor. For instance, in this respect credit will not be considered as irreparably disturbed when the creditors are willing to accept payment by instalments. Court interference in that case would therefore be unlikely.

11.4.2 JUDGMENT OF BANKRUPTCY

Bankruptcy may only be declared by means of a judgment of the commercial court and in the district where the debtor's domicile or registered office is located at the time when payments ceased. This judgment can be made on the court's own initiative, upon admission by the debtor, or upon request by one or more creditors. Furthermore, the bankruptcy order must establish that the conditions for bankruptcy were both present and met (Cass, 3 September 1981, Pas, 1982, I, 18).

11.4.3 ORGANISATION OF THE BANKRUPTCY

Having adjudicated on the bankruptcy the court will:

(1)   Nominate a judge-auditor (*rechter-commissaris—juge-commissaire*) from the ranks of the available commercial judges, to preside for the duration of the bankruptcy procedure. This judge is entrusted with the specific task of supervising the receiver and all the operations he undertakes during the management and liquidation of the bankrupt estate. In certain circumstances, this judge-auditor is required to act on his own initiative. For instance where it may be necessary to take urgent measures for the preservation and protection of goods within the bankrupt estate. In addition, the judge-auditor also has a reporting duty to the court with respect to any dispute which may have arisen during the bankruptcy procedure.

(2)   Order the affixing of seals other than for immediate inventory purposes.

(3)   Designate one or more receivers (*curateur—curator*) who will be responsible, with 'due diligence', for realising the estate's assets and for paying its debts. The receiver is invested with all powers necessary to enable him to carry out this exercise. Some acts of special importance must, however, be authorised by the judge-auditor and/or by the court (for instance permission is needed to keep the business running for a limited period, to sell the assets, etc. Thus in these circumstances, the judge-auditor could not act alone).

(4) Order the creditors to declare their claims within a period not exceeding 20 days after the judgment. But creditors who failed to file their claim within that period of time will still be eligible for examination of their claims to determine its acceptability (or otherwise) as a liability of the bankruptcy estate. This is done by suing the receiver if, the receiver unusually, in such cases, declines to appear in court voluntarily.

(5) Indicate the newspapers in which the judgment must be published.

(6) Designate the day and place for the examination of claims. Each claim will be examined before being accepted as an enforceable liability against the bankrupt estate.

11.4.4 CONSEQUENCES OF THE BANKRUPTCY JUDGMENT

Discharge from management ('dessaisissement'—'buitenbezitstelling')

The bankrupt party is automatically prevented from managing his assets and the receiver (under supervision of the judge-auditor) steps into the shoes of the bankrupt party to perform the management function, within the limits imposed on him by law. The bankrupt debtor, however, may start new activities, and realise profits out of this new activity. In some circumstances, however, these profits can be seized by the receiver.

The fact that the bankrupt is no longer in charge of the management of his affairs does not prevent him from taking legal action in matters which concern him individually. But any compensation he may receive from such legal action will have to be paid to the bankrupt estate (Cass, 26 May 1977, Pas, 1977, I, 985; Antwerp, 22 January 1988, RW, 1987–1988, 1100 with note by Mr Storme).

Suspended enforcement of legal actions

As a matter of principle, all actions and measures of enforcement by or against the debtor in his individual capacity are suspended as from the date of the bankruptcy judgment. Thus any legal action must be directed against the bankruptcy receiver. Likewise retention of title clauses will no longer be enforceable as from that date. Some creditors, however, will benefit from preferential legal treatment. After the period provided for examination of claims filed against the bankrupt estate has elapsed, creditors who have preferential rights over specific assets (such as lessors, pledgors or mort-gagors) will be entitled to enforce their claim notwithstanding the advent of bankruptcy. As a rule, financial (as opposed to operatio-nal) leasing companies will be able to recover any item leased, provided all conditions with respect to the valid recognition of financial leasing companies have been met.

Consequences for settlement prior to bankruptcy

Individual settlements made between the bankrupt and his creditors, after the bankruptcy will be invalid. Consequently settle-ments entered into prior to the bankruptcy, in turn, will be valid unless:

(1)   The enforceability of the settlement against third parties required the fulfilment of conditions which had not yet been met as at the date of bankruptcy. (As an exception to this rule, a legal mortgage in favour of the tax administration can, however, still be registered after bankruptcy has ensued.)

(2)   The settlement was entered into during the fraudulent period (see definition *below*).

(3)   The settlement was concluded with fraudulent intent.

Consequences for transactions during the fraudulent period

The commercial court determines when the bankrupt trader or company ceased to pay its debts (*cessation de paiement—staking van betaling*). Generally this is considered to have taken place no later than six months before the issue of the bankruptcy order. The period between the bankruptcy order and the date on which payments were deemed ceased is called the fraudulent period (*période suspecte—verdachte periode*). Under the bankruptcy act certain transactions carried out by the bankrupt during the fraudulent period will be set aside. Some transactions will automatically be null and void if made during the fraudulent period or during the ten days prior to it, such as for example transactions for no—or for less than due—consider-ation, and payments of debts which were not yet due. The effect of these operations is considered detrimental to the bankrupt estate.

Even seemingly, legitimate transactions, such as payments made by the bankrupt debtor in satisfaction of outstanding and due debts can be challenged in court in circumstances where payment occurred during the fraudulent period.

As a rule, mortgages and securities legally acquired can be

registered at any time before the bankruptcy order is made. However, in some circumstances, their registration may still be declared invalid. Case law shows that judges will not usually accept such cancellation of these registrations unless there has been some fraud (or serious negligence) on the part of the creditor, or unless the lateness of registration has not been detrimental to the bankrupt estate.

Consequences of bankruptcy for current agreements

As a rule, the current contracts will not be terminated as a result of the bankruptcy, unless the parties have clearly provided otherwise. (In fact rescission of contract clauses in the event of bankruptcy are frequently included in most agreements.) The contract will also be brought to an end if the contract was concluded *intuitu personae* (ie with reliance having been placed on the contract partner's personal or individual character).

Except in the above circumstances, it will be up to the receiver to continue or prevent the performance of the contract. If he decides to preserve the contract, the receiver will have to pay all sums due under the contract and the co-contracting party may even require payment of amounts outstanding to be made before he will resume performance of the contract. On the other hand, if the receiver decides to terminate the contract, the co-contracting party is entitled to claim damages for breach of contract.

Consequence of bankruptcy on overall activities

The general principle is that the activities of the bankrupt debtor will be terminated as a result of the bankruptcy order. In a limited number of cases, the Bankruptcy Act authorises the court to order the provisional continuation of the bankrupt's activities but only after having heard the receiver and after having received a report from the judge-auditor. Such continuation may be applied for by any interested party (the creditors, the receiver, or even the court) and then the court will authorise the continuation thus requested whenever the best interest of the creditors so requires.

If the continuation is granted, it will have to be carried out under the direction and the supervision of the receiver. The receiver may entrust a third party with this duty but he will still remain responsible for the actions of his appointee.

11.4.5 TERMINATION OF BANKRUPTCY

One of the major duties of the receiver consists in the realisation of the assets of the bankrupt estate and then in the distribution of the proceeds amongst the creditors. During this distribution, he must pay due respect to the creditors' right to be treated equally where they rank equally, and also to the legal rules governing priority of payment. Before the receiver is entitled to bring the bankruptcy procedure to an end, all creditors are invited to review the bankruptcy accounts and to make observations, if they so desire. Once these accounts have been approved, the bankruptcy is finalised and as a result, the creditors and the debtor will recover full freedom of activity.

11.4.6 REHABILITATION

Bankruptcy has severe consequences for the political and civil rights of the bankrupt. The bankrupt will fully recover those rights only where he is rehabilitated and he will only be entitled to obtain the necessary rehabilitation after he has paid all his debts, including principal debts as well as interests and costs. If the bankrupt has incurred criminal penalties, his rehabilitation will not be possible unless he has also previously been rehabilitated in the criminal context.

11.4.7 POST-BANKRUPTCY COMPOSITION

Before the receiver can start to realise the assets of the bankrupt's estate, he must offer the bankrupt the possibility of issuing proposals with a view to inducing a settlement with his various creditors. It is usually for the bankrupt to propose either deferred payment terms or to relinquish all assets of his estate to the benefit of the creditors. Whether or not the bankrupt intends to put forward any such proposals, a meeting of all creditors must be arranged. Approval of the proposals outlined *above*, if any are to be made, requires the agreement of more than 50 per cent of creditors who themselves represent at least 75 per cent of the total amount of all claims. Again, creditors who would normally have enjoyed preferential rights will lose the benefit of those rights if they cast a vote.

No post bankruptcy composition will be available to any

person who has been declared bankrupt pursuant to a finding of fraudulent trading. Likewise his rights to any such composition arrangement will also be restricted in circumstances where grounds exist for criminal measures to be taken against him for any reason.

11.5 RIGHTS OF CREDITORS

As a rule, the goods of the debtor constitute a common fund for all his creditors, and the proceeds of sale of these goods can thus be distributed among them on a *pro rata* basis. This will be the case when legal reasons for priority of certain creditors disturbs the equality which normally exists between them.

Such rights of priority can derive first from pledges (*gages—panden*) whether civil or commercial, pledges on goodwill (or even on invoice or warrant). Secondly, from rights of asset retention (ie, where the creditor is entitled to retain possession of assets belonging to the debtor, for as long as he has not received payment for release of those assets). Thirdly, from liens (*privilèges—voorrechten*, which grant a creditor priority over other creditors and even those whose claim is secured by a mortgage). And fourthly, rights of priority can derive from mortgages (*hypothèques—hypotheken*, whether legal, contractual or testamentary).

Liens (*privilèges—voorrechten*) can attach to movable assets (either to a specific asset or to all of the debtor's assets) as well as to real estate. By contrast, mortgages can only attach to real estate and to ships. In general, the validity of most privileges attached to movable assets will not require compliance with any publicity formalities, provided the assets are in the possession of the debtor. In some cases, however, the law has created publicity requirements, compliance with which will allow the creditor to enforce his lien against even the new owners of the asset which forms the basis of his security.

An interesting example of such a lien in trade is that which is granted by law to the seller over goods which he has sold but for which he has not yet been paid. Subsequent enforcement of that lien requires that the goods in question are in the possession of the purchaser, that they remain movable and can be identified. If, however, the purchaser has sold the goods, then the seller's security in them is transferred to the price, provided the price has not yet been paid. If the sale was made for cash, the seller may in addition claim back the goods sold provided they are still in the purchaser's possession. His claim, however, must be made no later than eight days after delivery and the nature of the goods must not have been transformed in any way. Once the purchaser has been declared a bankrupt, the seller loses his lien. A vendor of industrial equipment can, however, retain his security interest for a five year period after delivery, even if the equipment becomes immovable, and even if the purchaser becomes bankrupt. This will however, require the purchaser to comply with specific publication requirements, eg the deed of sale must be registered with the registrar of the court of commerce in the place of the debtor's domicile within 15 days of delivery of the goods.

The creation of any mortgage in favour of a creditor requires the fulfilment of publicity requirements, without which the mortgage will not give the creditor the desired right of priority. Priority rules as established by law vary on the one hand between liens of the same type, and, on the other hand, between liens of different types. The law also provides specific rules of priority between liens and mortgages, eg:

(1)   Secured creditors will take priority over unsecured.

(2)   Liens will effectively grant priority to the holder over all other creditors, including those with the benefit of a mortgage.

(3)   As a rule, debts secured over specific movable goods will take priority over debts simply secured over all the movable goods of any particular debtor.

(4)   As far as movable goods are concerned, the lien attaching to them will not affect the rights of third parties (for instance, the beneficiaries of a pledge) as long as those rights were created *before* the security interest itself was formalised.

(5)   Enforceability against other creditors of a lien attaching to specified real property requires compliance with specific publicity formalities.

As explained *above*, when a debtor is declared bankrupt, the commercial court will nominate a receiver to liquidate the bankrupt estate and to determine the rights of each creditor whose claim has been accepted. As a rule, the existence of liens would have been brought to the trustee's attention at the time when creditors filed their statement of claim against the bankrupt estate. If the creditor failed to state his preferential right or security interest, he will have the chance to correct his omission later on.

11.6 RESPONSIBILITIES AND LIABILITIES OF THIRD PARTIES

In exceptional circumstances, the corporate veil can be lifted and the real master of the business can be held responsible for discharge of the company's liabilities.

Of much more practical importance however is the particular liability incumbent on founders of any company adjudicated bankrupt within the first three years of its incorporation and whose capital is found to be 'obviously insufficient' to enable the company to carry out its activities during its first two years. The effect of this, is that the founders are rendered jointly liable *vis-à-vis* any interested person for the commitments undertaken by the company up to a definite proportion to be fixed by the judge.

Directors of a company, who fail to acknowledge the bankruptcy of their company within three days from the creation of the bankruptcy situation can also incur specific responsibility on the grounds of art 1382 of the Civil Code, and thus will be liable in full to compensate third parties for any losses they may have suffered as a result thereof. It is accepted, however, that the aggrieved plaintiff must succeed in proving that the directors were or should have been aware of the fact that the company was unable to continue its business. Directors can in addition incur responsibility in cases of serious negligence on their part where this contributes to the bankruptcy of the company (as defined by the legislator who took inspiration from the French *action en comblement de passif*). The conditions required for the directors to incur liability in this way, are, however, quite strict.

Finally any third party who contributed to a state of confusion as to the real situation of a trader may incur particular liability.

11.7 INTERNATIONAL ASPECTS

11.7.1 CONSEQUENCES OF A BELGIAN BANKRUPTCY ORDER

Belgium applies the principle of universality and unity of jurisdiction (ie one single court has jurisdiction to commence bankruptcy proceedings which simply extend to all the assets of the bankrupt trader, wherever they are located) as opposed to the principles of territoriality and plurality (under which there can be as many bankruptcies as there are countries in which assets belonging to the bankrupt trader are located). As a result of the principle of 'universality', a bankruptcy declared in Belgium will result in all creditors, both Belgians and non-Belgians, being treated in the same way.

Bankruptcy status will extend to all assets of the bankrupt estate whether located in Belgium or abroad. Thus, the receiver (*curateur—curator*), who is appointed to manage the bankrupt estate and to deal with the realisation of its assets, is necessarily entitled to carry out his duties in Belgium as well as beyond the Belgian borders. Even so, this will usually require him to obtain the recognition or *exequatur* of the bankruptcy order in the other countries concerned.

Nevertheless, the attitude of the Belgian courts towards foreign bankruptcies may, however, vary depending on the attitude taken to Belgian bankruptcy decisions imposed on them by their own national rules. In other words, implementation of the above-mentioned principle will only follow where there is reciprocity of attitude on the part of the foreign country concerned. However, bilateral recognition of bankruptcy is still only certain where Belgium has concluded treaties to that effect. Such is the case as far as France, The Netherlands and Austria are concerned. Practice shows, however, that even treaties do not prevent all the problems of enforcement and some foreign court decisions still ignore their provisions.

In parallel, according to the principle of 'unity' of jurisdiction applied in Belgium, one and the same court is competent to open bankruptcy proceedings and to hear the claims and disputes resulting therefrom.

11.7.2 CONSEQUENCES OF A FOREIGN BANKRUPTCY COURT DECISION

Belgium recognises the consequences of bankruptcy proceedings commenced abroad over the assets of a bankrupt estate which is located on Belgian territory. The judgment declaring the bankruptcy is even recognised in Belgium *ex officio*, ie without any prior specific recognition procedure (*exequatur*) being necessary. Forced execution (such as an executory attachment for example) by contrast requires prior compliance with the recognition procedure under art 570 of the Judicial Code, unless specific treaty provisions apply to the contrary. Most treaties, however, exclude bankruptcy matters from their sphere of application.

The principle of quasi-automatic recognition which applies only to strict bankruptcy situations will also apply to any proceedings aiming to prevent the occurrence of bankruptcy itself. Thus it may apply to the judicial composition (*concordat judiciaire—gerechtelijk akkoord*) earlier discussed, and to the various types of procedures for assisted management existing in other judicial systems.

12
FINANCING A BELGIAN COMPANY

12.1 INTRODUCTION

Generally speaking, Belgian companies can be financed in the same ways as their counterparts in most European countries. Most measures of protection provided by Belgian law relate in effect to the financing granted to individuals who are not acting within the framework of commercial or professional activities.

12.2 LOANS FROM A BANK

Except where expressly regulated by law, such as mortgage loans or credit agreements, as defined by the law of 12 June 1991 on consumer credit, which are concluded with an individual residing in Belgium with no commercial or professional purpose, loan agreements are not subject to specific legal provisions. The money lent will be made available to the customer either at once or in instalments (*ouverture de crédit—kredietopening*). Sometimes no contract will be concluded in respect of overdraft facilities granted. (Most Belgian banks will record the agreement in writing.) In that case, the bank can require the client to endorse a bill of exchange in its favour (*escompte—disconto*), in which event the bank will pay the corresponding amount under deduction of interests calculated until the due date and a commission.

In accordance with art 1905 et seq of the Belgian Civil Code, parties are free to determine the interest rate applicable to the loan agreement. If no such rate is provided in the agreement, the rate applicable will, as a rule, be as determined from time to time by law (*intérêt légal—wettelijk interest*)—at present, that rate is equal to 8 per cent. As far as overdraft facilities are concerned, any amount drawn will accrue interest by law, even when parties did not expressly provide for interest, at the rate usually applied.

Special rules have been provided with regard to:

(1) Compound interest: Belgian law does not permit the charging of compound interest (*anatocisme—rente op rente*) unless the interest upon which the interest is sought has been owing for a full year. The compound interest must, however, be provided in a specific agreement or in a writ of summons. Bank accounts are not subject to this rule.

(2) Usurious interest: according to art 1907*ter* of the Civil Code, if the lender takes advantage on the borrower's weakness, emotional state, needs or ignorance in order to obtain an interest rate or other advantages obviously in excess of the normal rate and the coverage of the risks involved, the borrower may petition the court in order to be authorised to reimburse the loan and pay an interest rate as provided by law. The court order may concern the payments already made, provided proceedings are initiated no later than three months after payment.

(3) *Indemnité de remploi—wederbeleggings–vergoeding*): total or partial anticipated reimbursement may not trigger the payment of compensation in excess of six months interest calculated on the amount reimbursed, at the rate determined by the agreement.

12.3 LEASING

12.3.1 FINANCIAL LEASING

Belgian law defines financial leasing as an operation which presents the following characteristics:

(1) The leasing must relate to equipment (eg trucks, computer equipment, furniture, etc) which the lessee shall exclusively use for professional purposes;

(2) The equipment must be bought by the lessor in accordance with the specifications given by the lessee. Usually the lessee will order the equipment himself, on behalf of the lessor.

(3) The leasing period must correspond to the assumed duration of economic use of the equipment in question.

(4) The rental must be established in such a way that the value of the equipment is depreciated upon expiry of the agreement.

(5) The lessee must be granted the right to acquire the ownership

of the equipment at the end of the leasing period for a price which corresponds to its residual value.

To conduct financial leasing operations requires the prior approval of the Ministry of Economic Affairs, failing which fines can be imposed.

The rent charged to the lessee is subject to VAT.

Financial leasing must be distinguished from other types of operations such as:

(1) Operational leasing, where the lessor merely rents the equipment to the lessee and usually takes care of the maintenance.

(2) Sale on deferred payment (*vente à tempérament—verkoop op afbetaling*), which the law of 12 June 1991 on consumer credit defines as an agreement which must, as a rule, result in the acquisition of movable tangible assets or in the performance of services and in which the price will be paid in at least three instalments in addition to the down payment. That type of agreement will usually contain a clause of retention of title in favour of the seller.

(3) Hire-purchase (*crédit-bail—financieringshuur*), which that same law of 12 June 1991 defines as the contract whereby the lessor undertakes to supply the lessee with movable goods at a fixed price which the lessee will pay in instalments. In accordance with the provisions of the law of 12 June 1991 on the consumer credit, the hire-purchase agreement must now mandatorily contain an offer to purchase.

12.3.2 LEASING OF REAL ESTATE

The leasing of real estate is a contract whereby a financier, in accordance with the instructions of his client, acquires real estate or causes a building to be erected and then leases it to that client who must use it for professional purposes. The lease agreement may be either a simple lease or a long lease (not less than 27 years, not more than 99 years).

If the conditions laid down by the VAT Code are complied with, the leasing operation will qualify as a service and as such the rent will be subject to VAT.

The leasing of real estate can present several advantages for the lessee such as the possibility of financing his investment up to 100 per cent which would not be possible should he finance it through a mortgage loan or any other type of loan.

In Belgium, real estate leasing operations can be financed in various ways: by the *Crédit Communal de Belgique*—*Gemeentekrediet van België*, when the operation involves a township (*commune*—*gemeente*), by institutional investors, by the leasing company itself through the issue of bonds or real estate certificates (*certificats fonciers*—*vastgoed*—*certificaten*).

12.4 FACTORING

In Belgium, factoring is not the subject of any specific legislation. A factoring contract is usually defined as a contract concluded between a factor and an individual or a company which undertakes to assign to the factor all claims arising from a delivery of goods or from the performance of services and embodied in invoices issued on Belgian or foreign clients. The title to the claim is assigned by endorsing the invoices in favour of the factor.

Factoring basically enables the individual or the company to entrust the management of his or its claims to a third party, the factor, and in addition to obtain provision by the factor against the possible insolvency of those clients and/or immediate payment of a certain percentage of the relevant invoices (usually 80 per cent) under deduction of the factoring fees charged by the factor.

In Belgium, in contrast with the situation in France, the transfer of the invoices to the factor will be operated by endorsing those invoices in his favour. Since indorsement may only be carried out in favour of banks or approved credit institutions, factors operating in Belgium must obtain prior approval. The transfer will be enforceable against third parties by the mere fact of the endorsement. Enforceability against the debtor from whom the invoice has been transferred, however, requires by law notification by registered letter with acknowledgement of receipt of a transfer notice reproducing the text of art 16, para 2 of the law of 25 October 1919 governing, among other things, the indorsement of invoices. In fact, factors usually content themselves with affixing a notice of transfer on the invoices. The enforceability of a transfer operated in those conditions, however, is somewhat doubtful.

12.5 CORPORATE FINANCE

12.5.1 DIFFERENT METHODS OF FINANCING

Different methods of financing are available to commercial companies:

(1) Direct funding of the capital by either private or public subscriptions. To call on the public to subscribe the capital of the company requires compliance with the rules laid down by the Company Act on the one hand and by Royal Decree no. 185 dated 9 July 1935 (recently modified by the law of 4 December 1990), which basically subjects the operation to the approval of the Banking Commission (*Commission Bancaire et Financière—Commissie voor Bank-en Financiewezen*).

(2) Issue of preferential shares: Belgian company law authorises joint stock companies (*sociétés anonymes—naamloze vennootschappen*) to issue preferential shares which do not represent corporate capital. They can be issued either in consideration for contributions made to the capital or not. In any event, preferential shares may not be issued without a contribution of some kind being made by their beneficiary to the company. In companies which call or have called for public subscription, preferential shares issued in consideration for contributions made in cash must be immediately paid up in full. The articles of incorporation will determine the rights attached to those shares. The transferability of preferential shares is strictly regulated by law.

(3) Issue of non-voting stock: since the last modification made to the Belgian Company Act, non-voting stock may be issued both in joint stock companies and in private limited liability companies (see chapter 3).

(4) Issue of bonds: Belgian Company law authorises joint stock companies (the issue of bonds in private limited liability companies is much more restricted) to issue the following types of bonds (*obligations—obligaties*):

    (a) The discounted bond, the issue of which is decided by the corporate body provided therefor in the company's articles of association. That bond is issued at a lower price than its face value. Special conditions are provided by law for the case where those bonds are reimbursable through drawing. Failure to comply with these conditions result in the bond being null and void.

(b)   The mortgage bond, the issue of which is decided as that of the discounted bond. A mortgage bond implies that the company mortgages one of its properties as a collateral for an existing loan or for a loan to be granted. The creation of the mortgage requires a notarial deed.

(c)   The convertible bond, the issue of which is decided by the company's general meeting in accordance with the rules applicable to alterations of the articles of association in some circumstances by the board of directors and which can, at the option of the holder, be converted into stock.

Since the modification of the Company Act brought about in July 1991, subscription rights (*warrants*) may also be issued in the absence of any bond issue. The issue of these subscription rights is, as a rule, decided as that of the convertible bonds. The subscription rights entitle their holder to subscribe to a future capital increase of the issuing company.

The issue of convertible bonds by the general meeting, as that of subscription rights, requires the board of directors to draft a special report which explains the purpose and the detailed justification of the operation proposed. If the issuing company calls for public subscription, a copy of that report must be supplied to the Banking Commission 15 days before the general meeting is convened. Existing shareholders have a preferential right of subscription to the bonds and rights of subscription.

The issue of convertible bonds and of the subscription rights may also be carried out by the board of directors when it takes place within the framework of the authorised capital, provided the board is duly authorised thereto in the issuing company's articles of association by the general meeting. When the Banking Commission is involved, as mentioned *above*, it will determine whether or not the report of the board is sufficiently complete. If the Commission considers that such is not the case or that the report is misleading, it shall inform the company and each of the directors. If the directors fail to comply with the remarks issued by the Commission, the latter may suspend the operation for a maximum period of three months.

The public issue, offer or sale of bonds is subject to specific regulations.

•   Loans obtained from banks or affiliated companies: when

borrowing money from related companies, attention must be paid to provide an interest rate commensurate with usual practices. Failure to enter into an arm's length loan agreement with a related company can have serious tax consequences.

12.5.2 CAPITAL INCREASE

In joint stock companies, as opposed to private limited liability companies whose capital may only be increased by a decision of the general meeting of shareholders, capital increases will be decided either by the general meeting of shareholders or by the board of directors. The board of directors, however, is entitled to increase the capital only within the framework of the authorised capital and provided it has been specifically authorised in the articles of association. That authorisation may not be granted for a period in excess of five years but it can be renewed one or more times by a resolution of the general meeting of shareholders. That resolution must be passed in accordance with the rules governing modifications to the articles of association. In any event, the board may not be authorised to decide on increases of capital to be chiefly completed through contributions in kind to be made by a shareholder who owns more than 10 per cent of the voting rights.

The formalities involved in an increase of capital decided by the general meeting differ depending on whether the capital is increased through a contribution in kind or through a contribution in cash. Those formalities, however, are identical to those to be complied with upon incorporation of the company. The resolution must be passed before a notary public and requires a majority of 75 per cent of the votes. In addition, if at the shareholders' meeting which will decide on the increase, less than 50 per cent of the capital stock is present or represented, a new meeting will need to be convened. At that second meeting, no quorum is required.

12.6 BANKING OPERATIONS

12.6.1 BANK ACCOUNTS

All traders and companies need to open a bank account with a bank established in Belgium. Companies undergoing incorporation will need to open a special bank account on which the shareholders will be able to transfer their contribution to the capital fund. After incorporation is completed, the notary public will issue a certificate acknowledging the incorporation and transmit it to the bank. The bank shall then transfer the money to a 'normal' bank account, which can then usually be operated from that moment on. The bank will require the persons authorised to operate the bank account to sign a signature card. The bank will also require a copy of the company's articles of incorporation and, as the case may be, of the board resolution which authorises the signatories to operate the account.

12.6.2 BANK FACILITIES

As a rule, overdrafts are subject to the prior approval of the bank and require a specific agreement to be entered into with the bank. Banks, however, sometimes informally authorise temporary overdrafts, provided the amount in question is reasonable. Interest rates charged on overdrafts are usually higher than those applicable to straight loans, probably with a view to discouraging excesses.

12.6.3 LIABILITY OF BANKS AND CREDIT INSTITUTIONS

The liability of banks and credit institutions is increasingly called into question. Banks have been held liable for having granted or maintained credit facilities to a company whose financial situation was in fact hopeless and where the credit facilities created an appearance of solvency likely to mislead third parties. It is, however, usually considered that only the bank's gross negligence will trigger its responsibility, although it has sometimes been argued that the slightest negligence of the bank should incur its liability. Sudden or unreasonable withdrawal of credit facilities can also result in the bank being held liable to compensate for the damage resulting from that withdrawal. The bank will also incur responsibility in connection with bank transfers, because the payment is made without instructions, on a false or falsified instruction, in error, etc.

As a rule, bankers are bound by a duty of confidentiality. However, they are obliged by law to disclose to the tax authorities all transactions whose object or consequence is a violation of the tax code. Likewise, a bank may not refuse to produce banking documents revealing information about its clients when a search warrant is issued by an examining magistrate (*juge d'instruction—*

onderzoekingsrechter). Finally, the bank must disclose the balance of a bank account which has been attached by a client's creditor.

12.7 NEGOTIABLE INSTRUMENTS

12.7.1 BILLS OF EXCHANGE ('LETTRES DE CHANGE— WISSELBRIEVEN')

Bills of exchange are governed by the law of 31 December 1955 which at present constitutes Title VIII of the Belgian Code of Commerce.

The validity of a bill of exchange is subject to it containing the following indorsements:

(1) the words 'bill of exchange' in the language in which the bill is drafted;
(2) the order to pay a sum certain;
(3) the name of the drawee;
(4) the due date for payment;
(5) the place where payment must take place;
(6) the name of the payee;
(7) the date and place of the issue;
(8) the signature of the drawer.

Except in specific circumstances listed by law, failure to include one of these indorsements on the bill will result in the bill being null and void. A bill without indication of the due date for payment is deemed to be a draft payable at sight. If the address for payment is missing, it is deemed payable at the place indicated next to the drawee's name. Likewise if the place of issue is missing the bill is deemed issued at the drawer's address. Only bills payable at sight or those payable at a fixed period after presentation may stipulate a specified interest rate. Any such provision in any other type of bill is void. As a rule, the drawer guarantees acceptance and payment, although he can release himself from the guarantee regarding the acceptance. Acceptance of the drawee may be sought until the due date. Sometimes the drawer will provide on the bill that acceptance must be sought either before or after a certain date.

Bills of exchange can be transferred by indorsement and can be guaranteed by a third party (*aval*) who will be held liable for payment in the same way as the drawer.

Payment of bills payable at a specific date or at a fixed period after presentation must be required upon due date, failing of which damages can be due. The drawer may not refuse partial payments but may not be forced to accept payment before due date.

Protests for refusal of acceptance or of payment must be recorded in a certified deed. Refusal may also be recorded by means of a declaration made on the bill of exchange itself and signed by the drawee, on condition that the drawer agrees to this. If acceptance is required before a certain date, the protest for lack of acceptance must be made before that same date. The same applies for bills payable at sight whose payment is refused. Protest for lack of payment of all other bills must be recorded within two working days of the date on which the bill is payable.

The relevant prescription periods are as follows:
(1) Three years after due date, for an action against the acceptor;
(2) One year after the protest, for an action against the indorsers or the drawers if it is brought by the holder;
(3) Six months after the indorsee has reimbursed the bill or has been sued, if it is brought by one endorsee against another one or against the drawer.

12.7.2 CHEQUES

In Belgium, cheques are governed by the law of 1 March 1961 which implemented the International Convention signed in Geneva on 19 March 1931 creating a Uniform Law on Cheques.

Like the bill of exchange, the validity of a cheque is subject to it showing a certain number of indorsements:
(1) the word 'cheque' in the language in which the document is drafted;
(2) the mandate to pay a certain sum;
(3) the name of the drawee;
(4) the place where payment must take place;
(5) the date and the place of the issue;
(6) the signature of the drawer.

Similar presumptions to those with regard to the bill of exchange will save the document from being invalid in the absence of some of these indorsements. Cheques are drawn on a bank where funds are available to the drawer, in accordance with an agreement which entitles the drawer to make use of those funds by means of a cheque.

Cheques are always payable at sight. If they have been certified by the drawee (usually a bank), the funds will be blocked in favour of the drawer until expiry of the presentation period.

Cheques issued in Belgium must be presented for payment within eight days after they have been issued. That period of time is extended to 20 or 120 days for cheques payable in Belgium but issued in or outside of Europe. Cheques issued in Belgium but to be paid in another country will also have to be presented either 20 or 120 days after they have been issued, depending on whether they are intended for a European or a non-European country. The banker may pay even after the presentation period has lapsed, unless the drawer has revoked the cheque.

The owner of a chequebook is by law liable for the cheques it contains and, for instance, will bear all the negative consequences resulting from their loss, theft or misuse unless he can prove the drawee's fraud or serious default, or that the loss, theft or misuse took place after its legitimate beneficiary received it.

Cheques may be crossed which means that they may be collected only by a banker or a client of the banker. A cheque which has been crossed without specifying the name of a particular banker may be collected by any banker. In contrast, a crossed cheque showing the name of a banker may be collected only by the banker named in the crossing. Cheques may also be issued with an indication that they must be paid into a bank account. Cheques may be indorsed and guaranteed (*aval*) in accordance with rules similar to those applicable to bills of exchange.

If a cheque bounces, the bearer will be able to seek redress from the drawer, possible indorsers and other parties who are bound on condition the cheque has been presented for payment in time and the refusal to pay recorded:

(1)   in a certified deed (*protêt*—protest);
(2)   in a statement of the drawee, dated and written on the cheque stating the date when it was presented;
(3)   in a statement by a clearing house (*chambre de compensation*—*verrekeningskamer*), dated and written on the cheque, stating that the cheque was presented in time and left unpaid.

In some circumstances, the bearer will be exempted from complying with the presentation period and the obligation to record the refusal. In addition, the issue of a bounced cheque, the withdrawal of the necessary funds before the presentation period has lapsed, etc expose the drawer to criminal penalties. Imprisonment for between one month and two years and a fine of BF 26–3,000 (to be multiplied by 80) may be ordered as a penalty for the issue of cheques which are not covered. In circumstances where the issue of a cheque induces the supplier to deliver, the offence will qualify as fraud (*escroquerie—oplichting*). Penalties may then be between one month to five years imprisonment and a fine of BF 26–3,000 (to be multiplied by 80). The law also expressly authorises the bearer to seek permission from the judge in charge of seizures to attach the movable assets of the drawers and the indorsers.

Failure to present the cheque or to record the refusal to pay on time will not deprive the bearer from his right to seek payment from the drawer unless the funds disappeared without any fault on his part after the presentation period lapsed. The bearer's right to seek redress from the drawer, the indorsers and any other obligated party is subject to a six month prescription period starting from the expiry of the presentation period. Prescription, however, does not ban the bearer from seeking payment from the drawer if the latter failed to provide funds, or from the drawer and the subsequent indorsers if they derived unfair enrichment from the non-payment of the cheque.

As in France, delivery of a cheque does not constitute payment which only takes place at the time when the funds are made available to the payee. In addition, except when parties provide to the contrary, delivery does not involve novation of the original debt, which means that any security provided for is unaffected.

Usually a bank card will be delivered by the bank. Bank cards aim to give the beneficiary of the cheque the certainty that he will be paid provided the cheque is not drawn for an amount in excess of BEF 7,000. Delivery of a bank card grants the holder of the card an immediate (and temporary) overdraft facility for an amount of BEF 50,000. As a rule, the drawee will require presentation of the bank card, or, if the amount is in excess of BEF 7,000 an identity card or other identification document.

12.7.3 PROMISSORY NOTES ('BILLETS À ORDRE'—'ORDERBRIEFJES')

Promissory notes are governed by the same law as the bills of exchange. Most rules applicable to the bills of exchange also apply to promissory notes.

A promissory note will be valid only if it contains the following, although presumptions similar to those indorsements provided for the bill of exchange will be acceptable:

(1)   the words 'promissory note' in the language in which the document is drafted;
(2)   the promise to pay a certain sum;
(3)   the due date;
(4)   the name of the beneficiary;
(5)   the place where payment must take place;
(6)   the date and the place of the issue;
(7)   the signature of the issuer.

12.8 GUARANTEES

12.8.1 PERSONAL AND REAL SURETIES

Generally speaking, sureties constitute a specific type of guarantee which seek to give the creditor more chance of obtaining the payment of his claim. As a rule, securities are ancillary to the claim they secure.

Sureties can be divided in two main categories:

(1)   On the one hand, personal sureties whereby the grantor commits himself to pay the debt of the main debtor and, as a rule, thereby commits the whole of his estate to that payment. *Cautionnement—borgtocht* is the main type of personal surety provided by Belgian law. Personal sureties granted as a security for commitments arising from a credit agreement governed by the law of 12 June 1991 on the consumer credit are subject to specific rules which aim to protect the consumer.
(2)   On the other hand, real sureties whereby the grantor commits a specific piece of property for the payment of his own debt or to that of a third party. The pledge (*gage—pand*) and the pledge of goodwill (*gage sur fond de commerce—pand op handelsfonds*) are, together with the mortgage, the main type of real sureties.

'Cautionnement'

In accordance, with art 2021 of the Civil Code, the *cautionnement* is a contract whereby the guarantor (*caution—borg*) undertakes in favour of a creditor to execute the debtor's obligations in the event that the latter fails to execute them. The *cautionnement* will be either civil or commercial, depending on the circumstances. Different rules will apply to commercial *cautionnement* as regards evidence and the guarantor will be presumed severally liable with the main debtor.

No specific formality needs to be fulfilled for the *cautionnement* to be valid. It must however be recorded in writing if it is not a commercial operation. A written document is, of course, always the safest course of action and in any event, the guarantor's will to act as such must be unequivocal.

The *cautionnement* can be granted either for all sums owed or to be owed by the debtor, or for a fixed amount. The guarantor will, as a rule, be entitled, prior to performing under the *cautionnement*, to require the creditor first to seek payment from the debtor (*bénéfice de discussion—voorrecht van uitwinning*) and/or to divide his action among the other guarantors, if they exist, and to reduce his claim to the portion each of them is bound to pay (*bénéfice de division— voorrecht van schuldsplitsing*). A guarantor may, however, waive those rights either expressly or tacitly, for instance by providing that he stands as (*caution solidaire—hoofdelijke borg*). As a rule, the guarantor is subrogated to the rights which the creditor he has paid holds against the main debtor. Article 2032 of the Civil Code also grants the guarantor, in certain circumstances, the right to act against the main debtor even before he has performed under the *cautionnement*. The guarantor can, however, renounce the right to make use of those rights before the creditor has been reimbursed in full.

Pledges

A pledge is a contract under which the debtor gives the creditor goods as collateral for his debt. The pledge will be either civil or commercial. When the commitment is made by a trader, the pledge is assumed to be commercial. This presumption can be rebutted only if, at the time the pledge was made, the creditor did not reasonably believe the secured claim relating to the debtor's trade. Pledges constituted as security for the payment of a commercial debt, will, as a rule, also be considered commercial.

Different rules apply to a civil pledge and a commercial pledge. Civil pledges are governed by arts 2073 to 2084 of the Civil Code, whilst commercial pledges are governed by the law of 5 May 1872, revising the provisions of the Code of Commerce relating to pledges and commission agencies. As a matter of principle, any claim can be secured by a civil pledge. The goods encumbered must be trade goods which are sufficiently identifiable. These goods can be intangible or future goods, on condition the creditor can be put into possession of the goods in question (eg clientele as such cannot be pledged), Money or fungible goods can also be the subject of a pledge.

The creation of a pledge, either civil or commercial, requires the fulfilment of several formalities. Failure to comply with them will usually result in the pledge being null and void. Authorisation to sell the subject matter of the pledge must first be obtained from the court. Sale is usually by (public) auction and is conducted by a bailiff. If the pledge is governed by the Civil Code, the pledgee can also request the court to grant him the subject matter of the pledge in satisfaction of the debt.

Pledge of goodwill

The law of 25 October 1919 relating to the pledge of goodwill, the discount and the pledge of invoices, provides the conditions to be complied with in order to pledge goodwill.

The beneficiary of such a pledge must be a bank or a credit institution approved by the government, and must comply with the approval conditions provided for that type of operation. Any credit operation may be covered by pledging goodwill, even if the operation is not a commercial one for the debtor.

Only an existing business may be pledged; the pledge must include the main assets of the business. As a matter of principle, all items constituting the business are covered by the pledge without any need to list them in the deed, although stock must be specifically indorsed in the deed if it is pledged. In no case, however, can the pledge extend to more than 50 per cent of the value of that stock. Likewise if claims, portfolio and cash, are to be included, they must be indorsed in the deed.

The pledge must be expressed in a written agreement, which does not need to be signed before notary.

The pledge is valid against third parties provided it is registered at the *bureau de la conservation des hypothèques* of the place where the business is located. Failure to register results in the pledge being void against third parties prejudiced thereby.

A pledge of goodwill has a duration of ten years and may be renewed.

Authorisation to sell the subject matter of the pledge must be obtained from the President of the Commercial Court and the sale is subject to the subject matter of the pledge being attached first since it will remain with the pledgor as opposed to the subject matter of other pledges.

12.8.2 FIRST DEMAND GUARANTEE

First demand guarantees (*garanties à première demande—waarborg op eerste verzoek*) can be required to cover several types of risks, such as those involved in bids, reimbursement of advance payments, performance of the contract, etc. As a rule, under a first demand guarantee, the guarantor, usually a bank, must perform upon the first request made by the beneficiary, without being able to require any justification whatsoever. In contrast with the *cautionnement*, the first demand guarantee, as with any other type of independent guarantee, is not ancillary to the underlying obligations. Possible causes of declaring the underlying contract null and void or other exceptions affecting the underlying obligations therefore will not affect the guarantee. Calls on a first demand guarantee, however, will be rejected in three cases:

(1) Where the underlying contract is unlawful.
(2) Where the underlying contract is cancelled or rescinded with retroactive effect.
(3) Where the call on the guarantee is obviously fraudulent.

13
ENVIRONMENTAL PLANNING

13.1 NATIONAL DEVELOPMENT

Originally national development was regulated at the national level by law dated 29 March 1962. As a result of the regionalisation process, jurisdiction over national development has been granted to the regions, so that one should now talk about regional development.

Development in the Flemish Region is still governed by the law of 29 March 1962, as supplemented by regional regulations. On the other hand, on 14 May 1984, the Walloon Region adopted a new code regarding regional and town planning. (This new code has already been substantially modified on several occasions.) Likewise, on 29 August 1991, the Brussels Region adopted a new ordinance regarding regional planning and town planning. The provisions of the law of 29 March 1962 are maintained in as far as they do not conflict with the new provisions enacted at regional level.

Planning in all three regions, is operated through various types of plans:
- regional plans;
- sector plans, which determine the allocation of each square meter of the sector;
- general and/or specific town plans.

13.2 ENVIRONMENTAL CONTROL LAW

13.2.1 REGIONALISATION AND COMPETENT AUTHORITIES

Regionalisation process

As explained in the Introduction, as a result of the regionalisation process started in 1970, Belgium is now composed of three regions:

- the Flemish Region;
- the Walloon Region;
- the Brussels Region;

All three regions have the same areas of jurisdiction. The central state retains only residual control for the matters which were not or not expressly granted to the regions or other bodies (provincial and local authorities).

Competences of the regions

The law of 8 August 1980 (as modified in 1988) implementing art 107*quater* of the Constitution defines the various powers of the regions.

As far as environmental matters are concerned, specific powers have been granted to the regions with regard to:

(1) development, monuments and sites;
(2) protection of the environment *sensu stricto*, including waste disposal policy as well as that of dangerous, unhealthy or insalubrious establishments;
(3) water policy;
(4) rural remodelling and preservation of nature;
(5) economic and energy policy with direct effects on the environment;
(6) scientific research.

The national state, however, still retains powers in the same fields when, for instance, there are no EC standards or when a specific sector has been entrusted with it (eg the national state controls the import, transit and export of waste, and radioactive waste; minimal technical norms regarding drinking water).

Regions are also granted power to claim compensation for services they render and to some extent to levy taxes (eg environmental tax on solid waste levied in Flanders).

The treaty-making power and the *ius legationis* still belong exclusively to the Crown, and thus to the central state. Since they have legal personality, the regions may conclude agreements and enter into contracts, provided these do not belong to the *droit des gens*. The regions, however, are also involved in the negotiation of international agreements when they relate to matters falling within their fields of competence, bearing in mind that the Crown is the only possible partner in the international field. In practice, regions are regularly consulted as far as EC matters are concerned.

Under Belgian law, it is up to the regions to implement directives issued at EC level in matters falling within the scope of their competence. However, if the regions fail to carry out their obligations in this regard, it is the national state which will be penalised pursuant to art 169 of the Treaty of Rome. At the present stage of the Belgian federalisation process, the state is nevertheless unable to force the regions to comply, nor is it entitled to substitute its action for theirs. A recently announced state reform will result in the regions having direct responsibility with regard to the implementation of directives.

13.2.2 NECESSARY PERMITS

As mentioned above, environmental protection is partially governed by the regions and the decrees they enact. The permits which are necessary to conduct industrial activities usually fall, therefore, within the jurisdiction of the regions. The permits required will also vary depending on the region concerned as well as on the activity envisaged. In some cases regions have not yet enacted specific legislation, in which event the rules initially provided at national level will still apply. Only those rules applicable to the Flemish and the Walloon Regions will be sketched *below*, since the Brussels Region is unlikely to be chosen when industrial activities are envisaged.

Flanders

Flanders (recently followed by the Brussels region) has recently replaced the previous multi-authorisation system for what could seem, at first sight, an easier system. In effect, it subjects most activities to the obtaining of one single authorisation so that, except in specific cases, only three major types of environment-related permits are now required to operate a potentially polluting site in the region:

(1) An ecological permit, which must be applied for in all circumstances where the site to be operated is classified as noxious. Three classes of establishments have been created depending on the potential pollution the activities represent. Applications for permits relating to first and second class establishments must be filed as a rule either with the Permanent Deputation of the Provincial Council or with the Board of Burgomaster and Aldermen where the business will be carried on. The exploitation of establishments that belong to a third class only require a declaration to the Board of Burgomaster

and Aldermen of the town concerned, prior to operating or converting it. When the establishment for which the authorisation is sought belongs to that category of sites which presents risks of major accidents, a safety report needs to be included in the application file to obtain environmental authorisation. Three months before starting the industrial activities concerned, the operator must supply the aforementioned body with an additional notice. This notice must be updated regularly, at least once every ten years.

(2) A building permit, which must be applied for whenever the project requires the construction of a building or facility.

(3) A licence to extract underground water, provided by the decree of the Flemish Executive of 27 March 1985 containing regulation and authority for the use of underground water and the delimitation of water catchment resorts and protection areas, where applicable.

An impact assessment study should precede any decision to grant an exploitation licence or a building permit for any project which could have an important impact on the environment. Such an environmental impact assessment study is required for those projects listed by directive 85/337/EEC, as well as for other projects whose characteristics, according to the Flemish authorities, require it. The need for such a study usually results from the importance of the project involved but may also result from its situation within the environment. Adjustments or modifications to existing installations may also be subject to a prior impact assessment study. In all cases, it is the possible impact of the project on the environment which is the determining factor as to whether such a study must be done.

Wallonia

In Wallonia there has not been a regrouping of the environmental authorisations as there has in Flanders; as a result, the operation of an industrial or semi-industrial site may require the obtainment of several authorisations, ie basically:

(1) An exploitation permit must as a rule be obtained prior to exploiting, modifying, or moving any establishment classified as dangerous, unhealthy or insalubrious.

Certain types of pollution sources are the subject of specific regulations, and therefore are not subject to the obtaining of an exploitation permit as provided by the General

Regulation for the Protection of Labour, but they have instead their own system (eg coal tips, mines, quarries, controlled dumping grounds). Other activities have always fallen beyond the scope of the regulations (eg nuclear power plants).

In addition, obtaining of an exploitation permit does not relieve the applicant of the obligation to obtain other authorisations in specific cases. It may be necessary, for instance, to get, in addition, a building permit or an authorisation to discharge used water.

Basically, the regulation divides establishments within the scope of its regulatory authority into two classes, first and second class, on the basis of their nuisance level. The authorities competent to decide on the granting of exploitation permits differ depending on the class concerned:

(a)　the Board of Burgomaster and Aldermen, for second class establishments;

(b)　the Permanent Deputation, for first class establishments and for establishments belonging to both classes.

The application procedure includes the conducting of a public enquiry by the Board of Burgomaster and Aldermen of the township(s) concerned.

(2)　A building permit must be obtained for most types of construction. The building permit is delivered by the Board of Burgomaster and Aldermen. In cases where the building permit departs from the development plans adopted pursuant to the Decree of 14 May 1984, a prior modification of that development plan will be required.

(3)　Licences are also required as regards the use of water:

(a)　licence to discharge into surface waters;

(b)　licence to extract water which can be made drinkable (ie underground water which is or can be made drinkable, as well as ordinary surface water classified in a protection area pursuant to the decree of 7 October 1985);

(4)　A licence must be obtained with regard to waste, either at national level (for the import, transit or export of waste) or at regional level. Regional decrees have, in effect, been adopted. They aim to prevent the creation of unauthorised general waste dumping and the unauthorised dumping on Walloon territory of foreign general and toxic waste. (The validity of these decrees have recently been challenged at EC level. A decision of the European Court of Justice has considered that 'waste' qualified as a good in the sense of the Treaty of Rome and that it must therefore be allowed to be moved freely).

The impact on the environment of projects subject to an exploitation or building permit, a waste processing permit, or other authorisations it lists, are subject to assessment either automatically (for the projects which are the subject of enclosure 2 of the decree) or upon examination of the prior assessment notice.

If no study is supplied, the application file must be considered incomplete and the procedure suspended. An insufficient study is cause for the authorities to refuse the authorisation applied for, to grant it with stricter conditions, to order a new study, or to carry out their own study.

13.3 ENVIRONMENTAL LIABILITIES: PENALTIES AND LIABILITY

13.3.1 PENALTIES

Infringements of the various laws or of the authorisations referred to above can give rise to:

(1) Administrative sanctions: fines, prohibition on using equipment in unauthorised ways or on operating the relevant plant, either temporarily or permanently, adoption of protective measures (this can also usually be done even where the danger does not result from any violation).

(2) Criminal sanctions: imprisonment and/or fines (in practice, imprisonment is seldom imposed, unless as a suspended sentence), direct measures (such as prohibition on use of equipment or installations, sealing or closure of the establishment, restoration, or payment of the profit gained as the result of an infringement) publication of the court decision, confiscation pursuant either to arts 42 and 43 of the Criminal Code or pursuant to other specific laws.

As far as criminal sanctions are concerned, it is important to note that, in Belgium, corporate bodies may commit infringements; this is in contrast to other countries, such as Denmark, the United Kingdom, The Netherlands or Ireland, where corporate bodies cannot incur criminal liability. Therefore, the court will determine whom in the enterprise must be considered at fault (judicial imputability). Sometimes the law itself will determine either implicitly or

explicitly, whom must be considered responsible (legal imputability). In other cases, the law may even deem a particular person
liable.

13.3.2 LIABILITY

Liability in tort

The principles governing liability in tort are to be found in art
1382 of the Belgian Civil Code. Basically, art 1382 of the Civil
Code obliges anyone whose fault results in harm to a third party to
indemnify the latter. Article 1384 of the Civil Code also attributes
liability for harm caused by persons or goods for whom one is
responsible (eg parents are responsible for their children, employers
for their staff, etc).

In order to obtain compensation pursuant to those provisions,
the victim is required to prove that the harm has been caused
through the fault of the defendant (ie, through behaviour which
does not coincide with that of a normally careful person in the same
circumstances). There can be fault either when a law or regulation is
violated or when the general duty of care is not complied with. It is
therefore not always sufficient to comply with the law of exploitation
or other authorisation: the general duty of care may impose higher
standards.

The harm must be certain, or at least sufficiently certain, and
personal. This, of course, limits the application of art 1382 of the
Civil Code in cases of ecological damage where the harm is often
uncertain or concerns the community. Courts, however, usually
conclude that the harm is personal when personal rights or assets are
indirectly damaged through damage to collective assets.

Indemnification on the basis of art 1382 of the Civil Code also
requires the proof of a link between damage and fault, which is not
always easy to establish. As a rule, compensation will be by restitution, monetary compensation will only be allowed if restitution is no
longer possible.

Provided a fault and potential harm can be proved with some
degree of certainty, art 1382 *et seq* of the Civil Code will also enable
the plaintiff to obtain a stop order for projects causing, or likely to
cause, damage. If, however, there is no underlying violation of the
law or the authorisation relating to the project, it is traditionally
considered that the powers of the court will be rather limited. In

these cases, the court may not impose remedies in conflict with the relevant authorisation and, in addition, the remedies may not jeopardise the activities authorised. This traditional approach is disputed by both courts and authors.

If the defendant fails to abide by the court decision ordering him to provide restitution or to carry out specific measures, the plaintiff may be authorised to carry out the necessary work and to obtain compensation from the defendant. The court may also accompany such a decision with daily penalties in the case where the defendant fails to comply with its decision.

Objective liability

The law provides several cases where the operator may be held liable even when he is not at fault. In some cases, it is sufficient to prove that the harm results from the activity carried out by the operator or by his behaviour. Such an objective liability has also been provided by specific laws, eg with regard to operation of nuclear plants, to toxic waste, sea pollution by oil, and reduction of the water table. The only remedy offered in those cases is compensation for the damage suffered.

Usually, the laws providing for such an objective liability also contain provisions aimed at ascertaining whether the operator will be able to meet his obligations in connection with any potential liability (either through compulsory insurance policies or through guarantee or compensation funds).

Abnormal neighbourhood disturbance

Pursuant to art 544 of the Belgian Civil Code, ownership is the right to enjoy and dispose of goods as one deems appropriate, provided that right is not exercised in contravention of laws or regulations. On that basis, and that of art 11 of the Belgian constitution, courts and doctrine have declared that there must be a sort of balance between neighbouring properties. As a result, when damage is caused to a neighbour, in excess of what is considered normal for a neighbour to stand, the latter is entitled to compensation.

In this case there is no need to prove fault. It is sufficient to prove that the harm suffered exceeds normal limits and that damage has resulted. This theory can therefore be very useful in the cases where no fault can be proved, for instance, where the operator fully complies with the licence he has been granted. However, it has been held that this theory, like art 1382 of the Civil Code, does not offer sufficient protection in all cases, for instance, where pollution results from several sources, such as in the case of acid rain.

As a rule, the only remedy for abnormal neighbourhood disturbance is the payment of money damages as compensation for the harm, although the current trend is also to allow compensation in kind to be ordered.

13.3.3 INSURANCE

The law seldom makes it a legal requirement to insure against one's environmental liability.

LUXEMBOURG

14
INTRODUCTION

14.1 THE COURTS

The state of Luxembourg is divided into two areas of jurisdiction, Luxembourg and Diekirch.

There are two Justices of the Peace in the area of Luxembourg, one in Esch/Alzette and one in Luxembourg City; and there is one in the area of Diekirch. This court has jurisdiction for minor cases as well as for cases on real estate rentals.

The District Courts are based in Luxembourg and in Diekirch. They have jurisdiction for other cases which are not in the jurisdiction of the Justices of the Peace, as well as rendering foreign judgements enforceable in Luxembourg. They also act as Court of Appeal for judgments given by a Justice of the Peace.

The High Court of Justice, the only one for the whole country, is the court of appeal for the judgments given by a District Court, as well as 'Cour de Cassation'.

The Justice of the Peace is a sole judge, whereas all chambers in the District Court and the Court of Appeal are composed of three professional judges. The *Cour de Cassation* is composed of five judges.

The President of the District Court has specific jurisdiction in certain matters.

The lawyers in Luxembourg have to apply, after a complete course of legal studies (minimum four years) at a university abroad, to be admitted to the Bar. After admission they have to serve as probationers for a period of three years and then have to sit a final examination. Successful candidates are finally admitted as fully fledged lawyers.

14.2 INTELLECTUAL PROPERTY

14.2.1 TRADEMARKS

A harmonisation of trademarks has been achieved through the so-called Benelux Convention and the 'Loi Uniforme Benelux'. The Convention came into force on 1 July 1969, and the *Loi Uniforme* on 1 January 1971.

The main objective of the regulations is to have a sole trademark on a sole territory.

The administration of the trademark system is centralised at the *Bureau Benelux des marques*, which is located in The Hague.

In order for a trademark to be registrable, it has to be a sign which is distinctive, legal and available.

Signs are illegal where they are contrary to public order in one of the three countries, where they mislead, or where they represent one of 'the countries' coat of arms.

The trademark must refer to a product or to services.

The exclusive rights for trademarks are obtained by first registration on Benelux territory, or by international registration. The date of the deposit is the date when the authorities issue the deed of deposit and this date determines the start of the exclusive rights.

The deposit is done either by the legal person itself or by its authority, with the *Bureau Benelux* in the Hague, or with the local administration.

However, the national authorities are only competent for the deposit of the trademark, for the confirmation of the deposit and for modifications thereof. The *Bureau Benelux des marques* is competent for the other services. The national authorities are located in Luxembourg, Brussels and The Hague.

The deposit is done by filing a specific form in French or Dutch.

A search to determine whether a deposit for such trademark has already been filed, has to be done before the applicant is admitted to confirm his deposit.

14.2.2 COPYRIGHT

The law of 29 March 1972 provides that the author of a 'literary or artistic work' has exclusive rights on his work. Such wording refers to a contribution in literature, science or art independently of the means of expression.

Unless otherwise provided for by the law, the exclusivity rights are granted for a period of fifty years after the death of the author to the benefit of the heirs or assigns. The right of reproduction or of disclosure to the public of the author's work is the author's exclusive right. This right may be transferred by way of the rules of the Civil Code.

The law also provides the rules for musical and theatre performances, for broadcasting and movies and for plastic arts.

Infringement of copyright is actionable in the criminal courts. The infringer or the person who has sold or imported into the Luxembourg infringed goods with full knowledge will be condemned to a fine ranging from LF 2,500 to 100,000. The infringed goods will be seized and in some cases imprisonment may be decided by the court.

Software is not specifically protected by that law. No specific legislation has been enacted for the protection of software. The Minister of Justice has however, expressed an opinion in answer to a question asked in Parliament by a deputy and according to the Minister the protection of software is guaranteed by the law on copyright, although it is not specifically provided.

15
COMPETITION

15.1 EEC COMPETITION LAW

The provisions of the Treaty of Rome relating to competition apply to the activities of any commercial business insofar as they are to affect trade between Member States of the European Community. In particular these provisions prohibit any agreement between undertakings which have as their objective or their effect the prevention, restriction or distortion of competition within the Common Market. In the same way, any abuse of a dominant position within the Common Market or in a substantial part of it is prohibited. Since a majority of Luxembourg businesses have significant trading relations with businesses in other EC Member States, those provisions apply to the whole of Luxembourg's economic activity.

15.2 LUXEMBOURG COMPETITION LAW

15.2.1 LAW OF 5 JULY 1929 ON UNFAIR TRADING

Article 4 which changed art 309 of the criminal code, provides that anyone who divulges a trade secret during his period of engagement or in the two years following the end of his contract with an objective of competition, will be punished by imprisonment for up to three years and a fine of LF 2,501–150,000. The same provisions apply to a person who knew such a secret and used it for competition.

15.2.2 LAW OF 27 NOVEMBER 1986 LISTING CERTAIN UNFAIR TRADING PRACTICES AND PENALISING UNFAIR COMPETITION

The provisions set out in the first chapter of the law governing clearance sales, winding-up sales, out-of-season sales, as well as end-of-lines sales. The provisions contained in the law of 5 July 1929 relate to unfair competition.

Luxembourg law (art 16) considers as unfair trading any act which is either contrary to the honest practices of industry or trade, or to a contractual engagement by which a business or individual trader attempts to win away part of competitor's custom or to reduce his competitiveness.

Competition is considered unfair where an individual:

(1) creates the belief in the general public that he sells his goods or provides his services at particularly favourable conditions, will have publicly announced false information about the destination, the quality, the quantity, the price or the fabrication process, *to deceive* the buyer or the recipient of services;

(2) creates by the addition, removal or a falsification of the commercial mark or the name of a product, a false origin or provenance;

(3) attempts to create confusion between his business and the person, the establishment, the products or services of a competitor;

(4) disseminates false information on the business of a competitor;

(5) uses without authorisation patterns, samples, technical combinations, or any indications or documents entrusted of a competitor;

(6) uses without authorisation the materials or wrappings of a competitor even without intention to acquire property in it or to create a confusion between his business and the competitor's one;

(7) offers, promises or grants price reductions on the acquisition of goods to buyers, due to their adherence to a group or an association.

Similarly, commercial advertising prompting unfair competition is strictly prohibited (art 18), and is considered unfair trading. If such advertising is placed by a Luxembourg non-resident, a stopping action may be instituted against the editor, the printer, the distributor or any person who has contributed to the realisation of the advertisement.

Sales with bonuses and sales at a loss are generally considered as unfair trading practices except in certain cases strictly limited by law (arts 19 and 20).

In cases of unfair practice a judge can dictate that the court's decision is displayed outside the premises of the business concerned or in a published newspaper.

15.2.3 LAW OF 5 JUNE 1970 ON RESTRICTIVE TRADING PRACTICES

Agreements between companies and the abuse of a dominant position in the Luxembourg market are prohibited when such agreements are exploitative and contrary to the public interest, or restrict or distort the competition.

This is not the case where authors are able to justify that an *amelioration* of the production or the distribution of products, or a promotion of the technical or economical progress is realised and users' interests are respected.

As no other definition is given, it is the role of an ad hoc commission to decide if undertakings, agreements are contrary to the object of the law as described above.

The commission is attached to the Minister of Economics and Middle Classes, and has only an advisory capacity. After having compulsorily heard the commission's opinion, the Minister can consider the matter closed, issue warnings or recommendations, or prohibit totally or partially the practices concerned. Appeal against the Minister's decision may be filed in the month following the notification with the State Council.

15.3 CONSUMER PROTECTION

The Luxembourg legislator has enacted special laws to redress the perceived contractual imbalance between professionals and non-professionals.

At first set of rules is to be found in the laws of 25 August 1983 and 15 May 1987 regarding consumer protection. They both aim at protecting the consumer. The 1983 law deals in general with any contractual clauses which create an imbalance of rights and obligations which are prejudicial to the consumer. Such clauses are null and void but the law only deals with Luxembourg residents. The persons protected are consumers who have acquired the services in a non-professional capacity. Article 2 of the law contains a non-exhaustive list of clauses which are deemed to be abusive and are as such to be regarded as null and void.

The following examples of such clauses may be mentioned:

(1) Provisions by which the amount of the claim is increased if the consumer files a litigation at court.

(2) Provisions exempting or limiting the legal guarantee in case of hidden faults (*vices cachés*).

(3) Provisions prohibiting a customer suspending payment of all or part of the amount due if the supplier does not fulfil its obligations.

(4) Provisions prohibiting the right of the customer to ask for the cancellation of the contract, when the supplied services are not rendered at the promised time, or without reasonable indication of a delay, within a reasonable period or time.

(5) Provisions entitling the supplier to determine the date of execution of his obligation, without special justification.

(6) Provisions forcing the customer to make any compensatory claims within an unreasonably short period.

(7) Provisions placing the burden of proof on the customer, when it normally devolves on the supplier.

(8) Provisions entitling the supplier to modify or to terminate the contract without good reason indicated in the contract.

(9) Provisions extending the term of the contract beyond one year, unless terminated by the customer.

(10) Provisions allowing the supplier to determine the price of services at the time they are rendered or giving him the right to increase the same, while the customer does not have the right to terminate the contract if the resulting increase is higher than the amount foreseeable at the time the contract was made.

In addition to controlling unfair clauses, the law completes the Civil Code by adding a new article 1135–1 which states in very general terms that any conditions of a contract that have been pre-established by one party will only be binding on the other party if the same can be considered to have been aware of them at the time the contract was signed. It is up to the judge to determine if this was the case. Furthermore, certain extra clauses must have been accepted expressly and especially in order to be binding. Such clauses include:

(1) limitation of liability clauses;

(2) clauses allowing the discretion to withdraw from a contract or to postpone its effects;

(3) arbitration clauses;

(4)   jurisdiction clauses.

It should be noted that unlike consumer protection legislation, these provisions govern any contractual relationship.

While the law of 1983 dealt primarily with unfair contractual clauses, the subsequent 1987 amendment changes certain basic concepts of the Luxembourg Civil Code. The following rules are particularly important:

(1)   Article 1118 states that any contract may be void if there is an obvious imbalance between the undertakings of both parties, or if such imbalance results from the abuse of a dominant position by exploiting the ignorance or inexperience of the other party.

(2)   Article 1907 of the Civil Code has been completed by a second paragraph stating that in the absence of a special clause or banking customs determining the interest rate, only the legal interest rate will be due and no additional commissions or charges may be claimed

(3)   Article 1907–1 is a restatement of the rule of art 1118–1 and empowers the courts to reduce abusive interest rates, which are defined as those rates that exceed the rate that would normally exist in light of the risks of the loan.

(4)   Articles 1152 and 1231 state that the judge may moderate or also increase the amount of the penalty clause if it is either excessive or insufficient.

16
BUSINESS ORGANISATIONS

16.1 INTRODUCTION

As in France and Belgium there are two principal ways under Luxembourg law to carry on business.

The first is as a sole trader. In this case no distinction is made between the assets of the business and those of the sole trader himself. The second is through a corporate body which has a legal personality which is separate to that of its members thus creating a distinction between the assets of the company and those of its participants. Luxembourg law recognises six different types of commercial companies or corporations.

Economic considerations such as the credibility of the company and legal considerations such as the extent of the members' liability or the transferability of shares, guide the choice of which category of company is chosen.

16.2 LEGISLATION

Two main laws relate to Luxembourg companies:
(1) The law of 10 August 1915 on commercial companies as subsequently amended. This law is largely based on the Belgian law of 1930. For any questions of interpretation, reference must be made to Belgian case law and commentaries.
(2) The general companies' rules of the Civil Code (Pt IX arts 1832–1864).

The first law only applies to commercial companies, whereas the second set of rules applies to both civil and commercial companies insofar as they do not conflict with the provisions of the 1915 law.

16.3 LIMITED LIABILITY COMPANIES

Companies may be divided into two categories, depending on the different level of liability of the participants. They may have unlimited liability for the debts of the company which corresponds to the partnership under British law. But the shareholders' liability may be limited to the business capital, in the case of limited liability companies, as with the public limited company and the private limited company.

16.3.1. PUBLIC LIMITED COMPANY (*SOCIÉTÉ ANONYME*)

The company must be established by articles of incorporation drafted by a notary and published. It is formed by at least two members, and all capital must be subscribed. The subscribed capital of a *société anonyme* must not be less than LF 1.25 million, of which at least one quarter must be paid up at the date the company is formed. Shares must normally be freely transferable, but the articles of incorporation may provide for certain restrictions.

The company is managed by a board of directors comprising at least three directors who may not be shareholders. An annual general meeting of shareholders must be held at least once a year.

Supervision of the company is entrusted to one or more auditors. If the company meets at least two of the following criteria, it must be audited by independent auditors:
(1) Balance sheet bottom line exceeding LF 77 million;
(2) Net turnover exceeding LF 160 million;
(3) Average number of salaried employees for the year is greater than 50.

Due to its rather elaborate construction, this type of company is used almost exclusively for larger business enterprises.

16.3.2 PRIVATE LIMITED COMPANY (*SOCIÉTÉ À RESPONSABILITÉ LIMITÉE* (SARL))

The company's articles of incorporation must be drawn up by a notary and published in full. The number of members may not be less than two or exceed 40.

The company's capital may not be less than LF 500,000, fully subscribed and paid up. The company is managed by one or more managers, who need not be members.

An annual general meeting is compulsory only if the company has more than 25 partners. In this case, accounting supervision of the company must be entrusted to one or more auditors, who may be members of the company. The company may not raise capital by a public issue of loan stock, nor may its shares be offered to the public.

Insurance, funding and savings institutions may not adopt the form of the SARL.

This type of company is in practice used for medium sized businesses of all types.

16.3.3 CO-OPERATIVE COMPANY WITH LIMITED LIABILITY (*SOCIÉTÉ COOPÉRATIVE*)

The *société coopérative* comprises members whose number and holdings may vary and whose shares are not transferable to third parties. Members of the *société coopérative* may decide whether liability is limited or unlimited.

Only a deed under private seal is required for its formation, but it must be published in full. The number of members must not be less than seven, and the articles of incorporation must state the manner in which the capital is to be paid up, and the minimum amount to be paid up initially.

The company is managed by one or more managers, who need not be members. Financial supervision is the responsibility of one or more auditors.

Shares are not transferable to third parties, and members may resign only as provided for by the law.

16.4 PARTNERSHIPS

16.4.1 GENERAL PARTNERSHIP (*SOCIÉTÉ EN NOM COLLECTIF*)

The *société en nom collectif* is formed by two or more persons, all of whom are personally, jointly, severally and indefinitely liable for the partnership's debts. It is formed by deed under private seal, published in short form.

Shares are normally not transferable, although the deed may provide for exceptions to this rule.

The SNC is managed by a manager. The partnership is not subject to tax under its own name, but personal income tax is charged on the partners in proportion to their share of the partnership's income.

In practice, partnerships of this type are most usually found in small to medium size family businesses.

16.4.2 LIMITED PARTNERSHIP (*SOCIÉTÉ EN COMMANDITE SIMPLE* (SECS))

The *société en commandite simple* is formed by one or more partners (the general partners) who are jointly, severally and indefinitely liable, plus one or more 'limited partners', who merely contribute to the share capital and whose liability is limited to their capital contribution. It is formed by a deed under private seal, which is published in short form.

Shares are normally not transferable, although the articles of incorporation may provide for exceptions to this rule.

Day-to-day management is carried out by a manager. A limited partner may not take part in the firm's management.

The firm is not subject to tax under its own name, but the partners are charged personal income tax relative to their share of the partnership's income.

There is also a derivative of the *societé en commandite simple* inspired by German law, a combined form of limited liability company and limited partnership (SARL and SECS). This kind of company offers the advantage of limiting the liability of the limited partner, while ensuring that the company is taxed as an entity separate from members.

16.4.3 PARTNERSHIP LIMITED BY SHARES—(*SOCIÉTÉ EN COMMANDITE PAR ACTIONS*)

The *sociéte en commandite par actions* is similar to limited partnership, the only difference being that the limited partners' shares are freely transferable. Most of the rules which apply to the public limited company also apply to the *sociéte en commandite par actions*.

16.4.4 CO-OPERATIVE COMPANY (*SOCIÉTE COOPÉRATIVE*)

In a *société coopérative* which has been described above, partners may decide to limit liability to their contribution.

16.4.5 CIVIL COMPANY

A civil company is a company formed in order to allow its members to carry out an activity which is considered by law as being a purely civil activity. There is normally no minimum share capital. The capital is not divided into non-negotiable shares and there is no minimum par value fixed by law.

The transfer of shares in a civil company must be made by written contract of sale and requires the unanimous prior consent of all members. The deed must also be served by bailiff on the company.

16.5 ECONOMIC INTEREST GROUP (*GROUPEMENT D'INTÉRÊTS ÉCONOMIQUES* (GIE))

The law of 25 March 1991 introduced the possibility of forming a Groupement d'Intérêts Économiques. Such a group is formed by two or more individuals or companies of the private or public sector, with the exclusive aim of facilitating or developing the economic activity of its members, and improving or increasing the result of that activity. The group's activity must be in line with the activity of its members, from which its object must not differ.

The group has it own legal identity, but it may not seek profit for itself. The group's members are jointly and severally liable for its debts, while the contract by which the group is formed must be drawn up by a notary or under private seal and published in short form.

The group is managed by one or more of its members on behalf of them all.

16.5.1 EUROPEAN ECONOMIC INTEREST GROUP (*GROUPEMENT EUROPÉEN D'INTÉRÊTS ÉCONOMIQUES* (GEIE))

A second law of 25 March 1991 implemented the EC Council Regulation 2137/85 of 25 July 1985 on the European Economic Interest Group (EEIG).

The EEIG is a legal entity inspired by the Groupement d'Intérêts Économiques. The aim of which is to facilitate cooperation between businesses situated in different member states of the EC. Membership is open to community persons, including individuals, partnerships and companies.

16.6 NON-PROFIT ORGANISATIONS

Non-profit organisations may be set up under the provisions of the law of 21 April 1928 (*Loi sur les associations sans but lucratif et les établissements d'utilité publique*).

16.6.1 *ASSOCIATIONS SANS BUT LUCRATIF* (ASBL)

Associations may be set up freely. This right is guaranteed by the constitution. No governmental approval is required, except in the case of acceptance of gifts and donations whose value exceeds LF 500,000.

In order to benefit from the legal personality, the ASBL must have its articles of incorporation, as well as the name, profession and address of its managers published.

Even if ASBL are non-profit organisations, they may undertake lucrative activities on condition that these activities are ancillary to the main activity of the association.

Associations are subject only to an annual tax on the net value of their immovable and movable properties owned in Luxembourg if this value exceeds LF 1 million. The tax rate is 0.14 per cent.

Associations are subject to corporation tax on profits which is assessed on the basis of the regulations governing personal income tax (at a rate of 20–34 per cent) and wealth tax on worldwide net worth (at a rate of 0.3–0.8 per cent). However, following a government decision, on the advice of the Finance Minister, some activities of non-profit making organisations are not considered industrial or commercial when the objects for which the association has been set up present a public interest, and the association does not aim to provide its members with a tangible profit.

16.6.2 *ETABLISSEMENTS D'UTILITÉ PUBLIQUE* (FOUNDATIONS)

Foundations may be set up under the law of 21 April 1928. They pursue exclusively philanthropic, religious, scientific, artistic, social, sporting or international aims.

Foundations may be set up by notarial deed or by will and must be authorised by a grand-ducal decree prior to obtaining their full legal existence.

Taxes levied on a foundation are close to those seen above for the associations.

16.7 INCORPORATION

16.7.1 THE MAIN RULES

For the general partnership (*société en nom collectif*), the limited partnership (*société en commandite simple*) and the co-operative society, the articles of association may be drawn up either by notary's deed or by deed under private seal.

A public limited company (*société anonyme*), a private limited company (*société à responsabilité limitée*) and a partnership limited by shares, may only be formed before a notary public, failing which it will be deemed null and void.

All these companies acquire their legal existence as soon as the articles of incorporation are signed. There is no public or judicial authority to control the regularity of the setting up of a company and once the articles of association are set up, they have to be published in full or in a short form, depending on the type of company.

Regarding the public limited company, the private limited company and the partnership limited by shares, the articles of incorporation have to be published in full, whereas a short form of these articles is sufficient in case of a general partnership, a limited partnership and a cooperative society.

Publication is carried out in two steps: firstly the documents are deposited with the registrar of the commercial court (*préposé du Registre de Commerce et des Sociétés*) within one month of the completion of the deed of incorporation, and are then published in the special companies and association edition of the official gazette (the *Mémorial*) within one month of the deposit with the registrar.

A deed of incorporation, or its short version, may be referred to in litigation only with effect from the date of publication in the *Mémorial*. Any subsequent amendment to the deed must be made in the form required for the formation of the company, failing which it will be deemed null and void.

The law makes no provision as to the language in which these documents may be drafted, but an opinion of the Conseil d'Etat restricts it to French, German and English. In practice, a French or German translation is required for registration purposes if the original is in English.

16.7.2 PRINCIPAL COSTS ON FORMATION

The founder members of a company are responsible for meeting the following charges on the company's formation:

(1) The fees of the notary, whether he is acting at the request of the parties or in fulfilment of legal provisions. The scale of charges is laid down by law.

(2) The registration duty or capital contribution, which is fixed at 1 per cent of the nominal capital.

(3) The registrar's fee for registration in the business register, and the costs of publication in the *Mémorial*.

16.8 SHAREHOLDERS' RIGHTS

Shareholders' rights are mainly pecuniary. They are entitled to receive the proceeds of the company's activity, to participate in the distribution of the share capital during the liquidation of the company and to receive a share in the surplus upon liquidation.

In order to guarantee their pecuniary rights, the shareholders have the right to vote at the shareholders' meeting. Access to information allows the shareholders to use their voting rights efficiently. They have the right to receive or to consult corporate documents in connection with the shareholders' meetings.

17
MERGERS AND ACQUISITIONS

17.1 MERGERS AND HIVE-OFFS

17.1.1 MERGERS

The provisions governing mergers are to be found in arts 257–283 of the company law of 10 August 1915. A merger is a transaction whereby one or more companies may transfer their undertaking to an existing company (*fusion absorption*) or newly formed company (*fusion réunion*). The provisions on mergers apply only to public companies. If other types of companies decide to merge, the absorbed company has to be dissolved and wound up and its assets have to be brought into the absorbing company, whereas there is no winding up under the provisions concerning public limited company mergers.

The provisions also set forth that the consideration for the transfer of the undertaking is the issue of shares in the absorbing company to the shareholders of the absorbed company. It is possible for up to one-tenth of the par value of the shares transferred to be paid in cash.

There is a preparatory phase which consists of negotiations between the companies' managers during which the financial conditions of the transaction are studied and the value of the companies' shares are estimated to establish an exchange value for the shares of the absorbed company. These negotiations may also concern the timing of the transaction or the perfecting of mergers' draft.

The merging companies' boards of directors have to establish in writing a merger draft which will be submitted to the shareholders meeting. This draft has to contain information such as:

(1) the form, name and registered office of each company involved;
(2) the exchange value of the shares;
(3) the date on which the operations of the merging company will

be deemed to be completed from an accounting point of view by the merged company;

(4)   the terms in which the shares of the merging company are handed over;

(5)   the date on which these shares give right to the profits;

(6)   any rights granted to shareholders holding special rights, as well as holders of any securities other than share and other special benefits granted to the shareholders.

This draft has to be examined by independent experts whose main task is to ensure that the fixed exchange value is reasonable and pertinent.

Under art 9 of the law on commercial companies, the draft of a merger plan has to be published at least one month before the shareholders' meeting which has to decide on that draft (art 262).

The draft will be dealt with in a written report by the boards of directors on each company involved, giving an explanation of the merger draft and particularly the exchange value of the shares (art 265), as well as in a written report for the shareholders which has to be established by one or more independent auditors (art 266).

With a few exceptions, the approval of the shareholders' meetings of the two companies is necessary to validate the merger (arts 263–264). Any shareholder has the right at least one month before the date of the shareholders' meeting to examine at the registered office, inter alia, the merger draft and the companies' annual accounts and last three business years' management report.

The minutes of the shareholders' meeting which decide on the merger are established by notarial deed; as is the merger draft, which must be approved by shareholders in all the companies involved in the merger (art 271).

The merger has automatically and simultaneously the following effects (art 274):

(1)   universal transmission of all the assets of the merged company into the merging company;

(2)   the merged company's shareholders become shareholders of the merging company;

(3)   the merged company no longer legally exists;

(4)   cancellation of the merged company's shares held by the merging company or the merged company or a person acting under his own name but on behalf of one of these companies.

The merger becomes effective from the date of the shareholders' meeting which finally approves the transaction and becomes effective against third parties as of the date of the publication of the decision to merge.

As a general rule, the merged company automatically acquires all the rights and obligations of the transferor arising from the reorganisation.

Any creditors of the companies involved in the merger have the right to petition the competent *tribunal de commerce* for an order requiring that the merged company give the necessary guarantees for the payment of the outstanding debts.

17.1.2 HIVE-OFFS

The provisions governing hive-offs are to be found in arts 285–308 of the law on commercial companies of 10 August 1915.

A hive-off is a transaction whereby one company may transfer its undertaking to one or more existing companies (*scission par absorption*) or one or more newly formed companies (*scission par constitution*). The provisions on hive-offs apply only to public limited companies.

The boards of directors of the merging companies have to establish in writing a hive-off draft, which will be subject to the proceedings of the shareholders' meeting. The document must contain the following information: (art 289):

(1) the form, name and registered office of each company involved;
(2) the trade-in value of the shares;
(3) the date on which the operations of the hiving-off company will be deemed to be completed from an accounting point of view by the hived-off company;
(4) the terms of shares' handing of the hiving-off company;
(5) the date on which these shares give right to the profits;
(6) any rights granted to shareholders holding special rights as well as holders of any securities other than share and other special benefits granted to the shareholders.

Under art 9 of the law on commercial companies, the hive-off draft has to be published at least one month before the date of the shareholders' meeting which expresses its opinion about the draft (art 290).

With a few exceptions, the approval by the shareholders' meetings of each of the companies is necessary to validate the hive-off (arts 291–292).

The boards of directors of each company involved establish a written and detailed report explaining and justifying from a legal and economic point of view the hive-off draft and particularly the trade-in value of shares. An independent expert has to examine the draft. Moreover a report on the checking of investments in kind has to be established by an independent auditor.

The creditors of the companies involved, whose claim is previous to the date of the publication of the draft, may seek the constitution of guarantees in case the transaction would reduce the general pledge of these creditors.

17.2 SHARE ACQUISITIONS

17.2.1 GENERAL

Private companies

Private companies are so-called because the personal consideration (*intuitus personae*) is very important for them. It refers generally to small companies, in which the partners trust each other and, in which it is possible to choose the other partners.

Main features of such companies are:

(1) The capital is divided into 'shares of interest' (*parts d'intérêts*) or 'partnership shares' (*parts sociales*).
(2) Shares of interest or partnership shares are in principle not transferable without the unanimous agreement of the other partners.
(3) Death, prohibition (the court decided that this concerned a person who can no longer exercise his rights for reasons of serious mental illness, bankruptcy or insolvency of a partner all entail the winding up of a company (unless otherwise provided for in the articles of association).

These concern two categories of company: the general partnership (*société en nom collectif*) and the limited partnership (*société en commandite simple*).

Public companies

In such companies the partners' personality is not so important. To raise capital, these companies appeal to the public and accept as a partner any person who agrees to offer their financial support.

Main features of such companies are:

(1) The capital is divided into 'shares of stock' (*actions*) or 'partnership shares' (*parts sociales*).

(2) The shares are freely transferable, without requiring the agreement of the partners.

(3) Death, prohibition, bankruptcy or insolvency of a partner does not entail the winding up of the company (unless otherwise provided for in the articles of the company).

These refer to two categories of companies, i.e.: the public limited company (*société anonyme*) and the partnership limited by shares (*société en commandite par actions*).

Limited companies and co-operative companies

As far as limited and co-operative companies are concerned, the difference between private companies and public companies is not so clear. The limited company belongs at one and the same time to the private companies' group, because of the personality of its partners and the limitation of its number as well as the limitations on its transfer of partnership shares; and to the public companies' group because of the limited liability of the partners.

From a fiscal point of view, limited companies are considered public companies.

The co-operative company has to be classified in the private companies' group because it is organised with regard to a partner's personality and not in consideration of the capital brought to the company.

The shares are also not transferable to third parties.

17.2.2 TRANSFER OF SHARES FOR EACH COMPANY

Private companies—general partnership

In principle, shares are not transferable, due to the fact that general partnerships are organised along lines of mutual trust and partners' personality. Nevertheless the transfer of shares is valid when:

(1) it is provided for in the articles of the company, or

(2) there is unanimity of vote on that subject.

If the transfer of shares is authorised, it generally will be stipulated that the co-partners will be able to buy the shares by preference. This transfer is only enforceable on the company when formal notice is given to the company or when it is accepted by the company in a notarial deed.

To be binding on third parties, the transfer must also be published in *Memorial*. The transferor is jointly liable for the debts of a company as long as the transfer has not been published.

Limited partnership (art 21)

The partnership shares or shares of interest are not transferable except where:
(1)　unanimous consent of the partners is obtained;
(2)　the transfer is authorised by the articles of the company;
(3)　the partner dies.

As for general partnerships, the transfer is only binding on the company when formal notice is given to the company or if it is accepted by the company in a notarial deed.

To be binding on third parties, it must be published in the *Mémorial*.

Public companies—public limited company

(1)　Bearer stock shares: the transfer of these shares occurs by handing over the certificate without the knowledge of the company.
(2)　Registered shares: the transfer of shares is valid, only after the final establishment of the company and the full payment of the legal minimum. A transfer may be realised:
　　(a)　by a notification of transfer listed in the registered shareholders' register, dated and signed by the transferor and the transferee or by their general representatives;
　　(b)　by the company which accepts and lists on the register a transfer stated by exchange of letters or other documents establishing the agreement of the transferor and the transferee;
　　(c)　by official document (notarial deed or document served by a process server) given formal notice to the company (art 1690 of Civil Code).
　　Finally, the company deletes from the registered shareholders' register the old registration in order to replace it with a new one in the name of the transferee who receives a new certificate.
(3)　Partly paid share transfer: as long as the shares are partly paid, they have to remain registered shares. As the representative

shares of investments in kind are subject to a previous examination, the limitations on their negotiability become
unnecessary. The state of registered capital will be published
once a year, following the balance sheet (art 48). It concerns:
(a)   the number of subscribed payments;
(b)   the information of actual payments;
(c)   the list of shareholders who have partly paid up their
      shares, with the indication of amounts of which they are
      indebted.

This allows third parties to have information about the
changes among the holders of partly paid shares and also about
actual transfers. Nevertheless the articles of association may
prohibit the transfer of party paid shares or subordinate it to the
authorisation of the board of directors or the general meeting.

(4)   Public sale of shares: must be preceeded by the publication of a
      dated and signed notice of the transferors, and be published in
      the *Mémorial*. This notice must contain the following informa-
      tion (art 33):
      (a)   names, professions and residences of the signatories;
      (b)   date of the articles of association and date of their
            amendments as well as the dates of their publication;
      (c)   object of the company, share capital and number of
            shares;
      (d)   amount of partly paid-up capital and amount remaining
            to pay for each share; number and rate of bonds issued,
            with the statement of possible mortgaged securities;
      (e)   composition of the board of directors and of the auditors;
      (f)   provisions contained in art 27, provisions concerning the
            investments which must be listed in the act of formation
            are not necessary if the company has existed for not less
            than five years;
      (g)   the last balance sheet and the last profit and loss accounts
            or mention of the fact that these have not yet been
            published.

Anyone who wishes to transfer shares has to inform the *Institut
Monétaire Luxembourgeois* at least 15 days in advance and in the
three months which precede the application for admission to
the official listing of the Luxembourg market. This provision
does not apply for the State of Luxembourg or the
municipalities.

Moreover the required publicity does not apply for the transfers ordered by judicial authorities or regulary organised by the *Commission de la Bourse et du Commerce* (arts 36 and 83).

Partnership limited by shares

The provisions concerning public limited companies apply to these companies.

Limited company (arts 189 and 190)

The transfer of shares is authorised:

(1) When it is to a partner (transfer *inter vivos*). If the transferee is not a partner, he has to be approved in advance by the shareholders' meeting; the agreement must be given by partners who represent three-quarters of the registered capital.

The transfer has to be given formal notice to the company by a document served by a process server, or has to be accepted by the company in a notarial deed.

(2) In the case of a partner's death, the shares can only be transferred to his heirs, if they manage to obtain the agreement of the surviving partners who represent three-quarters of the registered capital.

The redemption of shares can be decided by the shareholders' meeting, if a mutual agreement exists with an approved third party or with the company and all the conditions are fulfilled.

The price of the redemption is based on the profits of the last three years, if any, or the last two years' balance sheet. If there was no distribution of profits, and if no agreement has been made as to the way the purchase price is to be calculated, the court will determine the price if no agreement can be found.

17.3 ACQUISITION OF GOODWILL

Goodwill is often considered as the sum of intangible and tangible assets, linked together for a common purpose. The acquisition of goodwill concerns, unless otherwise agreed, all assets which contribute to the prosperity and working of the vendor's business.

Certain elements may be excluded by agreement of the parties, on condition that transferred assets permit the purchaser to take full advantage of goodwill. Thus the enjoyment of premises is considered a main element.

Goods are generally included in the transfer but they are often sold separately at a separate price, fixed at the moment of their actual delivery and according to the rates of the day.

The trademark is also included in the transfer, unless otherwise agreed.

The transfer of goodwill is generally linked with the right of the transferee to use the known business name to indicate the goodwill.

The law provides that the vendor of goodwill gives implied warranties as follows:

(1) he will not set up in business in competition with the goodwill. This warranty is implied by law, but it is common to make specific arrangements in the purchase agreement which may increase its ambit. However, like all non-competition clauses, it will only be enforceable if it is related to a limited territory and if it is for a reasonable period of time;

(2) the purchaser will have quiet enjoyment;

(3) there are no defects in any constituent part of the sold goodwill not discoverable by due diligence.

18
AGENCY

18.1 BACKGROUND

The Luxembourg constitution guarantees the freedom of commerce and industry. A business may be operated through intermediaries. The many categories of intermediaries in commerce and industry reflect the diversity of economic life. There exist in Luxembourg commercial agents, commission agents and brokers who are considered to be independents; and sales representatives who are employees and are considered to be subordinates to and controlled by their employers.

18.2 COMMERCIAL AGENTS

The commercial agent does business for consideration on behalf of a client and not in his own name. The commercial agent is self-employed, in which case he is qualified as a trader.

18.2.1 ABSENCE OF SPECIFIC LUXEMBOURG LEGISLATION

The commercial agent's profession is regulated by the Civil Code in art 1984 et seq. Luxembourg law has no particular rules which govern agency contracts. At the present time a Bill is pending in Parliament ('the Bill') which would clearly define the commercial agent, his rights and duties, his consideration and his relationship with the client. This draft is the result of harmonising the Luxembourg legislation with the Council Directive of 18 December 1986.

An agency contract is a contract whereby an independent agent handles the business of one or several clients in a specific territory. There is a Benelux Convention on agency giving detailed provisions for these particular contracts, but unfortunately it has not yet come into force.

18.2.2 PERFORMANCE OF THE CONTRACT

As there are no specific rules on agency, the parties determine their rights and duties contractually. The following are typical provisions of such agreements:

(1) assignment of a territory;
(2) exclusive or non-exclusive agency;
(3) confidentiality;
(4) description of products concerned;
(5) minimum quantities to be sold;
(6) use of trademarks and name;
(7) duration;
(8) amount and method of determination of commission (this will be regulated by the Bill. We would certainly talk about fixed sums, commission or consideration in accordance with commercial practice or a 'reasonable consideration');
(9) indemnities to be paid upon determination.

All these rights and duties, now determined contractually, will be regulated by the Bill. In his relationship with the client, the agent has to safeguard the client's interests and each party has to act honourably and in good faith.

Generally it is stipulated that the commercial agent may not compete with the client's business for a certain period of time after termination of the relationship. Such clause must be in writing. To be valid, the non-competition clause must:

(1) be restricted to specific activities that are similar to those of the employer:
(2) not exceed a period of 12 months after the date of termination of the agreement;
(3) be limited geographically to cities where competition with the employer is possible, but it can in no circumstances extend beyond the Luxembourg borders.

A non-competition clause is not binding if the employer has illegally terminated the agreement.

During the duration of the employment contract, the employee must perform his duties in good faith and respect the terms of his agreement. If he does compete with his employer, the latter may terminate the agreement with good cause.

The extent of client liability to acts of agents depends on the agent's relationship with his client. If the agent acts in the name of and on behalf of the client, then the latter is fully liable. Moreover if the agent acts beyond his authority, he can also be liable if the third party in good faith relied on the agent's 'apparent authority'.

18.2.3 TERMINATION OF AGENCY CONTRACTS

The termination of agency is regulated by the law of 1 July 1988. Unless otherwise agreed by the parties, an agency contract terminates by the dismissal or the resignation of the agent, the incapacity of adults, bankruptcy or similar proceeding, as well as the death of the agent or the client. Any party terminating the agreement unilaterally must respect a mandatory notice period.

The agreement may be terminated without notice for serious reasons, ie for acts or omissions making continuation of the employment contract impossible, as, for instance absence from work without a valid excuse, or refusal to execute orders given by the employer.

If the employer illegally terminates an employment contract the employee may sue for damages.

The Bill will certainly contain the right of eviction compensation (*garantie d'éviction*) with regard to the Council Directive.

18.3 COMMISSION AGENTS (*COMMISSIONAIRES*)

A commission agent is one who acts for another person, the client, but in his own name, without revealing the identity of the person for whom he acts.

18.4 BROKERS

A broker is a person who makes his living by bringing together persons who wish to enter into a particular kind of contract, without his further intervention.

18.5 THE COMMISSION AGENT'S CONTRACT

The commission agent may act as another trader's commissioned agent. He acts in the name of and on behalf of the trader from whom he received the commission. However, and unlike *commissionaire*, he reveals the identity of the person for whom he acts.

If the commissioned agent is not a trader, the contract is governed by the Civil Code. In practice, a person qualifying himself as a broker may in fact be a commissioned agent or a *commissionaire* too. It is therefore important to investigate the facts in detail for each operation in order to determine to which category an agent really belongs.

18.6 COMMERCIAL REPRESENTATIVES

A representative under an employment contract, supervised by his employer, is an employee whose rights and duties are regulated by labour law.

19
DISTRIBUTORSHIP

19.1 DEFINITION

The distributor is an independent trader, doing business for his own benefit, but he represents one or more suppliers or manufacturers.

19.2 LEGISLATION

As for agents, Luxembourg has no specific legislation on distribution agreements. Thus the same principle of freedom of contracts applies as for independent agents.

19.3 TERMS AND CLAUSES OF THE AGREEMENT

The supplier and the distributor often agree on exclusivity clauses, whereby the supplier commits himself to sell only the products of a particular supplier. Since a grand-ducal decree of 1965, clauses indicating that the distributor may not sell under a price notified by the supplier, are forbidden.

The distributor and the supplier may agree on minimum targets of sale to be achieved during the duration of the agreement, and on the notice period in case of termination.

19.4 TERMINATION

As a general rule, the termination of distribution agreements shall be in accordance with the provisions of the agreement. If the agreement is entered into for a fixed term, it ends with its term. If the agreement is for an undetermined period, either party may terminate it. But in accordance with the general principles of the Civil Code an agreement has to be executed at all times in good faith.

The rights of each party have to be respected without abuse. An agreement which is for an undetermined period may not be terminated by one party without sufficient notice. In cases where an agreement is illegally terminated, or the agreed notice period is not respected, damages may be claimed.

In such cases the courts are free to determine the appropriate notice period and the amount of damages. To do so the courts will take into consideration the share of total sales of the distributor's products, the turnover of those products and the profits thereof, and the opportunity for the distributor to find similar products elsewhere (Court of Appeal, 11 July 1972, Pasicrisie XXII, 194).

If the parties have agreed upon an amount of indemnification for the clients of the distributor, that amount has to be paid. If the parties had not come to an agreement, the court may find the supplier liable for payment thereof in cases where the distributor proves that the major part of his turnover results from the sale of the supplier's products.

20
FRANCHISING

20.1 LEGISLATION

Luxembourg law has no separate body of legislation relating to franchising. Franchising contracts are governed by contract law in general, as well as by a combination of rules which affect the contract, ie, contract law, employment law, or intellectual property law. The definition given by the draft regulation of the EC commission on certain categories of franchise agreements 1987 20CE No C 229/3 may be withheld.

A franchising agreement is defined as 'an agreement whereby a business enterprise ("the franchisor") grants to another business enterprise ("the franchisee") in exchange for monetary consideration, the right to operate a franchise for the sale of goods and the carrying out of services for end users'.

20.2 DRAFTING OF A FRANCHISE AGREEMENT

As no specific legislation on franchising exists in Luxembourg, no special registration or notification needs to be made by the franchisor or by the franchisee.

As there is no general provision on franchising, distribution or commercial agency in Luxembourg, the parties may freely arrange their respective rights and obligations, provided that they do not contravene Luxembourg public policy.

The laws of 17 June 1970 on restrictive commercial practice, and of 27 November 1986 listing certain unfair trading practices and penalising unfair competition (see chapter 15) must be kept in mind when a franchising contract is concluded.

A franchising agreement which could be regarded as a concerted practice affecting both free competition and public interests may thus be prohibited. The same may apply, in cases where dominant position implies an unfair advantage of affecting the public interest.

Provisions regarding trade restraints are generally valid if they are limited in space and time, otherwise they may be considered as violating the constitutional principle of freedom of trade, as well as the principle of free competition.

20.3 CHARACTERISTICS

According to civil law principles applicable in Luxembourg, a contract may be established for a definite or indefinite period of time. Contracting parties are bound to observe the contractual term, except in case of a mutual consent to terminate earlier than previously arranged. Contracts for an indefinite period of time may be unilaterally terminated by either party, subject to giving prior notice within a reasonable period.

No special regulation exists, other than that set out above, regarding transfer of know-how, royalty rates or management service fees, grant back of know-how in improvements, ownership of know-how, sales quotas, minimum sales requirement, the sale of the business or the franchise by the franchisee, exclusive territories, guarantee of corporate franchisee's obligations by an individual shareholder, or the transfer of shares in a corporate franchisee. Accordingly, normal contract and commercial law applies, as well as the relevant EC rules.

Compensation upon termination may only be granted to the franchisee in cases of an unfair termination by the franchisor, or if a penalty clause has been agreed upon.

21

REAL PROPERTY AND SUCCESSION

In this chapter we will try to give a general view of land transactions and the main provisions of succession law, while pointing out rules which will need to be kept in mind in commercial dealings with Luxembourg individuals and corporations.

21.1 REAL PROPERTY

Real property, eg, land and buildings, may be acquired by accession (increase of existing land by act of nature), contract, inheritance or prescription (adverse possession which must be continuous, public, unequivocal and peaceful).

21.1.1 SALE AND PURCHASE

Transfers of real property interests by contract must be made by notarial act and registered in the mortgage registry. No restrictions on ownership of real property for foreigners apply.

A contract for the sale of real property for building needs to be the *acte authentique* ie a notarial deed which should provide the following information:

(1) real estate and building owner's identity;
(2) date of issue and conditions affecting administrative permits;
(3) description of the part of the real estate sold;
(4) price and payment conditions;
(5) delivery date;
(6) completion guarantee by the terms of the contract. This guarantee is not required for buildings constructed by the State, a municipality, a public institution or a corporate controlled by one of these institutions.

A *compromis de vente* (sale compromise) generally precedes the conclusion of the contract before a notary whereby parties indicate the general terms of the contract and set a penalty in case of non-signature by one party. This agreement is totally binding on the parties to the contract. However it is not enforceable on third parties.

No general right of pre-emption exists in Luxembourg. However, in certain circumstances, a right of pre-emption is granted, for instance, for a farm tenant, or even a hirer when the leasing has lasted more than a certain period. Moreover, tax authorities may increase the purchase price when the purchase value has been excessively reduced in order to assess the proper registration duty due.

Notary fees and sales and registration duty expenses are usually paid by the purchaser. Notary fees depend on the amount of the transaction, and are determined in a schedule of charges. Registration duty (*droits d'enregistrement*) is assessed on the market value of property transferred.

Fixed rates ranging from LF 100 (the standard rate) to LF 100,000 are applicable in the case of acts which do not involve any obligation of money or money's worth, or the transfer of ownership, usufruct or enjoyment of real personal property; this is a duty levied for the preparation of the legal act, which is payable when the acts are registered.

A proportional duty, according to the nature and purpose of the legal procedure involved, is levied on any transfers between living persons for the ownership, usufruct or enjoyment of real property. Legal acts on which proportional duty is payable are not liable to the fixed duty.

The standard rate of taxation is 6 per cent on transfers of immovable property. However, this rate is increased to 50 per cent if the real estate is situated in the City of Luxembourg or in Esch/ Alzette. A transcription duty of 1 per cent is also levied by the registrar.

A reduced rate of 1.2 per cent applies for real estate sold in the case of bankruptcy, and under certain conditions for social real estate.

If the purchaser declares to the notary public at the signature of the deed that he purchases with the intention to resell, the registration duty is 7.2 per cent. In such case the buyer will obtain a reimbursement of 6 per cent if he resells within a five year period.

As there is no registration tax on sales of shares of a civil company (*société civile immobilière*) except a fixed duty to register the transaction, the practice of ownership of property by means of such a company has been furthered. To reduce tax advantages the legislator amended income tax rules so that for direct taxation purposes the sale of shares in a civil company is equivalent to the sale of real property, and subject to taxation following the rules applicable to capital gains.

Real property may be subject to easements which should also be revealed in the purchase deed. The vendor of real property gives two warranties by law: enjoyment (*garantie d'éviction*) and freedom from inherent defects (*garantis des vices cachés*).

The guarantee of quiet enjoyment may be excluded or specifically disposed of by the parties in a special clause, for instance in the case of goodwill for a clause of no reestablishment.

The vendor of real estate may omit the warranty of freedom from inherent defects, but this exclusion will not apply for apparent defects discovered before the expiry of a term of one month after the date occupation began. Also, this exclusion is prohibited if the vendor is a professional. If an operative hidden defect is discovered and if the vendor was a professional or did not know of the defects, he only will be liable to return the sale price and costs incurred by the sale. Damages could be claimed otherwise.

The vendor of real estate is liable for ten years from the completion of work for inherent defects as architects, constructors, and any person bound to the constructing authority are themselves liable under the rules relating to the ten-year guarantee.

The buyer must declare the defect to the seller within a short period of time, which is not further defined by the law. He must then start proceedings within one year of this declaration. If the price paid is very low (*rescision pour lésion*), the vendor may, within two years of completion and after registration of the sale, rescind the contract. He should prove that the price he received was less than five-twelfths of the fair market price at the time of sale.

21.1.2 BUSINESS LEASES

Immovable property or that part of the real estate to which the lease agreement either expressly forecasts such attribution, or which is intended for trade or industry, and where such activity is principally exercised is considered to be premises for commercial or industrial use.

The business tenant has a certain security of tenure. The law makes a compromise between rights of the lessee to preserve his clientele and his goodwill and the rights of the owner to dispose of his premises. Thus, art 1762 of the Civil Code states that all tenants on premises for commercial purposes who exploit a goodwill have the right to obtain the renewal of their contract without preference to any other person. The tenant loses this right after the 15th year of renting. To evict such tenants sooner, the owner must make a genuine and serious offer, and the tenant refuse to pay an amount equal to it.

The owner could object to the exercise of the preference right:

(1)   in cases of legitimate grievance at the discretion of the relevant judge,

(2)   for a personal occupation by the owner or his children etc,

(3)   in case of surrender of hiring for commercial purposes,

(4)   in the case of building or development of the property.

The legislator wished to restrict the tenant's right of preference to avoid limiting the right of the owner in creating an assessment.

Unlike normal lease contracts, the price is determined by the parties and an indexation clause is valid. The tenant must strictly respect the user convenant. In case of a transformation without the owner's agreement, the lease may be cancelled.

21.2   SUCCESSION

Succession law is quite close to French law, as they share the same model: the French Civil Code. The same rules apply for a deceased person if he has children. If he has one child, half his estate must go to that child; if he has two, two-thirds must go to them equally, and in the case of three or more, three-quarters of the estate passes to them in equal shares. It is in fact impossible to disinherit a child.

Where there is no will a surviving spouse has the right to at least a quarter of the estate or the life-long interest (*usufruit*) of the real estate commonly occupied by the spouses and movables included, provided that the real estate was owned by the deceased in whole or conjointly with the surviving spouse.

In a few words, we would like to point out the lower rates of taxation available in Luxembourg. There is no tax due in cases of inheritance in direct line and the maximum rate is 15 per cent with certain increases depending on the amount of the succession.

Finally, a few remarks relating to the notion of marriage contracts which still have an influence in business dealings. It is not necessary for a couple to enter into a marriage contract, but if a couple does not, the partners are deemed to be married under the regime of community on the acquired assets which means broadly that they each have a half share in the assets acquired during the marriage, except for assets received by gift or inheritance by one of the spouses. If another regime is chosen, typically the separation of goods, each spouse keeps the assets brought to the marriage and any assets acquired thereafter.

22
IMMIGRATION AND EMPLOYMENT

22.1 IMMIGRATION

22.1.1 NON-EC NATIONALS

Right to reside

(1) In principle, all the non-EC nationals who intend to reside in Luxembourg for less than three months must present themselves to the competent local authority in the area in which the individuals intend to reside in order to submit a notification of entry within eight days of their entry into Luxembourg.

(2) All non-EC nationals who intend to reside in Luxembourg for more than three months but not exceeding one year, and who have kept in their home country their own residence, must go to the relevant local authority in the area in which the individuals intend to reside, in order to make a notification of entry within eight days of their entry into Luxembourg.

Moreover they have to present to the Ministry of Justice an application for authorisation of temporary establishment. Documents giving details of their financial means of support in Luxembourg and the purpose of their stay have to be attached to the application.

The authorisation for temporary residence is delivered against the payment of a tax. Thus, it is not necessary to ask for an identity card of a foreign person.

All non-EC nationals who are more than 15 years old and who intend to reside in Luxembourg for more than three months must, within eight days of their entry into Luxembourg if they come from a foreign country, or as soon as they are 15 years old if born in Luxembourg (or if they have come to Luxembourg before reaching fifteen), present themselves to the competent local authority in the area in which they intend to reside in order to ask for an alien's identity card. The delivery of this card is equivalent to an authorisation of residence.

In order to obtain the identity card, they have to prove that
(1)   they have paid the legal tax;
(2)   they have entered Luxembourg lawfully;
(3)   they have adequate accommodation.

Moreover they have to provide a medical certificate (see below).

The document delivered by the local authority will be equivalent to an authorisation of temporary residence. It is the Ministry of Justice which is exclusively competent to deliver identity cards to foreigners. The card will be equivalent to an authorisation to reside permanently in Luxembourg. In principle the authorisation is valid for five years, with effect from the day of delivery and is renewable thereafter. As an exception to this rule, a foreign worker employed by a foreign firm and seconded to Luxembourg for the completion of work for a foreseeable period of one year or less, is excused from applying for an alien's identity card.

Right to work

The engagement of foreign labour is governed by the provisions of the law of 28 March 1972 on the right of foreigners to enter and stay in Luxembourg, their medical examination, and the employment of foreign labour.

Employee

An employer wishing to employ a non-EC national to work in Luxembourg on a regular basis as a salaried employee must obtain authorisation for him to do so from the Minister of Labour or his deputy, before the employee arrives in Luxembourg and make the relevant social security declarations. When making his application, the employer must give to the Department of Employment, having jurisdiction over the employer's place of work, information about the person he wishes to employ.

The Department of Employment examines the application. The document it delivers operates as a provisional work permit. Work permits are issued by the Minister of Labour or his deputy on the recommendation of the Department of Employment, which takes into account the situation, tendency and pattern of the labour market. Delivery and renewal of permits are liable to a legal tax.

Under the regulation, there are four types of work permit:

(1) Permit A, is allowed for a maximum of one year, and is valid in principle only for a fixed profession and for a fixed employer.

(2) Permit B is available to all non-EC nationals who can prove uninterrupted residence and employment in the Grand Duchy for not less than one year. It is valid for four years and only for a fixed profession, but for any employer.

(3) Permit C is available to:
   (a) all non-EC nationals who can prove uninterrupted residence and employment in the Grand Duchy for not less than five years; or
   (b) all workers who were born in Luxembourg and who have resided in Luxembourg without interruption for two or more years before asking for a work permit.

   This permit is valid for any profession and for any employer and its duration of validity is not limited.

(4) Permit D concerns apprentices and trainees and it is valid only for the duration of apprenticeship or training period.

A work permit of whatever category becomes invalid if its holder is away from Luxembourg for any uninterrupted period of more than six months.

Self-employed

A Ministry of Economic Affairs' written authorisation is necessary to undertake or exercise (—for either the principal or a subsidiary purpose of business—), one of the following independent professions:

(1) sole traders and manufacturers;

(2) sales representatives, commission agents, brokers and commercial travellers;

(3) haulage contractors and passenger transport operators or the holders of machines or engines, the purpose of whose business is to lease their equipment;

(4) craftsmen;

(5) independent architects and engineers;

(6) landscape painters and such persons who act on behalf of others;

(7) independent qualified accountants.

Authorisation is necessary for individual and corporate entities. If an alien wishes to undertake an activity which may prejudice the national economy, the authorisation may be refused.

The authorisation's duration of validity is unlimited only if the home country of the worker grants the same rights to Luxembourg nationals in that country.

Note In principle, any alien who intends to reside in Luxembourg for more than three months in order to undertake an activity as an employee or as a self-employed person, is subject to a medical examination within eight days of his entry into Luxembourg.

22.1.2 EC NATIONALS

Under the provisions of the Grand Ducal Regulation of 28 March 1972 on the 'conditions of entry and stay of certain categories of aliens covered by international convention', a national of any of the Member States of the EC needs only to produce a national identity card or a passport which is valid and the validity of which is for at least five years in order to enter Luxembourg territory.

If he wishes to stay for more than three months in Luxembourg, authority to do so is granted by virtue of being issued with a residence permit for a national of a Member State of the European Community.

Application for a permit has to be made to the local authority which is responsible for receiving notifications of entry. The permit is valid for five years and is initially renewable for ten years automatically.

As far as employment is concerned, Luxembourg nationals and the nationals of other Member States of the EC are treated alike.

22.1.3 FRONTIER WORKER'S CARD

All EC nationals who work in Luxembourg but who reside in their home country, from where they commute every day or at least once a week, must ask the local authority in which they work for a frontier worker's card. This document is issued by the Ministry of Justice for a period of five years is renewable.

22.2 EMPLOYMENT

22.2.1 LEGISLATION

Relations between employees and employers are governed by the law of 24 May 1989 and by art 1779 et seq of the Civil Code.

22.2.2 EMPLOYMENT CONTRACT

A labour contract is a contract by which a legal person undertakes to put its activity at the disposal of another one, under the orders of which it is placed, for consideration. Under Luxembourg law, the relationship between employees and employers is an individual one. The employer must enter into a contract in writing with each of his employees and their mutual rights and obligations are governed by art 1979 et seq of the Civil Code, as well as by the law dated 24 May 1989.

To be valid, the contract must have the consent of the parties who must have legal capacity and the agreement must be for good and proper cause and consideration. A contract of service must always be produced in writing and in duplicate. It must contain:

(1)   the type of employment and the nature of the work;
(2)   the starting salary and, where applicable, the periodic increments and the agreed commissions or share offers;
(3)   any agreed clauses which are more favourable to the employee than these statutorily required.

Fixed term contracts are unusual. All employment contracts have to be concluded for an indefinite term and exceptionally for a fixed term, only in specific circumstances such as:

(1)   where a permanent employee is temporarily absent and he must be replaced;
(2)   where a particular job is of a seasonal nature;
(3)   where there is a need to fulfil a specific task;
(4)   where there is a need to fulfil an exceptional order;
(5)   where there is a temporary increase in business;
(6)   where it is usual for certain contracts to have recourse to fixed term contract.

In principle the duration of a fixed term contract may not exceed 24 months including any renewal.

A contract of service can be terminated at any time by one of the parties. Unilateral termination is lawful only if its conforms to the prescribed procedure and time limits.

A worker can resign from the contract after giving notice in writing or orally. The employer is bound to release the worker from his contract by registered letter.

Moreover the employer must inform the Department of

Employment and, if the worker is dismissed, state the reasons therefor if he so requests.

A contract of employment cannot be terminated by an employer during the employee's absence on sick leave for a period not exceeding 26 weeks. It is also forbidden to terminate the contract of a female worker immediately following her marriage, during pregnancy or during the 12 weeks following childbirth.

A party revoking the contract without complying with the prescribed time limits has to pay compensation to the other party equivalent to the wage payable during the period of non-compliance. A dismissed worker is entitled by law to receive a severance payment granted according to the length of service.

In the event of gross misconduct by one of the parties, the law recognises the right of the other party to terminate the contract. To be valid, the termination must be communicated by registered letter within three clear days of the misconduct and must state the grounds for termination.

Termination of a contract owing to gross misconduct entitles the innocent party to damages with interest.

22.2.3 WORKING CONDITIONS

The statutory working day in Luxembourg is eight hours. The working week is a standard one of 40 hours.

Hours of work are defined by law as the length of time during which the employee is at the disposal of his employer(s). Under the law of 22 April 1966 all employees in the private sector receive a standard period of annual leave. This holiday is set at 25 days, irrespective of the age of the employee. The qualification for this leave is three months' uninterrupted service with the same employer.

If the employee has been absent for more than 10 per cent of the time when he should have been at work during the previous year without good reason, the employer is entitled to refuse leave.

The following are considered good reasons:
(1) absence authorised by the employer;
(2) absence due to accident:
(3) absence due to illness;
(4) absence during a public holiday;
(5) lawful strike;

22.2.4 MATERNITY LEAVE

This is governed by the law of 3 July 1975. Maternity leave applies whether the mother is married or single. Such leave does not interrupt the contract of service. The contract comes back into force when the reason for its suspension ceases to exist.

Maternity leave is divided into two categories:

(1) pre-natal leave consists of the eight weeks prior the expected date of confinement, with extension if necessary, to the actual date;

(2) post-natal leave consists of the eight weeks after the confinement, with extension if necessary:
   (a) in the case of premature birth:
   (b) in the case of a multiple confinement;
   (c) in the case of a breast-feeding mother.

22.2.5 WORKER REPRESENTATION

Luxembourg law provides for two main categories of worker representation.

Staff representatives

Businesses employing 15 or more paid employees must appoint staff representatives.

In businesses where the employees do not exceed 100 workers, manual workers and staff elect jointly a single staff committee. When businesses have more than 100 employees, including at least 15 manual workers and 15 staff, separate committees are elected.

When businesses employ five or more young workers aged under 21, the workers elect their own representatives.

Staff committees consist of a number of representatives in proportion with the total number of employees in the firm. The staff representatives are elected for a five-years' period and may be re-elected. Their job is to defend the interests of the employees concerning questions of working conditions, job security and social legislation.

Representatives must have time to carry out their duties. Moreover, there are special legal provisions protecting staff representatives from dismissal.

Joint works councils

The law of 6 May 1974 provides for joint works councils which are composed of an equal number of management and of employees' representatives, which varies according to the number of persons employed by the establishment concerned.

All businesses employing 150 salaried employees during a period of three years are obliged to appoint a works council. Works councils have to be set up in the month following the publication of the result of the election for the personnel delegation.

In the case of a newly established firm, the works council comes into being within three months. The same applies when the number of employees reaches the point at which the provisions begin to apply.

The employer's representatives are appointed by the head of the concern on any basis he chooses. The employees' representatives are elected by proportional representation in a secret ballot of the personnel delegates; to be elected they have to be employed in the firm for not less than one year.

Labour unions

Labour union freedom is guaranteed under art 11 of the Constitution.

Luxembourg workers are organised on a voluntary basis into three main labour unions, whose principal task is to negotiate collective agreements.

Employers are similarly organised into a number of professional and trade groups.

22.2.6 SOCIAL SECURITY

The social security system is built around a series of independent public institutions, each insuring a particular kind of risk, and organised into socio-professional categories.

The social security system covers sickness insurance including maternity insurance and insurance payable upon death, invalidity insurance, old age insurance, insurance for the surviving members of a family, accident insurance, unemployment insurance and payments to the family.

23
TAXATION

23.1 INTRODUCTION

The Luxembourg system of taxation bears some similarity to the German system and tax decisions given by the German courts are a useful guide to the interpretation of Luxembourg tax law. It also shares common features with the French and Belgian systems.

The three most significant dates in Luxembourg's fiscal history are the following:

1839 : Treaty of London which proclaimed Luxembourg's independence. Adoption of the Netherlands' direct taxation legislation applicable prior to 1830, indirect taxation legislation being an inheritance of the French Revolution.

1921 : Luxembourg concludes with Belgium the Belgian-Luxembourg Economic Union (BLEU) which provided for a customs union and imposed special tax on certain products (excise duties).

1940 : During the Occupation, German legislation replaced that of Luxembourg.

After the Liberation, the Luxembourg legislator re-established provisions of law applicable prior to the War, relating to the circulation of goods and provisions of the BLEU. However, German legislation which related to direct taxation was temporarily maintained, and is still applicable today except for personal income tax (*Einkommenssteuer*) and corporate tax (*Körperschaftssteuer*) which were abolished in 1967 and superseded by the law of 4 December 1967 on income tax.

Under the law of 5 August 1969, value added tax replaced turnover tax, in order to fulfil community requirements.

In conclusion, Luxembourg tax law has been directly or indirectly influenced by several foreign legal systems. However, the Luxembourg legislator has adapted and brought in the necessary modifications without being bound by the evolution of legislation in these countries. In addition, to develop Luxembourg as an attractive financial centre, some specific laws have been implemented to attract foreign investors.

23.2 VALUE ADDED TAX

This is a tax payable by any entity who, or which (on a regular basis) performs independent activities connected with an economic activity and by importers.

The tax is due when goods or services are supplied against payment within Luxembourg by a taxable person in the course of his business, or when goods are imported or produced by the undertaking for its own purposes which would not give right to total VAT deduction if they were bought by an external supplier. Certain supplies of services are however subject to specific rules with regard to the territoriality of the tax.

The basis of assessment for goods and supplies of services is on the remuneration received (exclusive of VAT). In the case of private use, the normal value is used. For imports, the basis available is the purchase price or normal value plus all charges, duties (other than VAT) and incidental expenses involved up to the first point of destination of the goods within Luxembourg.

The tax charged on goods and services used for business purposes may be deducted by the taxable person from the tax payable by him in respect of taxable transactions carried out by him.

The tax rates were, prior to 1 January 1992: 3, 6 and 12 per cent. In order to meet the community requirements, the rate of 12 per cent will be progressively replaced by a rate of 15 per cent, whereas the rate of 6 per cent should be abolished in favour of the rate of 3 per cent.

23.3 PERSONAL TAX

Individuals resident in Luxembourg are taxable on their worldwide income. An individual is resident if either his main residence is in Luxembourg, or if he spends more than 183 days a year in

Luxembourg otherwise than for merely temporary purposes. Credit for foreign taxes is given up to the amount of the Luxembourg income tax payable on that foreign income. Non-resident individuals are taxable only on specific types of Luxembourg-source income.

Taxable income in the hands of an individual is calculated by reference to eight categories, according to different rules, though losses made in one category may generally be set off against income from another:

(1) commercial profits (including income from commerce, industry, handicraft and transferred income);
(2) agricultural and forestry profits;
(3) independent profession profits;
(4) net wages and salary income;
(5) net pensions and annuities income;
(6) net investment income;
(7) net rental income;
(8) miscellaneous income.

In addition, short term capital gains (within two years for real estate and six months for other property) are taxed as ordinary income. Gains on real estate held for longer than two years are taxed at 50 per cent of the effective overall income tax rate. A deduction of LF 2,000,000 (LF 4,000,000 for married taxpayers) on capital gains is available once every ten years. Main residences are exempt. Certain additional rebates are available for inherited property.

In general the method of assessing and collecting the tax due is the same for non-residents as for residents, except that only income accruing in Luxembourg is taxable, and no deduction is made for certain special expenses or for extraordinary charges. Income tax for non-residents only is collected by withholding at source tax due on income from self-employed literary and artistic activities (10 per cent of gross receipts), and company directors' fees (8.2 per cent of gross fees). Tax is withheld at source on wages, salaries, pensions and annuities, and directors' fees paid by employers.

Progressive rates of income tax apply to both residents and non-residents ranging from 0 to 50 per cent (on 1992 income). For 1992, the tax charge is increased by an unemployment contribution of 2.5 per cent. The income tax burden is lowered for taxpayers with dependant children.

Deductions may be claimed for expenses incurred in generating income. A standard deduction of LF 21,000 is available for salary-related expenses, excluding travel expenses. In addition, a flat deduction for travel expenses between home and the place of work is granted amounting to LF 3,900 per unit with a flat minimum deduction of LF 15,600 per annum and a maximum of LF 117,000.

Compulsory social security contributions are fully deductible. In addition, various kinds of insurance premiums and interest on loans are deductible subject to certain ceilings.

23.4 CORPORATE INCOME TAX

23.4.1 COMPUTATION OF TAXABLE PROFIT

Luxembourg corporation tax (*Impôt sur le revenu des collectivités* (IRC) is levied on profits made by the *sociétés de capitaux* (*sociétés anonymes, sociétés en commandite par actions, sociétés à responsabilité limitée*), *sociétés coopératives* and by permanent establishments owned by a non-resident company.

The rate of corporate income tax on resident and non-resident corporations is 33 per cent plus a 1 per cent surcharge for unemployment contributions.

The following are generally exempted from the IRC: professional associations which do not directly or indirectly carry on an economic undertaking, 1929 holding companies (see below) and investment funds.

Sociétés de personnes which have a corporate structure are nevertheless regarded as fiscally transparent for tax purposes. *Sociétés civiles, sociétés en commandite simple* and *sociétés en nom collectif* are not directly taxed but the partners' shares of profits corresponding to the partnership share in the company are aggregated with global income for income tax purposes.

In addition, municipal business tax is levied, partly based on trade income and partly on trade capital. Municipal business tax is imposed on businesses situated in Luxembourg regardless of their legal form of ownership. The tax rate is 9.09 per cent on taxable income.

A net worth tax is also payable by corporations, non-residents and branches owning assets in Luxembourg. The tax is assessed on the total value of property at the beginning of the year less debts, with a minimum of LF 500,000. The tax rate is 0.5 per cent.

23.4.2 CORPORATIONS HAVING FAVOURABLE TAX REGIMES

Luxembourg holding companies, under the law of 1929 which are normally set up as a *sociétés anonyme*, operate in a special tax regime, but the company's objects must be limited to the holding of and the management of investments. No commercial, or industrial activity may be conducted. Luxembourg holding companies are exempt from all income and capital taxes, and no withholding tax rates apply on income distributed to non-residents.

The only taxes payable are the contribution duty of 1 per cent on the issue and further issue of share capital, and the subscription tax at 0.2 per cent per annum on capital, with a minimum of LF 2,000.

Billionaire holding companies are standard holding companies which have a minimum share capital of LF 1,000 million. The only difference between these companies and standard holding companies is that in place of the subscription tax, an income tax of a minimum of LF 2 million per annum is assessed on the amount paid in respect of (i) interest paid to the holders of bonds and transferable securities, (ii) dividends distributed to shareholders and (iii) fees and salaries paid to directors, statutory auditors and liquidators residing less than six months a year in Luxembourg.

Luxembourg participation companies (*Soparfi*) are, unlike 1929 holding companies, covered by tax treaties and therefore limited withholding tax rates apply. A *Soparfi* is subject to taxation as an ordinary corporation under the common tax law as described in 23.4.1. However, they enjoy a tax exemption for both dividends received and capital gains made upon disposal of shares held in other companies.

Dividends received from a domestic or foreign shareholdings are exempt, provided that the shareholding held is at least 10 per cent or the acquisition cost was at least LF 50 million, and has been owned for 12 months preceding the year of receipt.

Capital gains from the disposal of a domestic or foreign shareholding are exempt if the shareholding held is of at least 25 per cent or the acquisition cost was at least LF 250 million, and the holding was owned for 12 months preceding the year of disposal. To obtain these tax exemptions, the subsidiary must be subject to an income tax similar to that of Luxembourg.

Unlike the 1929 holding companies, *Soparfis* are subject to dividend withholding tax at the standard rate of 15 per cent in Luxembourg. However, no withholding tax is due when dividends are paid from a Luxembourg corporation to another Luxembourg corporation, provided the provisions of the dividend exemption outlined above are met and a reduced withholding tax rate applies to dividends distributed to shareholders located in jurisdictions that have concluded a double taxation agreement with Luxembourg. Moreover, as the EC Parent and Subsidiary Directive has been implemented by Luxembourg legislation, dividend payments to a parent company in another EC country will be exempt from Luxembourg withholding tax, if the parent holds at least 25 per cent of the capital of the Luxembourg subsidiary, and the relevant holding was held without interruption for at least two years at the date the dividend is paid.

Captive insurance companies have to take the form of a public limited liability company with a minimum capital of LF 50 million.

Reinsurance companies are subject to standard Luxembourg taxes (see 23.4.1) but are entitled to create generous reserves which are deductible against losses from taxable income. As captive insurance companies in Luxembourg are fully taxable, they have in principle access to the double tax treaties to which Luxembourg is a party.

Investment funds based in Luxembourg are exempt from income tax, municipal business tax, tax on capital gains and withholding tax on dividends distribution. Consequently, double tax treaties are not applicable. A minimum capital of LF 50 million is required. The only tax payable is the contribution duty of 1 per cent on incorporation and a subscription tax of 0.06 per cent per annum on the net asset value of the fund.

Shipping companies are liable to common corporation tax applicable to any Luxembourg corporation except the municipal business tax. Moreover, shipping companies may benefit from tax reductions available to Luxembourg companies for structural investments (ie a tax credit up to 14 per cent of the investment).

Non-resident sailors are subject to a withholding tax of 10 per cent on their gross salary income, less a flat rate deduction of 10 per cent and a monthly deduction of LF 35,000.

23.4.3 INDIRECT BUSINESS TAXATION

In addition to indirect taxes which are not covered in this book such as the insurance tax, the following registration taxes are applicable:

(1)   a capital contribution duty (*droit d'apport*) of 1 per cent on incorporation based on the capital raised or the value of real or personal estate invested. In the case of capitalisation of reserves, a fixed duty of LF 100 is due. The capital contribution duty is not charged under certain conditions in the case of a merger. For family businesses (*sociétés familiales*), the duty is reduced to 0.5 per cent;

(2)   subscription tax is only levied on holding companies and investment funds under the conditions described in 23.4.2;

(3)   no registration tax is due in the case of the transfer of shares of associates. A fixed duty of LF 100 is due if parties want the benefit of a certain date for any document.

23.5 TAX ON LEGAL ENTITIES

Corporate income tax is levied on the worldwide income of resident companies and to the Luxembourg service income of non-resident companies.

Taxable profits are based on profits disclosed in the annual accounts approved by the shareholders, adjusted for tax purposes. Taxable profits are calculated on the difference between net assets at the beginning and the end of the year as shown in the company accounts.

Main adjustments relate to non-deductible items such as directors fees, corporate income tax and net worth tax, or non-business expenditures.

Capital gains are taxed as ordinary income. Tax on gains from certain fixed assets (real estate and permanent investment) which have been held for at least five years may be deferred by reinvestment in business assets.

Capital gains from the disposal of a shareholding and dividends received may be tax exempt provided the conditions described in 23.4.2 are fulfilled.

Losses can be carried forward indefinitely except for losses incurred prior to the tax year 1991 which may be carried forward for five years only. No carry back of losses is permitted.

Foreign income, unless exempted by treaty provisions, is fully taxable in Luxembourg. A tax credit may be granted for foreign taxes paid, limited to the amount of Luxembourg tax due on the foreign income. Excess foreign tax which does not qualify for tax credit is deductible from taxable income.

A withholding tax of 15 per cent is levied on the distribution of dividends unless the affiliation privilege or tax treaty provisions available provide for an exemption or a limitation of the tax rate.

23.6 TRANSFER PRICING

No specific regulations such as the *Aussensteuergesetz* in Germany or Art 209B of the *Code General des Impôts* in France exist in Luxembourg. Generally, the problem is inverted. Luxembourg tries to attract foreign investors by offering specific advantages based on common law rather than granting specific personal tax exemptions which as a consequence give effect to internal anti-avoidance regulations, and therefore produce an adverse effect in the country of residence of the investor. In 23.4.2 we saw that this objective has been reached with *Soparfi*, captive reinsurance companies and maritime companies. However, although the above is to foreign investors this does not mean that the Luxembourg tax authorities do not fix certain rules to control their application.

Thus, for example, the ratio of debts to equity in a holding company may not exceed 3:1. In addition, as Luxembourg legislation is very close to the German model, the same principles apply, especially the principle of 'arm's length'.

In conclusion, it is worth remembering the independence of the Luxembourg auditor (*réviseur d'entreprises*) and the highly formalised way in which accounts need to be kept.

24
INSOLVENCY

24.1 INTRODUCTION

Besides ordinary bankruptcy (*faillite*), Luxembourg law recognises two types of bankruptcies with penal consequences:
(1) bankruptcy resulting from recklessness, gross extravagance or other irregularities (*banqueroute simple*);
(2) fraudulent bankruptcy resulting from falsification of books, hiding of money or other fraudulent activities (*banqueroute frauduleuse*).
Luxembourg law provides for two kinds of arrangements:
(1) composition before bankruptcy, which is an arrangement between the debtor and his creditors in order to avoid bankruptcy;
(2) composition after bankruptcy, which is an arrangement between the debtor, his creditors and the court in order to allow the debtor to pay his debts by instalments.
These compositions are only available in cases of ordinary bankruptcy.

24.2 BANKRUPTCY

24.2.1 COURT'S JURISDICTION

The subject matter of bankruptcy is determined by the district court sitting in commercial matters for the debtor's registered office or home address. In the case of bankruptcy resulting from recklessness, gross extravagance or other irregularities or of fraudulent bankruptcy, the bankrupt may be tried by the criminal section of the court.

24.2.2 DECLARATION OF BANKRUPTCY

A business is considered to be in a state of bankruptcy when it has ceased meeting due payments and when its credit is wavering or when it is insolvent. In this case, any business must, within a month, petition the appropriate court.

A bankrupt who presents himself voluntarily must file a statement of his financial situation with the clerk of the commercial court of his registered office or home address.

Bankruptcy may also be declared by the court of its own accord or upon the petition of one or more creditors. In cases of arbitrary bankruptcy (*faillite d'office*), the court may, with a few exceptions, declare the bankruptcy only after a hearing with the bankrupt in the chambers.

24.2.3 ORGANISATION

One or more trustee(s) representing the creditors are appointed by the court to liquidate the bankrupt estate. The court also appoints the 'judge-commissioner' who is charged with supervising the trustee(s). Such a judgment divests the bankrupt of the right to administer his property.

24.2.4 CONSEQUENCES

From the date of the judgment, all debts owed by the bankrupt mature and, as far as the creditors are concerned, all interest on debts ceases to run, except for debts secured by lien, pledge or mortgage.

The trustee is charged with conserving the bankrupt's rights over his debtors and requesting the registration of any mortgage on the real property of his debtors.

An inventory of all the bankrupt's assets is also drawn up by the trustee. He may consolidate all disputes involving creditors.

Finally, if no composition takes place, the trustee liquidates the estate by selling the property and paying debts with the proceeds. The creditors will be paid after payment of the costs and expenses of the processing and administration of the case, sums necessary for expenses of the bankrupt and his family, and secured creditors.

All acts of the bankrupt after the date of bankruptcy are null and void. Moreover, the judgment of bankruptcy fixes within the six months preceding the bankruptcy a date which corresponds to a fraudulent preference period.

The following acts are null and void if executed during this period or within the ten days preceding it:

(1) gifts of real and personal property;
(2) transfer of property when the gross consideration is less than the real value;
(3) payment of unmatured debts;
(4) payment of debts at maturity, other than in cash or negotiable instruments;
(5) mortgages and pledges created on the property of the debtor in order to secure debt previously contracted.

24.2.5 REHABILITATION

If all these debts are fully paid, the bankrupt may ask to be discharged. But for so long as the rehabilitation is not approved by the court the bankrupt's forfeiture of political rights continues and he is prohibited from exercising certain civil and commercial functions.

24.2.6 POST-BANKRUPTCY COMPOSITION

The composition is proposed by the debtor. The latter must file an application with the appropriate court of his domicile, submit a statement of his financial situation and set forth the facts on which his demand is based.

The court examines the proposition and the creditors vote on the composition. If the majority of creditors, representing two-thirds of the amount of the admitted claims, votes in favour of the composition and if the court confirms the vote, the composition will come into force and will bind all creditors. Secured creditors are not entitled to vote, unless they waive their secured interest. If there is a breach of this agreement, bankruptcy ensues.

24.3 RIGHT OF CREDITORS

The creditors must file with the clerk of the commercial court a declaration of their claims and rights within the period fixed by the judgement establishing the bankruptcy. The creditors are informed by publication, advertisements and personal letters.

Each declaration must contain the full name, profession and domicile of the creditor, the amount of the claim and the consideration for the debt, and all pledges, liens and mortgages concerning the debt. The trustee then examines all the declarations. Those creditors whose claims are disputed, are called and heard.

24.4 RESPONSIBILITIES AND LIABILITIES OF THE MANAGEMENT OF AN INSOLVENT BUSINESS

If the bankrupt or the managers 'in law or in fact', whether shareholders or not, paid or not, of a business considered to be in a state of bankruptcy, have contributed to the bankruptcy by serious misconduct, the commercial court which has declared the bankruptcy, may prohibit these persons from carrying on a business, directly or indirectly, and from exercising directorship or managership, auditing or holding any job granting the power to binding a company.

This prohibition must be imposed on a bankrupt condemned for simple failure (bankruptcy resulting from recklessness, gross extravagance or other irregularities) or fraudulent bankruptcy. The duration of this prohibition cannot be less than one year and not more than 20 years.

Luxembourg law extends the sanctions which may be applied to the managers of the business 'in law or in fact', paid or not, or natural or legal persons who are liable for serious misconduct.

A manager may be required to make up, in whole or in part, any deficit arising on a liquidation, if he has committed errors in management that led to that deficit. This procedure may be instigated by the trustee.

The court may also make an order of personal bankruptcy against any manager 'in law or in fact', paid or not, legal entity if:

(1) he has used company assets as his own;
(2) he has engaged in trade activities for his personal interest under the cover of the business;
(3) he continued the business to further his own interest where such continuation could only lead to the insolvency of the business.

The manager must contribute to the losses of the business to the extent determined by the court.

A manager 'in law or in fact' may also be subject to criminal penalties where, in bad faith:

(1) has made use of the assets or the credit of the business in a way

adversely affecting its interests, in his interest, or with a view to favouring another business in which he holds a direct or indirect interest;

(2) has made use of his powers or his votes in a way adversely affecting its interests, in his interest or with a view to favouring another business in which he holds a direct or indirect interest,

Punishment is by imprisonment for one to five years, and by a fine of 10,000 to 250,000 LUF.

24.5 INTERNATIONAL ASPECTS

When a foreign person is interested in an adjudication of bankruptcy in Luxembourg, Luxembourg law is applicable and makes no distinction between a Luxembourg and a foreign bankrupt. The foreign creditors have the same rights as those of Luxembourg creditors.

The principle of unity of bankruptcy provides that a foreign judgment establishing a bankruptcy originated abroad is effective in Luxembourg without the necessity of being declared enforceable. However it is limited by the requirements of Luxembourg's public policy.

When positive steps to enforce execution by the Luxembourg authorities are required, enforcement by the court is necessary.

25
FINANCING A LUXEMBOURG COMPANY

The various ways in which a Luxembourg commercial undertaking may obtain finance are very similar to those available in the United Kingdom and the Latin countries.

25.1 LOANS FROM A BANK

There are no special rules relating to a loan contract from a bank to a company. The legislator considers that it is not necessary to protect the commercial undertakings, as opposed to the normal consumer. These contracts are governed by Civil Code principles.

25.2 LEASING

Financial leasing may be defined as a financial service rendered by a bank or a finance company which purchases goods at the customer's behest and leases them to him at an agreed amount, with an option to purchase at the end of the contract term.

Contrary to financial leasing, operating leasing are contracts concluded for a short term and generally may be terminated at any moment.

Non-full payout leases are contracts which do not provide that the acquisition price will be fully paid during the leasing period.

Sale-and-lease-back leases are characterised by the fact that the lessor himself buys goods that he sells to a leasing company to lease back.

Hire-purchase contracts (*location-vente* or *Mietkaufverträge*) may also be characterised as leasing contracts. The lessee has the right to acquire the object leased at an undetermined moment. Acquisition costs take into account rentals paid before the option is exercised.

Leasing contracts institute a legal relationship between the user and the financing company and also the producer of the equipment. The user makes the choice of the goods and the producer lets the goods to him. The finance company purchases the goods, and rents them to the user in accordance with the contract.

The subject matter may be movable or immovable property. No specific rules govern leasing contracts in Luxembourg, except tax provisions for the attribution of a tax credit for investment.

25.3 FACTORING

A factoring contract (*contract d'affacturage*) is a commercial contract whereby a factoring company, known as the factor, agrees to pay to his client, who is a seller of goods or services, the claim he has on his own debtors. The factor then has to collect his clients' debts.

The law of 27 November 1984, on the provision of the financial services, as amended, considers factoring operations as financial operations, and which can only be undertaken by financial institutions. As the mechanism is well-known, we would like to point out the partial possibility for holding companies and coordination centres to conduct such operations.

Compensation of accounts receivable in different foreign currencies, carried out by a qualifying Luxembourg coordination centre, only implies that multi-currency receivables can be compensated.

Debt factoring (*prise en pension de factures*) may be carried out by finance holding companies.

Debt factoring is similar to factoring operations except when the receivable is sold. Indeed, the holding company cannot accept the charge of the risk. If the receivable is not recovered, the risk will be borne by the seller of the receivable.

Debt factoring may only be performed for the benefit of group companies. Group companies are all companies grouped under the same name, which constitutes their logo of reciprocal dependance, and where all companies in these groups have a cumulated investment of at least 25 per cent of the share capital. In addition, a continuing trade or business link needs to exist within the group.

Debt factoring is subject to certain conditions:
(1) payment may not exceed market rates;
(2) debt should be entered in the accounts as a movable asset—
     short term receivable.

25.4 CORPORATE FINANCE

25.4.1 DIFFERENT METHODS OF FINANCING

In addition to the issue of ordinary shares, there are four principal ways in which a *société anonyme* may obtain finance:

The issue of *non-voting preferred stock* (*actions privilégiées sans droit de vote*)

Non-voting preferred stock may be issued when the company is set up, the capital is increased, or when ordinary shares are converted into privileged shares.

The issue of such stock is only possible if it does not exceed half of the share capital, and if a preferred dividend is distributed corresponding to a percentage of the accounting or the nominal value to be determined in the articles of incorporation.

A preferred right to the reimbursement of the capital must also be granted. If one of these conditions is no longer fulfilled, these shares would be granted the right to vote.

The issue of *bonds* (*obligations*)

A company may issue several kinds of loans. Luxembourg commercial practice recognises, in addition to ordinary bonds, convertible, or bonds coupled with a stock warrant.

As holders of convertible bonds have the opportunity to participate in a capital increase, such issue is governed by the rules relating to the issue capital, although no specific formalities are necessary at the time of the conversion.

Negotiable debentures may be issued even if the share capital has not been fully subscribed. The only restriction aims at prohibiting such an issue before the actual setting up of the company.

For a public share offer, a prospectus published in the *Mémorial* is prepared and distributed. Once the issue has been taken up, the debenture holders of each particular issue constitute a legal entity (*masse des obligataires*) prerogative exercised by the representatives of the group.

The issue of *founder's* shares

As opposed to ordinary shares which represent a share in the share capital, founder's shares represent the counterpart of contributions which have not been capitalised. However, these contributions are subject to a contribution duty of 1 per cent and in order to protect shareholders and creditors, an estimate of the value of such an interest must be carried out by an independent auditor.

Loans

In the case of a loan made by a shareholder to a *société anonyme*, the interest paid on such a loan is normally deductible by the corporation if the 'arm's length' principles are followed, and if the transaction is not considered by the tax administration as being a hidden distribution of dividends.

25.4.2 CAPITAL INCREASES

Luxembourg law traditionally distinguishes capital increases by the issue of new shares from an increase by the incorporation of reserves. The latter is a simple change in writing. The reserve account is decreased, insofar as the subscribed share capital is increased. This operation does not require unanimity but, as the articles will need to be amended, such an operation may only be enacted in a notarial deed and in fulfilment of the provisions relating to a quorum to amend the articles of incorporation.

The legal requirements that must be fulfilled for an increase in capital are similar to those for the setting up of a company. The decision to increase the capital is reserved for the shareholders at an extraordinary general meeting. However, the shareholders may delegate to the board of directors the power to make capital increase(s) for a maximum term of five years ('authorised capital').

Basically the shares must be subscribed for and at least 25 per cent paid up. Shareholders may renounce their preferential right of subscription.

25.5 BANKING OPERATIONS

25.5.1 BANK ACCOUNTS

One of the formalities to be complied with in setting up a company is the presentation of a certificate attesting to the fact that at least 25 per cent of the subscribed share capital has been paid into a bank account.

25.5.2 BANK FACILITIES

As already described, art 1907 of the Civil Code provides that unless otherwise agreed, only the legal interest rate will be due and no additional commissions or charges may be claimed.

Article 1907–1 empowers the courts to reduce excessive interest rates, which are defined as those rates that exceed the rate that would be normal in the light of the risks of the loan.

The liability of the bank for its activities may be owed *vis-à-vis* its clients, ie, the borrower and *vis-à-vis* third parties, the borrower's creditors or co-contractors.

25.5.3 LIABILITY OF BANKS AND CREDIT ESTABLISHMENTS

Banks may be held responsible in tort (*responsabilité délictuelle*) which is governed by arts 1382 and 1383 of the civil code or in contract (*responsabilité contractuelle*) which is governed by art 1134 of the Civil Code.

Under tort, the plaintiff must cumulatively prove that the bank committed a wrongful act or omission, that he suffered a loss and that a causal link exists between such act or omission and his loss.

Under contract, the party must prove that either the contract has not been properly complied with if the bank is bound to guarantee a result, or that the bank is at fault and did not act with due diligence.

Limitations of liability clauses are recognised, but not in case of an intentional act or omission, or gross negligence. Furthermore, if the exclusion clause deprived the contract of an essential element it would not be upheld. The courts decide at their discretion on the basis of the facts whether banks are liable in tort. Thus, it has been held, for example, that executing a falsified instruction does not make the bank liable if the signature appearing on the instruction appeared to be genuine.

25.6 NEGOTIABLE INSTRUMENTS

25.6.1 BILL OF EXCHANGE

The rules relating to bills of exchange are contained in a coordinated text published in the *Mémorial* which includes the

Geneva Convention of 1930 approved by the law of 8 January 1962 and amended by the law of 15 December 1962.

No definition of a bill of exchange is given by the law, but to be valid, it must contain:

(1) the wording 'bill of exchange', in the language in which it is drafted,
(2) an order to pay a certain sum;
(3) the name of the payee;
(4) the due date for payment;
(5) the place where payment is to take place;
(6) the name of the drawee;
(7) the place and date of the issue;
(8) the signature of the drawer.

If one of the above mentioned formalities is not met, the bill is considered null and void. However, a bill without a date of payment is deemed to be a valid draft. If the address for payment is missing it is deemed payable at the drawee's address on the bill and similarly if the place of issue is missing the bill is deemed issued at the drawer's address. Only sight bills or these payable at fixed period after presentation may stipulate a specified rate of interest. Any such stipulation in any other type of bill is void.

Bills of exchange are transferable by indorsement, which can be to a named indorsee or bearer. Indorsees are generally liable for acceptance and payment of a bill.

Holders of a bill may request its acceptance by the drawee until maturity. Acceptance results from the drawee's signature on the bill. By accepting a bill, the drawee assumes a personal commitment to pay, at maturity.

A surety may be given to guarantee the payment. Without indication of the guaranteed party, a guaranty will be deemed to be for the benefit of the drawer. Refusal of acceptance or payment must be established by a formal deed (*protêt faute d'acceptation ou de paiement*). The holder must inform the drawer and his indorsee of such refusal. Each indorser will have in turn to notify his own indorser.

Drawer, drawee, indorser or guarantors are jointly and severally liable *vis-à-vis* the holder, who may sue each of them separately or jointly, but in respect of the following time-limits:

(1) within three years following maturity against a drawer who has accepted;

(2)   within one year from date of formal protest or maturity date against an indorser and a drawer;

(3)   within six months after payment for actions of the indorsers against each other.

25.6.2 CHEQUES

A coordinated text of the legislation available has been published in the *Mémorial*. It includes the Geneva Convention of 1931 as such approved by the law of 14 March 1968, and amended by laws of 4 July 1968 and 16 January 1987.

As with the Bill of Exchange Act, no definition of a cheque is given by the law, only a list of matters that must be included in a cheque for it to be valid. The following matters are required:

(1)   the word 'cheque' in the language used;

(2)   an order to pay a determined sum;

(3)   the name of the payer,

(4)   the place and date of the issue,

(5)   the signature of the drawer.

If even one matter is missing, the instrument will not be considered as a cheque. However, if the place of payment is not mentioned, it is deemed payable at the drawee's address. Any interest provision inserted in a cheque is deemed void.

The cheque may be a crossed cheque (*cheque barré*) which means that it may be collected only by any banker. A cheque which has been crossed generally may be collected by one banker, whereas a specially crossed cheque may be collected only by the banker named in the crossing.

As regards payment, a cheque must generally be presented within eight days of its issue. If not, payment is still due by the bank until the expiry of the limitation period, which is equal to one year for an action by the holder against the drawee and six months for any other actions.

The owner of a cheque is responsible for consequences flowing from it. He particularly bears any consequences, which result from its loss, theft or unlawful use, unless he can prove either that the drawee acted fraudulently or committed a gross negligence, or that the cheque was lost, stolen or altered only after its reception by the legitimate recipient.

If a bank accepts a cheque after a stopping action has been

commenced by the drawer, the act of gross negligence will have been proved. Although, as in the eurocheque system, a guarantee of payment must be given by the bank even in the case of loss or theft, a bank which would have paid in spite of a stopping action properly requested would not have committed an act of gross negligence.

If payment is refused, the holder may file an action against the indorser, the drawer and his creditors, either, by a certified instrument (*protêt*), or by a drawee's declaration on the cheque, or by a declaration at the chamber of compensation.

The drawing of a cheque on an account where insufficient funds are available constitutes a criminal offence. The same is true if funds are withdrawn, while the cheque may still be presented for payment, or even after the expiration of the time period provided for by law for presentation of the cheque if the drawer fraudulently or in bad faith stops payment or withdraws funds necessary for payment.

25.6.3 PROMISSORY NOTES

A promissory note (*billet à ordre*) is quite similar to a bill of exchange. The rules relating to the note are the same.

A promissory note is subject to strict formal requirements and must contain the following matters otherwise it is void:
(1) the words '*billet à ordre*';
(2) the obligation to pay a determined amount;
(3) the issue date;
(4) the date where the payment must be made;
(5) the designation of the person to whom it is payable;
(6) the place and the date of subscription;
(7) the drawer's signature.

The purpose for which a promissory note is used determines its civil or commercial nature and as a consequence the court at which any claim may be pursued.

25.7 GUARANTEES

25.7.1 *CAUTIONNEMENT*

A *cautionnement* is a unilateral contract whereby the guarantor (*caution*) undertakes to execute the debtor's obligations in the event that the latter fails to execute them.

Such a guarantee may be given for a determined or undetermined sum. If the guarantor has not specified the exact debt to be guaranteed, the guarantee covers not only the underlying debt, but all incidental costs, charges and expenses relating thereto. Where the guarantor is called upon to perform under a guarantee, he has the right to require the creditor to first proceed against the property of the principal debtor, unless he has specifically waived such right. This right is known as the *bénéfice de discussion*.

Where there are several guarantors of the same debt, each one of them is, as a general rule, deemed to guarantee the entire debt. Nevertheless, each guarantor has the right to require the creditor to commence a separate action against him for his pro rata share of the principal debt (*bénéfice de division*), unless he has specifically waived such right.

When, however, the guarantor has agreed to be jointly and severally liable with other guarantees and the debtor (*cautionnement solidaire*), which is common practice, he does not benefit from these rights. If the principal debtor fails, such a guarantor may be sued by the creditor for the entire amount of the debt.

Where the guarantor has performed under the guarantee, he is subrogated to all of the rights of the creditor against the debtor.

An *office du ducroire* was created by the law of 25 November 1961 to encourage foreign trade by the granting of warranties in order to decrease risks and more especially, credit risks. Guarantees granted by the office may be applicable for:

(1)　any contract which has as a consequence Luxembourg debts, as soon as the economic interest of the transaction justifies the risks incurred;

(2)　the import of goods which offer a general interest in the field of government economic policy.

The office may contribute in cases of loss or damages resulting from:

(1)　non-execution of contractual engagements by a foreign contractor;

(2)　insolvency of a foreign contractor;

(3)　general measures taken by the contractor State or any political event which will prohibit the execution of transactions guaranteed by the office.

25.7.2 SECURITY INTERESTS IN REAL PROPERTY

A mortgage is a right to immovable property which guarantees the execution of obligation. A mortgage is attached to the real property (*droit réel*) and follows it in case of change in the ownership.

The mortgage may be legal, judicial or by agreement. Legal mortgages may result from operation of law, a judicial mortgage will result from a registration based on a judgment, and concensual ones from an agreement.

The exact nature and the location of each element of real property mortgaged must be specified in the notarial deed. Furthermore, the debt guaranteed has to be determined in advance. To be valid, a mortgage needs to be registered. A mortgage tax is due on registration and renewal of registration on the principal amount of the debt registered.

Mortgage tax is collected when the relevant legal documents concerning the mortgage are presented at the rate of 0.5 per cent in the case of registration and renewal of registration (in principle every ten years). A special duty (register fee) ranging from LF 50 to 500 depending on the amount of the mortgage debt to be registered or cancelled is levied by the government.

25.7.3 FIRST DEMAND GUARANTEE

A first demand guarantee is the contract whereby a bank undertakes to pay the amount of the guarantee if the other party does not execute its obligations.

The Luxembourg Court of Appeal considers that this contract is independent from the contract binding the parties to execute or provide a service. There is no question of 'discussion' or 'division' and the bank must pay in the place of the debtor in accordance with the terms set out in the guarantee.

26
ENVIRONMENTAL PLANNING

26.1 INTRODUCTION

Environmental planning has become one of the major challenges facing governments in the latter part of the Twentieth century. Environmental issues often create the news headlines and few people are unaware of the occurence of disasters such as the *Amoco Cadiz* and *Exxon Valdez*.

Environmental protection, started in the seventies and eighties, by a multitude of laws. This area of law is much too large to be subject to detailed coverage in this work, and the following paragraphs shall be treated only as a general outline of the applicable laws.

26.2 AREA PLANNING LAW

26.2.1 TYPES OF DEVELOPMENT PLANS

According to the law of 11 August 1982, governing the conservation of nature and natural resources, every construction which is to be erected for the purpose of habitation, trade, industry, or sports is subject to authorisation of the Ministry of Environment. Authorisation will only be granted if the construction falls within the rubric of the laws of 12 June 1937 (which governs town planning) and 20 March 1974 (which governs national planning). Operating plans define the special areas where constructions can be erected.

Where municipalities do not have a land-use plan, the construction will only be authorised if erected in an agglomeration, ie, in the centre of a circle having a radius of 100 metres within which are situated at least five habitations permanently occupied.

Besides the above mentioned constructions, which serve the

purpose of habitation, trade, industry, or sport, the law distinguishes agricultural, gardening, market gardening, sylvicultural, wine growing, piscicultural installations, or public utility undertakings. These constructions may be erected in a natural environment, provided their purpose meets with the requirements of the surrounding site. The Minister of Environment will refuse authorisation if the construction is a risk for the conservation of nature.

According to the law of 12 June 1937 every municipality subject to an operating plan, ie with more than 10,000 inhabitants, must have a building regulation (*règlement des batisses*). The law of 20 March 1974 extended this obligation to all municipalities. The building regulation will determine the character of the constructions and will provide for measures concerning the conservation of sites and monuments from an aesthetic point of view. Any construction must meet with the provisions of the building regulations of the relevant municipality.

The building regulations will also define monuments of artistic, historic or archaeological value and the places the land-use plans designated as having a special character from a landscape point of view. In the neighbourhood of these sites, new constructions, extensions, posters and other advertising facilities will be authorised, only if they do not harm the beauty of the site. Beside these authorisations it is understood that every construction needs a separate building permit from the mayor (*bourgmestre*).

26.2.2 SANCTIONS

The law of 1982 on the conservation of nature provides for a fine of up to one million LF and imprisonment from eight days to six months. The court must compulsorily confiscate the machinery and tools used by the contravener as well as the vehicles used to infringe the law. The court must also order, at the expense of the contravener, the restoration of the site within one year.

In practice the court will order, besides a fine, the confiscation of the building equipment and the demolition of the construction illegally erected. The restoration of the site in its previous state constitutes the civil compensation of the prejudice suffered by the community.

Infringements of building regulations are punished by the

sanctions provided for by the law of 12 June 1937, ie, a fine up to LF 500,000 and imprisonment from eight days to three months. The court may also order the demolition of the executed works and the restoration of the site, at the expense of the contravener.

The municipalities or, in their stead, the State may claim damages for prejudice suffered (*partie civile*). Although the law governing land-use only gives the courts the *possibility* of ordering the restoration of the site, the courts always order the restoration, it being considered as the only way to redress the infringement.

The municipalities may also ask the courts to order the abolition of the illegal works in penal proceedings; they also have the right to issue a direct writ of summons (*citation directe*) against the contravener.

26.3 ENVIRONMENTAL LAW

Pursuant to art 1 of the law of 9 May, 1990 installations are subject to licensing requirements if they are potential source of risk or nuisance or may be harmful to health. Industrial or commercial installations whose establishment or operation may involve a risk or have an adverse effect on the safety, health or well-being of the general public, the neighbourhood, its employees or the environment are also subject to these requirements. Furthermore, every facility, activity or manufacturing process that may lead to similar risks is subject to licensing.

Determination of the authorities responsible for granting the licence depends on the classification of the installation into one of three categories specified by the law according to the degree of risk involved.

Installations falling under category 1, such as chemical factories, must be licensed by the Minister of Environment and the Minster of Labour and are subject to the '*enquête commodo et incommodo*' (see below).

Installations under category 2, such as a bakery, are licensed by the mayor (*bourgmestre*), whereas installations falling under category 3 such as a hotel, must be licensed by the above mentioned ministers, but without being subject to the '*enquête commodo et incommodo*'.

The application submitted to the competent authority must include, in addition to the name, occupation and residence of the applicant, the nature and location of the installation, the purpose of its operation and details of the extent of production or the nature of materials to be stored there. The applicant must also provide an estimation of the number of employees and list the potential risks for their safety and health.

Additionally, he must supply information on the use of water, air, water and soil pollution, noise levels, vibrations, radiation, the nature, amount, treatment and disposal of wastes and other by-products engendered during production. He must also provide an evaluation of all other harmful effects on the environment. The application must contain approximate data on measures designed to prevent or reduce harmful effects as well as potential risks for the employees, the surrounding neighbourhood, the public and the environment.

The authorisation of the Minister of Environment and the Minister of Labour will specify the requirements to ensure protection for the safety, health and well-being of the public, the surrounding neighbourhood, the employees and the environment (air, water, soil, noise level and wastes).

The authority issuing the authorisation may require that the installation be checked and approved on initial operation and in regular periods thereafter. The requirements of the initial authorisation may be subject to a continual review.

Subsequently imposed directives are possible.

Notification of the project must be posted for two weeks in the office of the mayor at the location of the installation and in the surrounding municipalities. It must also be published in four daily newspapers.

Objections can be filed by every citizen. A public discussion (*enquête de commodo et incommodo*) is held in the community of the location of the installation, during which all objections will be heard.

Within 40 days of notification of the authorisation (or non-authorisation) decision, any affected party, ie, any person living in the immediate vicinity of the installation, who can thereby claim a personal and direct interest in the decision, may appeal against the decision.

Associations for the protection of the environment, which have been approved, have been recognised by the Conseil d'Etat (highest administrative jurisdiction) in respect of their right to defend the collective interests of affected individuals, provided the association has got the required approval by ministerial order.

Immediate neighbours and approved environmental associations also have the right subsequently to ask the competent authority to impose requirements on installations. They may even require a deadline for fulfilling the requirements already imposed.

26.4 CONSERVATION LAW

The conservation of nature is governed by a general law of 11 August 1982 and many other laws on air or water pollution, waste or noise.

The objectives of the law of 1982 are the conservation of the environment's character, variety and integrity, protection and restoring of landscapes and natural spaces, conservation of flora and fauna and their biotopes, upholding and improvement of biological balances, protection of natural resources against any damages, and improvement of the structures of the environment.

The law also deals with waste disposal, the protection of woods and their biotopes.

For new installations subject to licensing requirements, the authorisation will only be granted if the installation meets all requirements provided for by statutes governing waste disposal, pollution etc.

LEGISLATION TABLE

Belgian Legislation   *Page*
Bankruptcy Act 128, 131, 135
CIR
    art 24 ....125, 126
    art 46 125
    art 250...125, 126
Codes
Civil Code 22, 43, 71, 89, 91, 92, 99, 100, 156
    art 544.. 165
    art 1122..57
    art 1382 ....19, 139, 164, 166
    art 1384 164
    art 1690 62–4
    arts 1832–73..42
    arts 1882–4 ....28, 29
    art 1905 102
    art 1907 143
    art 2021 154
    art 2032 155
    arts 2073–84... 155
Commercial Code 53, 156
    art 437... 131
    Title VII..70, 150
Criminal Code 19
    arts 42, 43... 163
Judicial Code 11
    art 570... 141
    art 728... 5
    art 755... 4
    art 758... 5
    art 1138(2).. 4
Income Tax Code.. 117
    art 3.. 114
    art 94 118
    art 148 122

Napoleonic Code 2
Commercial Lease Act
    art 11 64
Company Act 20 July 1991 .... 33, 36, 38, 42, 47, 49, 52, 131, 146, 147
Constitution
    art 11 165
    arts 95–7 4
    art 104 3
    art 107 159
Consumer Credit Act 1991
    art 26 64
Copyright Act 17, 23
Decrees
Decree of 28 December 1948 110
Decree of 14 May 1984 162
Decree of 7 October 1985 162
Decree of the Flemish Executive 27 March 1985 161
Décret d'Allarde 10 November 1795 24
Royal Decree No 135 9 July 1935 .... 34, 47
Royal Decree No 185 9 July 1935 .... 61, 146
Royal Decree 30 November 1935 33
Royal Decree 12 December 1969 60
Royal Decree 10 April 1989 62
Royal Decree 8 November 1989 .... 60, 61
Royal Decree 9 January 1991 60
Royal Decree 30 December 1991 55
Fair Trade Practices Act 19, 24, 29, 30
Laws
Law at 16 March 1803 6
Law of 18 April 1851 131
Law of 24 May 1854 8
Law of 5 May 1872 155
    arts 12–17 70
Law of 22 March 1886 15
Law of October 1919 .... 34, 45, 50, 156
    art 2 46
    art 16(2) 145
Law of 5 March 1921
    art 38 15
Law of 27 June 1921 .... 34, 44, 47, 50
Law of 30 April 1951 .... 93, 94
Law of 27 July 1953 15
Law of 31 December 1955 150
Law of 11 March 1958
    art 21(b) 15
Law of 27 May 1960 24
Law of 27 July 1961 .... 66, 75–9, 83, 85, 86

art 6...81
art 4(1) 81, 82
art 4(1), (2) 81
Law of 29 March 1962.. 158
Law of July 1964 34
Law of 8 April 1965.. 108
Law of 27 June 1969 110
Law of 1 December 1970..17
Law of 30 December 1970...62
art 36 59
Law of 13 April 1971 86
Law of 17 August 1973 ....60, 62
Law of 17 July 1975 ....25, 34
Law of 19 July 1975 84
Law of 3 July 1978.. 72, 105
Law of 12 July 1979 43
Law of 8 August 1980... 159
Law of 28 March 1984...8, 9
Law of 14 May 1984.. 156
Law of 25 July 1985 30
Law of 8 August 1986...12
Law of 14 July 1987 111
Law of 2 March 1989 ....60, 62
Law of 12 July 1989 ....33, 44
Law of 17 July 1989 ....34, 44
Law of 10 January 1990...17
Law of 4 December 1990.. 146
Law of 20 February 1991 92
Law of 1 March 1991 92
Law of 12 June 1991.......................................30, 142, 144, 154
Law of 14 July 1991 .... 28, 29, 31, 32
Law of 20 July 1991 39
Law of 5 August 1991..25, 27
Law of 29 August 1991 156
Law of 4 August 1992...96
Law on Employment Contracts 19
Mortgage Act
art 5..63
Uniform Benelux Law 12, 17, 18, 21, 23

Luxembourg Legislation
Bills of Exchange Act.. 234
Codes
Civil Code 171, 197
art 1118... 176
art 1134... 232
art 1135–1... 175

art 1152... 176
art 1231 176
art 1382, 1383.. 232
art 1690 190
art 1762 205
art 1779 210
Pt IX
arts 1832–64.. 177
art 1907 232
art 1907–1 ....176, 232
arts 1979 *et seq* 211
art 1984 194
Criminal Code
art 309.. 172
Constitution
art 11... 214
Laws
Law of 10 August 1915 177
art 9..186, 187
art 21 190
arts 27, 33.. 191
art 36 192
art 48 191
art 83 192
art 189 192
art 190... 192
arts 257–283.. 185
arts 262–266.. 186
art 271 186
art 274... 186
art 285–308... 187
Law of 21 April 1928 182
Law of 5 July 1929
art 4... 172
art 16 173
art 18–20... 173
Law of 12 June 1937 ....238, 239
Law of 25 November 1961 236
Law of 8 January 1962 233
Law of 15 December 1962.. 233
Law of 22 April 1966 212
Law of 4 December 1967 215
Law of 14 March 1968 234
Law of 4 July 1968... 234
Law of 5 August 1969... 215
Law of 5 June 1970 174
Law of 17 June 1970 200

Law of 28 March 1972 .... 208, 210
Law of 29 March 1972 170
Law of 20 March 1974 .... 238, 239
Law of 6 May 1974 213
Law of 3 July 1975 213
Law of 11 August 1982 .... 238, 239, 242
Law of 25 August 1983
   art 2 174
Law of 27 November 1984 229
Law of 27 November 1986 .... 172, 200
Law of 16 January 1987 234
Law of 15 May 1987 174
Law of 1 July 1988 196
Law of 24 May 1989 .... 210, 211
Law of 9 May 1990
   art 1 240
Law of 25 March 1991 181
Uniform Benelux Law 170

International Legislation
Belgian-Luxembourg Economic Union 215
Benelux Convention on Agency 170, 194
Benelux Convention on Designs and models 25 October 1966 17
Berne Convention 9 September 1886 15–17
Brussels Convention of Enforcement of Judgments in Civil and
   Commercial Matters 110
   art 17 81
Convention of Munich 5 October 1973 9
European Convention on the International Commercial Arbitration
   of Geneva 84
Geneva Convention 1930 233
Geneva Convention 1931 234
Hague Convention 5 October 1961 54
International Geneva Convention on the Uniform Law on Cheques 151
Munich Convention 5 October 1973
   art 64(1) 12
New York Convention 10 June 1958 84
Rome Convention on the Law Applicable to Contractual Obligations 82
   art 7 83
Treaty of Luxembourg 9
Treaty of Madrid 12, 14
Treaty of Washington (Patent Co-operation Treaty) 19 June 1970 9
Union Convention of Paris 20 March 1883 9
Universal Convention of Geneva 6 September 1952 15

European Community Legislation
Treaty of Rome 163, 172

art 85 .... 56, 75, 76, 86
    (1)..20, 24
    (3)..26
art 86 ....24, 86
art 169.. 160
Directives
Directive 84/450 13
Directive 85/337 161
Directive 85/577 32
Directive 86/653 69
Directive 89/104 12
Directive 89/666 55
Parent and Subsidiary Directive..................................... 220
Product Liability Directive...30
Regulations
Regulation 1612/68.. 104
Regulation 1983/83...75
Regulation 1984/83...75
Regulation 4987/83...87
Regulation 2349/84..20, 22
Regulation 2137/85.. 33, 43, 181
Regulation 3842/86...12
Regulation 3077/87...12
Regulation 556/89 22

INDEX

Acquisitions—
  goodwill. *See* Goodwill, acquisition
    of shares. *See* Shares
Agency—
  background, 66
  Belgium, 66–74
  brokers, 71–2
  commercial agent. *See* Commercial
    agent
  commercial representatives, 72–4
  commission agent, 70–1
  Luxembourg, 194–7
Agreement—
  partnership, 43
Annual meeting—
  joint stock company, 37
Banking operations—
  Belgium. *See* Belgium
  Luxembourg. *See* Luxembourg
Bankruptcy—
  Belgium. *See* Belgium
  Luxembourg, 223–5
Belgium—
  acquisitions—
    goodwill. *See* goodwill,
      acquisition of *below*
    shares. *See* share acquisitions
      below
  agency—
    background, 66
    brokers, 71–2
    commercial agent. *See*
      commercial agent *below*
    commercial representatives, 72–4
    commission, 70–1
  banking operations—
    bank accounts, 148–9

Belgium—*contd*
  banking operations—*contd*
    bank facilities, 149
    liability of banks, 149–50
  bankruptcy—
    conditions, 131–2
    consequences of order, 139–40
    foreign court decision,
      consequences of, 140–1
    generally, 131
    judgment of, 132
    judgment, consequences of,
      133–5
    organisaiton of, 132–5
    post-bankruptcy composition,
      136
    rehabilitation, 136
    termination of, 136
  branches—
    commercial, 54–5
    generally, 53
    representative offices, 53–4
  brokers, 71–2
  business organisations—
    branches, 53–5
    directors' rights and liabilities,
      52–3
    economic interest grouping, 43–4
    generally, 33
    incorporation. *See* incorporation
      below
    legislation, 33–4
    limited liability company. *See*
      limited liability company *below*
    non-profit. *See* non-profit
      organisations *below*
    partnership. *See* partnership *below*

Belgium—*contd*
  business organisations—*contd*
    shareholder's rights and liabilities,
      51–2
    sole trader, 53
  co-operative company—
    limited liability, with, 39–40
    unlimited liability, with, 42
  commercial agent—
    absence of specific legislation,
      66–7
    determinate duration, 68
    duration, 67
    future orientation, 69–70
    indefinite duration, 68–9
    performance of contract, 67
    self-employed, 69–70
    termination, 67–8
  commercial representatives,
    72–4
  commission agent, 70–71
  communities, 2
  community dimension, 56
  competition—
    economic, law on protection of,
      25–8
    franchising and, 87
    generally, 24
    present legal situation, 24–5
    unfair. *See* unfair competition
      below
  confidential information, 19–20
  copyright—
    definitions, 15–16
    exploitation, 16
    generally, 15
    licensing, 21–2
    protection, 16
    remedies, 16
    semiconductors, 17
    software, 17
  corporate finance—
    capital increase, 148
    different methods, 146–8
  courts, 3–4
  credit institutions, liability of,
    149–50

Belgium—*contd*
  designs—
    definition, 18
    exploitation, 18–19
    generally, 17–18
    licensing, 22
    procedure, 18
    protection, 18–19
    remedies, 18–19
  directors' rights and liabilities, 52–3
  distribution agreement—
    conclusion, 84–5
    enforcement of protection, 81–4
    exclusive, 76–81
    generally, 75–6
    other types, 85
      quasi-exclusive, 76–81
  EC law, impact of, 2–3
  economic interest grouping, 43–4,
    50–1
  environmental planning—
    control law, 158–63
    insurance, 166
    liability, 164–6
    national development, 158
    necessary permits, 160–3
    penalties and liabilities, 163–4
    regionalisation and competent
      authorities, 158–60
  federalisation process, consequences
    of, 2
  financing company—
    bank loans, 142–3
    banking operations, 148–50
    corporate finance, 146–8
    factoring, 145
    generally, 142
    guarantees, 154–7
    leasing, 143–5
    negotiable instruments, 150–4
  franchising—
    certificate of distribution, 87–8
    characteristics, 86–7
    competition law, and, 87
    definitiion, 86–7
  goodwill, acquisition of—
    formalities, 62–5

Belgium—*contd*
  goodwill, acquisition of—*contd*
    generally, 62
    VAT implications, 65
  guarantees—
    first demand, 157
    personal sureties, 154–7
    real sureties, 154–7
  heart of Europe, as, 1
  immigration—
    EC nationals, 103–4
    generally, 102
    non-EC nationals, 102–3
  income tax—
    corporate, 118–21
    individual, 114–18
    non-resident, 123–5
  incorporation—
    EEIG, 50–51
    EIG, 50–51
    limited liability company, 47–9
    non-profit organisation, 50
    partnership, 49–50
  insolvency—
    concordat judiciaire, 128–31
    creditors, rights of, 137–9
    generally, 127
    international aspects, 139–41
    third party, responsibilities and
      liabilities of, 139
    tracing enterprises in difficulty,
      127–8
  intellectual property—
    confidential information, 19–20
    copyright. *See* copyright *above*
    designs. *See* designs *above*
    generally, 8
    invention made by employee,
      22–3
    know-how, 19–20
    licensing. *See* licensing *below*
    models. *See* models *below*
    patents. *See* patents *below*
    trade secrets, 19–20
    trademarks. *See* trademarks
      below
  invention of employee, 22–3

Belgium—*contd*
  joint stock company—
    annual meeting, 37
    capital, 34–5
    control, 37
    duration, 35
    generally, 34
    management, 36–7
    name, 35
    publicity requirements, 37
    shareholders, 35
    shares, 35–6
    winding up, 38
  know-how, 19–20, 22
  labour relations—
    applicable law, 110–11
    appropriate courts, 110–11
    employment contract, 105–8
    international, 110–11
    labour protection, 110
    language, use of, 108–9
    legislation, 104–5
    mandatory bodies, 109
    social security, 110
    temporary secondment, 111–12
    working regulations, 108
  lawyers, 5–6
  leasing—
    financial, 143–4
    real estate, 144–5
  legal entities, tax on, 122–3
  legal issues, approach to, 6–7
  licensing—
    copyright, 21–2
    designs, 22
    know-how, 22
    models, 22
    patents, 20
    trademarks, 20–21
  limited liability company—
    co-operative company with
      limited liability, 39–40
    incorporation, 47–9
    joint stock company, 34–8
    private, 38–9
  mergers—
    Community dimension, 56

Belgium—*contd*
  mergers—*contd*
    generally, 56–7
  models—
    definition, 18
    exploitation, 18–19
    generally, 17–18
    licensing, 22
    procedure, 18
    protection, 18–19
    remedies, 18–19
  negotiable instruments—
    bills of exchange, 150–51
    cheques, 151–3
    promissory notes, 153–4
  non-profit organisations—
    ASBL, 44–5
    incorporation, 50
    institutions of public utility
      (foundations), 47
    international association, 45–6
    taxation, 122–3
    VZW, 44–5
  partnership—
    agreement, 43
    civil company, 42–3
    co-operative company, 42
    general, 41
    incorporation, 49–50
    limited, 41
    shares, limited by, 41–2
    temporary, 43
  patents—
    definition, 9
    European patent, 12
    exploitation, 10–11
    generally, 8–9
    licensing, 20
    procedure, 9–10
    protection, 10–11
    remedies, 10–11
  political structural organisation, 1
  private limited liability company—
    capital, 38
    generally, 38
    management, 39
    name, 39

Belgium—*contd*
  private limited liability
    company—*contd*
      participants, 38
      shares, 39
  public take-over bids, 61–2
  real property—
    civil lease, 92
    commercial lease, 93–6
    generally, 89
    mortgage, 96–9
    residential lease, 92–3
    sale and purchase, 89–92
  regions, 1–2
  share acquisitions—
    goodwill, acquisition of, 62
    private, 60–61
    privately owned stock, 57–60
    public, 61–2
    shares publicly held or quoted, 60–62
    transparency of corporations, 62
  shareholders' rights and liabilities, 51–2
  sole trader, 53
  succession, 99–101
  taxation—
    corporate income tax, 118–21
    individual income tax, 114–18
    legal entities, 122–3
    non-profit organisations, 122–3
    non-resident income tax, 123–5
    transfer pricing, 125–6
    value added tax. *See* value added
      tax *below*
  trade secrets, 19–20
  trademarks—
    definition, 13
    exploitation, 14
    generally, 12–13
    international registration, 14–15
    licensing, 20–21
    protection, generally, 14
    protection procedure, 13–14
    remedies, 14
  transfer pricing, 125–6
  unfair competition—
    Articles 1382–1384 of Belgian
      Civil Code, 28–9

Belgium—*contd*
  unfair competition—*contd*
    information and protection of
      consumer, 29–31
    regulated practices, 31–2
    sanctions, 32
    sellers, fair competition
      involving, 29
    trade practices, law of 14 July
      1991, 29–32
    unfair trade practices, 32
  value added tax—
    exemptions, 114
    foreign entrepreneurs, 113–14
    general, 113
    mechanism, 113
    rates, 114

Bills of exchange—
  Belgium, 150–51
  Luxembourg, 232–4
Branches—
  Belgium, 53–5
  commercial branch, 54–5
  representative offices, 53–4
Brokers—
  Belgium, 71–2
  Luxembourg, 196
Business lease—
  Luxembourg, 204–5
Business organisations—
  Belgium, 33–55
  branches, 53–5
  directors' rights and liabilities,
    52–3
  Economic Interest Grouping, 43–4
  incorporation. *See* Incorporation
  legislation, 33–4
  limited liability company. *See*
    Limited liability company
  Luxembourg, 177–84
  non-profit. *See* Non-profit
    organisation
  partnership. *See* Partnership
  shareholders' rights and liabilities,
    51–2
  sole trader, 53

Capital—
  joint stock company, 34–5
  private limited liability company, 38
Cheques—
  Belgium, 151–3
  Luxembourg, 234–5
Civil lease—
  Belgium, 92
Co-operative company—
  limited liability, with, 39–40, 179
  unlimited liability, with, 42, 180
Commercial agent—
  Belgium, 66–70
  duration, 67
  future orientation, 69–70
  Luxembourg, 194–6
  performance of contract, 67
  self-employed, 69–70
  termination—
    determinate duration, 68
    general rules, 67–8
    indefinite duration, 68–9
Commercial lease—
  Belgium, 93–6
Commercial representative—
  Belgium, 72–4
  Luxembourg, 197
Commission agent—
  Belgium, 70–71
  Luxembourg, 196–7
Company—
  civil, 42–3
  financing—
    Belgium. *See* Belgium
    Luxembourg. *See* Luxembourg
  joint stock. *See* Limited liability
    company
Competition—
  Belgium, 24–32
  economic, law on protection of,
    25–8
  franchising and, 87
  Luxembourg, 172–4
  sellers, involving, 29
  unfair. *See* Unfair competition
Computer software—
  protection of, 17

Confidential information—
Belgium, 19–20
Conservation law—
Luxembourg, 242
Consumer protection—
Belgium, 29–31
Luxembourg, 174–6
Contract—
employment, 105–8, 211–12
transfer of, 63–5
Copyright—
Belgium, 15–17, 21–2
definitions, 15–16
exploitation, 16
licensing, 21–2
Luxembourg, 170–71
protection, 16
remedies, 16
semiconductors, 17
software, 17
Corporate finance—
Belgium. *See* Belgium
Luxembourg. *See* Luxembourg
Corporate income tax. *See* Income tax
Courts—
Belgium, 3–4
Luxembourg, 169
Creditors—
Luxembourg, rights in, 225–6

Debts—
transfer of, 63
Designs—
Belgium, 17–19, 22
definition, 18
exploitation, 18–19
licensing, 22
procedure, 18
protection, 18–19
remedies, 18–19
Directors—
Belgium, 52–3
rights and liabilities, 52–3
Distribution agreement—
Belgium, 75–85
enforcement of protection—
arbitration, 83–4

Distribution agreement—*contd*
enforcement of protection—
contd
rules provided by 1961 Act, 81
special cases, 81–3
exclusive—
enforcement of protection, 81–4
scope of protection, 76–8
termination, consequences of,
78–81
Luxembourg, 198–9
quasi-exclusive. *See* exclusive *above*
scope of protection—
categories covered, 76–7
fixed duration, 77–8
generally, 76
indefinite duration, 77–8
termination, consequences of—
compensation in lieu of notice
period, 79–80
complementary indemnity, 80–81
generally, 78
reasonable notice period, 78–9
Economic Interest Grouping—
Belgium, 43–4, 50–51
European, 43–4, 50–51, 181
incorporation, 50–51
Luxembourg, 181
Employee—
invention of, 22–3
Employment—
Belgium, 104–12
contract, 105–8, 211–12
labour relations. *See* Labour
relations
Luxembourg, 210–14
Environmental planning—
Belgium. *See* Belgium
Luxembourg, 238–42
European Community—
EEIG, 43–4, 50–51, 181
immigration. *See* Immigration
mergers, 56
patent, 12
share acquisitions, 56
Exclusive distribution agreement. *See*
Distribution agreement

Factoring—
  Belgium, 145
  Luxembourg, 229–30
Flanders—
  environmental control law, 160–61
Franchising—
  Belgium, 86–8
  certificate of distribution, 87–8
  characteristics, 86–7
  competition law, and, 87
  definition, 86–7
  Luxembourg, 200–201

Goodwill, acquisition of—
  Belgium, 62–5
  formalities—
    claims, transfer of, 62–3
    contracts, transfer of, 63–5
    debts, transfer of, 63
    generally, 62
    mortgage, transfer of claims
      guaranteed by, 63
  Luxembourg, 192–3
  value added tax, 65
Guarantees—
  Belgium, 154–7
  Luxembourg, 235–7

Hive-offs—
  Luxembourg, 187–8

Immigration—
  Belgium, 102–4
  EC nationals—
    generally, 103–4
    professional card, 104
    residence permit, 104
    work permit, 104
  Luxembourg. *See* Luxembourg
  non-EC nationals—
    professional card, 102–3
    residence permit, 103
    work permit, 102–3
Income tax—
  Belgium, 114–21
  corporate—
    favourable tax status, corporation
      with, 121

Income tax—*contd*
  corporate—*contd*
    general, 118
    Luxembourg, 218–21
    non-resident, 124
    tax rates, 120–1
    taxable income, 118–20
  double taxation treaties, 124–5
  individual—
    general, 114–15
    Luxembourg, 216–18
    mechanism, 115–17
    non-resident, 123–4
    rates, 117–18
  non-resident—
    corporate tax, 124
    double income tax treaties, 124–5
    individual tax, 123–4
Incorporation—
  Belgium, 47–51
  EIG, 50–51
  limited liability company—
    articles of incorporation, 47–8
    directly, 47
    formalities, 48–9
    founders, 49
    pre-incorporation operations, 49
    public subscription, by, 47
  Luxembourg, 183–4
  non-profit organisation, 50
  partnership, 49
Industrial property. *See* Intellectual
  property
Information—
  confidential, 19–20
  consumer, protection of, 29–31
Insolvency—
  Belgium. *See* Belgium
  Luxembourg, 223–7
Insurance—
  environmental liability, 166
Intellectual property—
  Belgium, 8–23
  copyright. *See* Copyright
  designs. *See* Designs
  Luxembourg, 170–71
  models. *See* Models

Intellectual property—*contd*
    patents. *See* Patents
    trademarks. *See* Trademarks
International labour relations. *See*
    Labour relations
Invention of employee—
    Belgium, 22–3

Joint stock company. *See* Limited
    liability company

Know-how—
    Belgium, 19–20, 22
    licensing, 22

Labour relations—
    employment contract, 105–8
    international—
        applicable law, 110–11
        competent courts, 110
        labour protection, 110
        language, use of, 108–9
        legislation, 104–5
        mandatory bodies, 109
        social security, 110
        temporary secondment, 111–12
        working regulations, 108
Lawyers—
    Belgium, 5–6
Lease—
    business, 204–5
    civil, 92
    commercial, 93–6
    residential, 92–3
Leasing—
    Belgium, 143–5
    financial, 143–4
    Luxembourg, 228–9
    real estate, 144–5
Legal entities. *See* Non-profit
    organisation
Legal issues—
    Belgium, approach in, 6–7
Liability—
    environmental, 164–6
Licensing—
    Belgium, 20–2

Licensing—*contd*
    copyright, 21–2
    designs, 22
    know-how, 22
    models, 22
    trademarks, 20–1
Limited liability company—
    Belgium, 34–40
    co-operative company, 39–40
    incorporation—
        articles of incorporation, 47–8
        Belgium, 47–9
        directly, 47
        formalities, 48–9
        founders, 49
        pre-incorporation operations, 49
        public subscription, by, 47
    joint stock company—
        annual meeting, 37
        capital, 34–5
        control, 37
        duration, 35
        generally, 34
        management, 36–7
        name, 35
        publicity requirements, 37
        shareholders, 35
        shares, 35–6
        winding up, 38
    Luxembourg, 178–9
    private—
        Belgium, 38–9
        capital, 38
        management, 39
        name, 39
        participants, 38
        shares, 39
Loans—
    mortgage, 96–7
Luxembourg—
    acquisitions—
        goodwill, 192–3
        share. *See* share acquisitions *below*
    agency—
        background, 194
        brokers, 196
        commercial agent, 194–6

Luxembourg—*contd*
 agency—*contd*
  commercial representatives, 197
  commission agent, 196–7
 banking operations—
  bank accounts, 231–2
  bank facilities, 232
  liability of banks, 232
  loans from bank, 228
 bankruptcy—
  consequences, 224–5
  court's jurisdiction, 223
  declaration of, 223–4
  organisation, 224
  post-bankruptcy composition, 225
  rehabilitation, 225
 brokers, 196
 business organisations—
  Economic Interest Group, 181
  generally, 177
  incorporation, 182–4
  legislation, 177
  limited liability company, 178–9
  non-profit organisations, 182
  partnership. *See* partnership *below*
  shareholders' rights, 184
 commercial agent—
  generally, 194
  performance of contract, 195–6
  specific Luxembourg legislation, absence of, 194
  termination of contract, 196
 commercial representatives, 197
 commission agent—
  contract of, 196–7
  generally, 196
 competition—
  EC law, 172
  restrictive trading practices, 174
  unfair trading, 172–4
 consumer protection, 174–6
 cooperative company—
  limited liability, 179
  unlimited liability, 180
 copyright, 170–1
 corporate finance—
  capital increases, 231

Luxembourg—*contd*
 corporate finance—*contd*
  different methods of financing, 230–31
 corporate income tax—
  computation of taxable profit, 218–19
  corporation with favourable tax regimes, 219–20
  indirect business taxation, 221
 courts, 169
 credit establishments, liability of, 232
 distribution agreement—
  distributor, meaning, 198
  legislation, 198
  termination, 198–9
  terms and clauses, 198
 Economic Interest Group—
  European, 181
  generally, 181
 employment—
  contract, 211–12
  legislation, 210
  maternity leave, 213
  social security, 214
  worker representation, 213–14
  working conditions, 212
 environmental planning—
  area planning law, 238–40
  conservation law, 242
  environmental law, 240–42
  generally, 238
 factoring, 229–30
 financing company—
  bank loans, 228
  banking operations, 231–2
  corporate finance, 230–31
  factoring, 229–30
  guarantees, 235–7
  leasing, 228–9
  negotiable instruments, 232–5
 franchising—
  characteristics, 201
  drafting of agreement, 200–201
  legislation, 200
 goodwill, acquisition of, 192–3

Luxembourg—*contd*
  guarantees—
    cautionnement, 235–6
    first demand, 237
    real sureties, 236–7
  hive-offs, 187–8
  immigration—
    EC nationals, 210
    frontier worker's card, 210
    non-EC nationals, 207–10
  incorporation—
    main rules, 182–3
    principal costs on formation,
      183–4
  insolvency—
    creditors, right of, 225–7
    generally, 223
    international aspects, 227
  intellectual property—
    copyright, 170–71
    trademarks, 170
  leasing, 228–9
  legal entities, tax on, 221–2
  limited liability company—
    co-operative company, 179
    generally, 178
    private limited company, 178–9
    public limited company, 178
  loans from bank, 228
  maternity leave, 213
  mergers, 185–7
  negotiable instruments—
    bills of exchange, 232–4
    cheques, 234–5
    promissory notes, 235
  non-profit organisations, 182
  partnership—
    civil company, 181
    co-operative company, 180
    general, 179–80
    limited, 180
    shares, limited by, 180
  real property—
    business lease, 204–5
    generally, 202
    sale and purchase, 202–4
  restrictive trading practices, 174

Luxembourg—*contd*
  share acquisitions—
    co-operative company, 189
    limited company, 189
    private company, 188
    public company, 188–9
    transfer of shares for each
      company, 189–92
  shareholders' rights, 184
  shares, partnership limited by, 180
  social security, 214
  succession, 205–6
  taxation—
    corporate income tax, 218–21
    generally, 215–16
    individual tax, 216–18
    key dates of fiscal history, 215
    legal entities, tax on, 221–2
    transfer pricing, 222
    value added tax, 216
  trademarks, 170
  transfer pricing, 222
  unfair competition, 172–4

Management—
  joint stock company, 36–7
  private limited liability company, 39
Maternity leave—
  Luxembourg, 213
Mergers—
  Belgium, 56–7
  Community dimensions, 56
  Luxembourg, 185–7
Models—
  Belgium, 17–19, 22
  definition, 18
  exploitation, 18–19
  licensing, 22
  procedure, 18
  protection, 18–19
  remedies, 18–19
Mortgage—
  Belgium, 96–9
  loans, 96–7
  power of attorney to, 97–8
  promise, 98
  transfer of claims guaranteed by, 63

Mortgage—*contd*
  undertakings not to alienate or,
    98–9

Name—
  joint stock company, 35
  private limited liability company, 39
Negotiable instruments—
  Belgium. *See* Belgium
  Luxembourg, 232–5
Non-profit organisation—
  ASBL, 44–5
  Belgium,, 44–7, 50
  incorporation, 50
  institutions of public utility
    (foundations), 47
  international association, 45–6
  Luxembourg, 182
  taxation—
    assessment of income, 122
    assets, 122
    Belgium, 122–3
    generally, 122
    inheritance tax, tax in lieu,
      122–3
    Luxembourg, 221–2
    tax rates, 122
  YZW, 44–5
Non-resident income tax. *See* Income
  tax

Partnership—
  agreement, 43
  Belgium, 41–3, 49–50
  civil company, 42–3
  co-operative company, 42
  general, 41
  incorporation, 49–50
  limited, 41
  Luxembourg, 179–81
  shares, limited by, 41–2
  temporary, 43
Patents—
  Belgium, 8–12, 20
  definition, 9
  European, 12
  exploitation, 10

Patents—*contd*
  licensing, 20
  procedure, 9–10
  protection, 10–11
  remedies, 10–11
Penalties—
  environmental liabilities, 163–4
Private limited liability company. *See*
  Limited liability company
Professional card—
  Belgium, 102–3, 104
Promissory notes—
  Belgium, 153–4
  Luxembourg, 235
Property—
  intellectual. *See* Intellectual
    property
  real. *See* Real property
Publicity—
  joint stock company, requirements
    relating to, 37

Quasi-exclusive agreement. *See*
  Distribution agreement

Real property—
  Belgium, 89–99, 144–5
  civil lease, 92
  commercial lease, 93–6
  leasing, 144–5
  Luxembourg, 202–5
  mortgage—
    generally, 97
    loans, 96–7
    power of attorney to, 97–8
    promise, 98
    undertakings not to alienate or,
      98–9
  residential lease, 92–3
  sale and purchase—
    costs of sale, 91–2
    generally, 89–90
    practical procedure, 91
    registration duties, 90–1
    value added tax, 91
Remedies—
  copyright, protection of, 16

Remedies—*contd*
  designs, protection of, 18–19
  models, protection of, 18–19
  patents, protection of, 10–11
  trademarks, protection of, 14
Residence permit—
  Belgium, 103, 104
Residential lease—
  Belgium, 92–3

Sellers—
  fair competition involving, 29
Semiconductors—
  topography, protection of, 17
Shareholders—
  Belgium, 35, 51–2
  joint stock company, 35
  Luxembourg, 184
  rights and liabilities, 51–2, 184
Shares—
  acquisitions—
    Belgium, 57–62
    Luxembourg, 188–92
    private, 60–1
    privately owned stock, 57–60
    public, 61–2
    shares publicly held or quoted,
      60–2
    transparency of corporations, 62
  joint stock company, 35–6
  partnership limited by, 41–2
  private limited liability company, 39
Social security—
  Belgium, 110
  Luxembourg, 214
Software—
  protection of, 17
Sole trader—
  Belgium, 53
Succession—
  Belgium, 99–101
  Luxembourg, 205–6

Take-over bids—
  public, 61–2
Taxation—
  income tax. *See* Income tax
  legal entities, on, 122–3

Taxation—*contd*
  Luxembourg, 215–22
  non-profit organisation, on, 122–3
  value added tax. *See* Value added
    tax
Trade practices—
  Belgium, 29–32
  unfair, 32
Trade secrets—
  Belgium, 19–20
Trademarks—
  Belgium, 12–15, 20–1
  definition, 13
  exploitation, 14
  international registration, 14–15
  licensing, 20–1
  Luxembourg, 170
  protection—
    generally, 14
    procedure, 13–14
  remedies, 14
Transfer pricing—
  Belgium, 125–6
  Luxembourg, 222

Unfair competition—
  Articles 1382–1384 Belgian Civil
    Code, 28–9
  Belgium, 28–32
  information and protection of
    consumer, 29–31
  regulated practices, 31–2
  sanctions, 32
  sellers, fair competition involving,
    29
  trade practices, 29–32
  unfair trade practices, 32

Value added tax—
  Belgium—
    exemptions, 114
    foreign entrepreneurs, 113–14
    general, 113
    mechanism, 113
    rates, 114
  goodwill, acquisition of, 65

Value added tax—*contd*
   Luxembourg, 216
   real property, sale and purchase of,
     91

Wallonia—
   environmental control law, 161–3

Winding up—
   joint stock company, 38
Work permit—
   Belgium, 102–3, 104